THE SIGNS OF THE LAST DAYS

A Scriptural Guide to the Future

By
Vicki Alder

Printed in the United States of America.

First Printing, May 1990

ISBN 0-9626559-0-2

Distributed by: Wellspring Publishing
P. O. Box 1113
Sandy, UT 84091
1-801-566-9355

DEDICATION

To my husband, Bruce, whose encouragement and support helped make this book possible.

Another book coming from the same author:

MYSTERIES IN THE SCRIPTURES

Enlightenment Through Ancient Beliefs

INTRODUCTION

For many years, I have had a fascination for studying the events that will occur during the last days and at the second coming of the Lord. In my research, it was difficult to really understand and comprehend all the many scriptures and statements about the last days without becoming confused. So I began compiling a list of each sign that the scriptures mentioned. Under each of these signs, I would list all the scriptures and many of the statements by Church leaders that had to do with that particular event. By studying all that had been written on a particular sign of the Last Days, a much more comprehensive understanding of what will transpire can be gained.

In this book, I have been very careful to use only the most authoritative quotations and statements. The vast bulk of the book is taken directly from the four standard works of the Church and the teachings of the prophets with only a few necessary exceptions.

I have wanted to present in the most understandable and factual manner possible, the signs of the last days and the second coming of our Lord. I have two main goals in mind in writing this book. The first goal is to encourage others to study the scriptures by trying to make them easier to understand and by demonstrating how fascinating the scriptures really are. My second goal is to motivate others to be prepared for what is coming in the last days by showing how critical this preparation is.

Anyone who wants to understand the signs of the last days must have inspiration from the Holy Ghost. He is a Revelator of spiritual knowledge, Who can enlighten our understanding and help us know the difference between truth and falsehood. "And by the power of the Holy Ghost ye may know the truth of all things." (Moro. 10:5) Any study of the scriptures and words of the prophets should always be prefaced by a prayer to God that we may have guidance and understanding from the Holy Ghost.

THE AUTHOR

ILLUSTRATIONS

Title **Page**

The Heavens Are Opened..................29

The Likeness of Creatures...............40

The Wheel...............................43

A Cherub................................45

The Glory of the Lord...................55

The Hollow Earth.......................128

Helicopters............................171

Airplanes..............................174

KEY TO ABBREVIATIONS

Old Testament

Gen.	Genesis
Ex.	Exodus
Lev.	Leviticus
Num.	Numbers
Deut.	Deuteronomy
Josh.	Joshua
Judg.	Judges
1 Sam.	1 Samuel
2 Sam.	2 Samuel
1 Kgs.	1 Kings
2 Kgs.	2 Kings
1 Chr.	1 Chronicles
2 Chr.	2 Chronicles
Neh.	Nehemiah
Esth.	Esther
Ps.	Psalms
Prov.	Proverbs
Isa.	Isaiah
Jer.	Jeremiah
Lam.	Lamentations
Ezek.	Ezekiel
Dan.	Daniel
Obad.	Obadiah
Hab.	Habbakkuk
Zeph.	Zephaniah
Hag.	Haggai
Zech.	Zechariah
Mal.	Malachi

New Testament

Matt.	Matthew
Rom.	Romans
1 Cor.	1 Corinthians
2 Cor.	2 Corinthians
Gal.	Galatians
Eph.	Ephesians
Philip.	Philippians
Col.	Colossians
1 Thes.	1 Thessalonians
2 Thes.	2 Thessalonians
1 Tim.	1 Timothy
2 Tim.	2 Timothy
Philem.	Philemon
Heb.	Hebrews
1 Pet.	1 Peter
2 Pet.	2 Peter
1 Jn.	1 John
2 Jn.	2 John
3 Jn.	3 John
Rev.	Revelation

Book of Mormon

1 Ne.	1 Nephi
2 Ne.	2 Nephi
W of M	Words of Mormon
Hel.	Helaman
3 Ne.	3 Nephi
4 Ne.	4 Nephi
Morm.	Mormon
Moro.	Moroni

Doctrine and Covenants

D&C	Doctrine and Covenants

Pearl of Great Price

Abr.	Abraham
JS-M	Joseph Smith--Matthew
JS-H	Joseph Smith--History
A of F	Articles of Faith

HC	History of the Church
JST	Joseph Smith Translation
I.A.	Italics Added

TABLE OF CONTENTS

INTRODUCTION

ILLUSTRATIONS

KEY TO ABBREVIATIONS

TABLE OF CONTENTS

CHAPTER		PAGE
1.	**THE SIGNS OF THE TIMES**	**1**
	The Seven Seals	1
	Many Churches	3
	The Restoration of the Gospel	3
	The Prophet Elijah to Return	4
	Iniquity to Abound, the Love of Many Shall Wax Cold	5
	The Rise of an Evil Power	6
	Secret Combinations	7
	The Jews to Be Gathered	8
	Men Shall Say that Christ Delays His Coming	8
	Earthquakes in Divers Places	9
	Wars and Rumors of War, Earth in Commotion	9
2.	**PREPARATORY TRIALS**	**11**
	The Saints Are Tested	11
	The Times of the Gentiles Fulfilled	12
	The Missionaries Are Called Home, God Preaches His Own Sermons in Calamities	13
	Punishments First on Saints Who Have Been Unfaithful	14
	God Will Change the Times and the Seasons	15
	A Rainbow Not Seen in a Year Will Precede Destruction	17
	The Day of Wrath Comes As a Whirlwind	17
3.	**A WORLDWIDE EARTHQUAKE DURING THE SIXTH SEAL (BEFORE A.D. 2000)**	**19**
	Great Destructions Upon the Wicked	21

The Earth Trembles and Reels To and Fro, Thunderings, Lightnings, Tempests, Tidal Waves and Fear 21
A Hailstorm Destroys the Crops of the Earth 22
Blood, Fire and Vapors of Smoke 24
Those Who Call on the Lord Will Be Saved 24
The Powers of Heaven Will Be Shaken 25

4. **THE SIGN OF THE SON OF MAN DURING THE SIXTH SEAL (BEFORE A.D. 2000)................ 27**
The Heavens Are Opened 27
The Sign of the Son of Man Is Seen in the Heavens 31
The Parable of the Fig Tree 34

5. **WHAT IS A "CLOUD" FROM HEAVEN?............... 36**
The Prophet Ezekiel 38
The Likeness of Creatures 38
A Wheel Within a Wheel 41
The Cherubims 44
Coals of Fire 46
The Spirit Was in the Wheels 47
The Speed of the Cherubims 51
The Noise of Their Wings-- As the Voice of the Almighty 52
The Glory of the Lord 54
A Pillar of a Cloud by Day, A Pillar of Fire by Night 62
Clouds 67
Chariots 73
The Star 75
Joseph Smith's First Vision 76
Other Descriptions of God's Chariot 79

6. **DESTRUCTION IN AMERICA AND JERUSALEM......... 83**
New York, Albany and Boston Destroyed 83
The Destruction of the Wicked in America 84
Some Righteous Will Die, But Most Will Survive 87
A Plague of Flies 87
A Desolating Sickness and and an Overflowing Scourge 88

TABLE OF CONTENTS

The Wicked Will Kill Each Other 91
The Lamanites Will Tread Down the Gentiles in America 94
The Bands of the Abomidable Church Made Strong 95
The Constitution Will Hang by a Thread 96
Unparalleled Affliction on the Jews and Jerusalem 97

7. **FALSE CHRISTS AND FALSE PROPHETS............. 99**
Go Not Forth to See Them 99

8. **FAMINE.. 102**
A Year's Supply and Gardens 102
Excuses for Disobedience to Counsel 103
Do It Now 105

9. **THE NEW JERUSALEM............................. 107**
The Saints Return to Help Build the New Jerusalem 107
What Will the New Jerusalem Be Like? 109
Jesus Christ Will Be Seen in the Midst of the New Jerusalem 111

10. **THE CALLING OF THE 144,000 DURING THE SIXTH SEAL (BEFORE A.D. 2000) AFTER THE RETURN OF THE TEN LOST TRIBES................ 113**
144,000 Are Sealed 113
John Sees the Faithful in Heaven 115
The Ten Tribes to Return 116
Background Information on the Lost Tribes 118
God Will Bring the Ten Tribes Back 120
The Ten Tribes Come to America and Zion 121
The Sons of Levi Make a Righteous Offering 123
The Scriptures of the Lost Tribes 124
The Ten Tribes Return to Israel 124

11. **ARE THE TEN TRIBES UNDER THE EARTH?.......... 126**
Are They in the North Countries? 126
The Hollow Earth Theory 127
Scriptural Evidence 129

Physical Evidences 135
Pictorial Evidence from Other Planets, Suns and Moons 137

12. **THE FUTURE OF THE LAMANITES.................. 140**
They Will Have the Gospel Preached to Them 140
They Shall Blossom as the Rose 140
They Shall Become a Righteous Branch 141

13. **THE SEVENTH SEAL--THE GATHERING OF THE RIGHTEOUS.............................. 142**
Silence in Heaven 142
A Temple Built at Jerusalem 145
The Gospel Preached in All the World 146
The Gathering of Israel and the Saints 146
The People of Zion Will Be the Only People Not at War 149
The Waters Will Be Cursed 149
The Righteous Will Be Separated From the Wicked 150

14. **THE CHURCH AND KINGDOM OF GOD, THE CHURCH AND KINGDOM OF THE DEVIL.............. 154**
Symbols and Interpretations 152
The Church of God 154
The Kingdom of God 157
The Church of the Devil 158
The Kingdom of the Devil 161
The Victory 163

15. **THE SEVEN JUDGMENTS........................... 164**
The First Judgment--Hail and Fire 165
The Second Judgment--A Burning Mountain 166
The Third Judgment--A Burning Star 166
The Fourth Judgment--Partial Darkness 167
The Fifth Judgment--Mankind Is Tormented 168
The Sixth Judgment--One Third of Mankind Is Killed 172
Two Prophets in Jerusalem 175
The Seven Final Plagues 176
The First Vial and Plague 177

The Second Vial and Plague 177
The Third Vial and Plague 178
The Fourth Vial and Plague 178
The Fifth Vial and Plague 179
The Sixth Vial and Plague--Armageddon 180
The Two Prophets Are Killed 181
War Casualties in Israel 182
The Two Prophets Resurrect 182
The Messiah Stands on the Mount of Olives 183
The Jews Are Converted to Christ 183
The Seventh Judgment--It is Done 184
The Seventh Vial and Plague 185
Destruction of Five-Sixths of the Gentile Armies 186

16. BABYLON AND THE WICKED ARE BURNED............ 187
The End of the World 187
All Corruptible Men and Creatures Are Consumed 190
The Tithed Are Not Burned 192

17. THE KINGDOM OF GOD REIGNS OVER THE EARTH..... 193
The Council at Adam-ondi-Ahman 193
The Saints Are Given the Kingdom 195

18. THE MARRIAGE SUPPER OF THE LAMB.............. 197
He Comes as a Thief in the Night 197
The Ten Virgins Are Called to Attend the Supper 198

19. CATACLYSMIC EVENTS AT THE LORD'S APPEARANCE.. 202
The Mountains Are Broken Down 202
The Heavens and Earth Shake 203
One Land Mass 204
The Sun and Moon Withhold Their Light 204

20. THE RIGHTEOUS ARE CAUGHT UP TO BE WITH CHRIST 205
The Heavens Are Opened 205
The Righteous Who Are Alive Are Caught Up to Meet Him 205
Some Saints Are Gathered by Angels Prior to the Second Coming 206

Quickened 208
The Dead Are Caught Up to Meet Him 209

21. **THE FIRST RESURRECTION.......................... 211**
The Resurrection of the Just 212
The Heathen Will Be Redeemed 213
Those Who Are Not Part of the First Resurrection 213

22. **JESUS CHRIST'S SECOND COMING................. 214**
His Red Apparel 214
His Apostles Will Be on His Right Hand 215
He Will Come in His Glory with the Angels in the Clouds of Heaven 215
Every Knee Will Bow 217
The Secret Acts of Mankind Revealed 218
There Will Be Time No Longer 219
Satan Will Be Bound 219
The City of Enoch Returns 221
The Lord Reveals All that Has Been Hidden 222
The Savior Will Reign Personally Upon the Earth 223

23. **GLORIOUS CONDITIONS DURING THE MILLENIUM..... 224**
A New Heaven and a New Earth 224
The Earth Changed From a Telestial to a Terrestrial Planet 226
Enmity Ceases, No Sorrow and No Death 228
The Earth Is Full of the Knowledge of God 229

24. **WILL PEOPLE ON THE EARTH BE TRANSLATED BEINGS DURING THE MILLENIUM?................. 231**
Five Evidences That They Will 231
Translation is Part of the Restoration of All Things 234
The Conclusion 235

BIBLIOGRAPHY 237

INDEX 239

THE SIGNS OF THE TIMES

We live in the last days before the end of the world. Jesus Christ has said that those who reverence Him will be very interested in the signs that precede His second coming. "And it shall come to pass that he that feareth me shall be looking forth for the great day of the Lord to come, even for the signs of the coming of the Son of Man." (D&C 45:39 I.A.)

The best way to study the many signs that have been prophesied will occur is to list each specific event and then study all the scriptures in the four standard works on each particular sign. Our dispensation is so fortunate to have the scriptures from the Book of Mormon, Doctrine and Covenants and Pearl of Great Price in addition to the Bible to study. The Savior has promised His latter-day saints, "And unto you it shall be given to know the signs of the times, and the signs of the coming of the Son of Man;" (D&C 68:11 I.A.).

THE SEVEN SEALS

It would certainly be marvelous to know when all of these signs of the last days will occur. But only in the Book of Revelation do we receive a definite order given by the Lord to John the Revelator as to the sequence of the events that will transpire. The Book of Revelation reveals many events that occur in seven different seals that are on the back of a book that John is shown. (Rev. 5-22) Joseph Smith explained what the seven seals represented: "Q. What are we to understand by the book which John saw, which was sealed on the back with seven seals?

A. We are to understand that it contains the revealed will, mysteries, and the works of God; the hidden things of his economy concerning this earth during the seven thousand years of its continuance, or its temporal existence." (D&C 77:6 I.A.)

THE SIGNS OF THE LAST DAYS

Thanks to revelation given to the prophet Joseph Smith, we know that each of the seven seals on the book represents one thousand years of the earth's temporal existence: "Q. What are we to understand by the seven seals with which it was sealed? A. We are to understand that the first seal contains the things of the first thousand years, and the second also of the second thousand years, and so on until the seventh." (D&C 77:7 I.A.)

The following is a representation of the seven time periods and the basic things that John saw in each of them except for the seventh time period where there are too many events to list here.

The first seal (Rev. 6:1-2) covers about 4000 B.C. to 3000 B.C. and John sees a warrior conquering.

The second seal (Rev. 6:3-4) covers about 3000 B.C. to 2000 B.C. and John sees what represents human contention and death.

The third seal (Rev. 6:5-6) covers about 2000 B.C. to 1000 B.C. and John sees representations of famine.

The fourth seal (Rev. 6:7-8) covers about 1000 B.C. to A.D. 1 and John sees death through war, famine and beasts.

The fifth seal (Rev. 6:9-11) covers about A.D. 1 to A.D. 1000 and John sees those who die for Christ in the early Christian era.

The sixth seal (Rev. 6:12-17, 7:1-17) covers about A.D. 1000 to A.D. 2000 and John sees a worldwide earthquake when many mistakenly fear it is the end of the world and 144,000 are sealed and heavenly rewards for the faithful.

The seventh seal (Rev. 8-20) covers about A.D. 2000 to A.D. 3000 and John sees many events that occur before the second coming. He also receives background information on some of the events he is seeing and he views the second coming and the millenium. (The Ensign, Oct. 1983, pp. 50-53.)

It becomes readily apparent that the vision John received had its main emphasis on the sixth and seventh seals or time periods. We, of course, are presently at the end of the sixth seal and neither the worldwide earthquake nor the sealing of the 144,000 has taken place yet.

Before we discover what lies ahead in the future according to the prophesies in the scriptures and by the prophets, we will take a brief look at what prophesies have already been fulfilled.

MANY CHURCHES

God knew that there would be many churches built up in the last days that would cause people to stumble and be confused about His doctrines. The Lord condemns the churches for putting down the power and miracles of God. Miracles were wrought by the power of God in both the Old and New Testaments. God has warned that in our day the churches will teach to get gain and to receive the praise of the world but not to help the poor or for the welfare of Zion. "And the Gentiles are lifted up in the pride of their eyes, and have stumbled, because of the greatness of their stumbling block, that <u>they have built up many churches</u>; nevertheless, <u>they put down the power and miracles of God</u>, and preach up unto themselves their own wisdom and their own learning, that they may get gain and grind upon the face of the poor. And there are many churches built up which cause envyings, and strifes, and malice. He commandeth that there shall be no priestcrafts; for, behold, priestcrafts are that men preach and set themselves up for a light unto the world, <u>that they may get gain and praise of the world;</u> but they seek not the welfare of Zion." (2 Ne. 26:20-21, 29 I.A.)

THE RESTORATION OF THE GOSPEL

Because of the apostasy of the earth Christian Church that was founded by Jesus Christ, it was necessary for the Lord to restore His gospel to the earth. (Acts 3:19-21, Dan. 2:26-45) The heavens were opened in the spring of 1820 with God the Father and His Son Jesus Christ appearing to a new prophet, Joseph Smith. The prophet Joseph Smith received revelations from God and many angels who were sent from heaven to usher in a new dispensation of the gospel. Through divine means and revelation, Joseph Smith gave us the Book of Mormon, the Doctrine and Covenants and the Pearl of Great Price as companion scriptures to the Bible. Through the administration of angels, the Priesthood power was again restored to the earth. On April 6, 1830, the Church founded by Jesus Christ was once again found on the earth. (JS-H 1, Rev. 7:1, D&C 77:8) The name given to His Church to distinguish this latter-day Church from the earth Christian Church was The Church of Jesus Christ of Latter-day Saints. (D&C 115:4)

The prophet Joel foresaw that revelations from the Lord would be poured out upon mankind in the last days. Peter quoted the prophesy of Joel, "And it shall come to pass in the last days, saith God, I will pour out of my Spirit upon all flesh: and your sons and your daughters shall prophesy, and your young men shall see visions, and your old men shall dream dreams: And on my servants and on my handmaidens I will pour out in those days my Spirit; and they shall prophesy:" (Acts 2:17-18 I.A., Joel 2:28-29) Those who say that there are no more revelations, visions and prophesies in our day, but that the Bible contains them all, have not understood what Peter and Joel foretold.

THE PROPHET ELIJAH TO RETURN

Malachi prophesied that before the second coming of the Lord, the prophet Elijah would return. "Behold, I will send you Elijah the prophet before the coming of the great and dreadful day of the Lord: And he shall turn the heart of the fathers to the children, and the heart of the children to their fathers, lest I come and smite the earth with a curse. (Mal. 4:5-6 I.A.)

The prophesied return of the prophet Elijah was fulfilled in the Kirtland Temple on April 3, 1836. "After this vision was closed, another great and glorious vision burst upon us; for Elijah the prophet, who was taken to heaven without tasting death, stood before us, and said: Behold, the time has fully come, which was spoken of by the mouth of Malachi--testifying that he [Elijah] should be sent, before the great and dreadful day of the Lord come-- To turn the hearts of the fathers to the children, and the children to the fathers, lest the whole earth be smitten with a curse-- Therefore, the keys of this dispensation are committed into your hands; and by this ye may know that the great and dreadful day of the Lord is near, even at the doors." (D&C 110:13-16 I.A.)

Since that visit from Elijah, there has been a worldwide movement by many people to search out the records of their ancestors. Countless people, both members and non-members of the Church, have been moved upon by the Lord and their deceased ancestors to compile a genealogy of their forefathers. Numerous temples have been built in many countries for the purpose of redeeming the living and the dead. Millions of the dead have had their temple ordinance work done for them vicariously by the living. This great work of the redemption of the dead goes forward and will continue into the millenium. The prophet Elijah has truly been instrumental in turning the hearts of the fathers to the children and the hearts of the children to their fathers in many cases.

INIQUITY TO ABOUND, THE LOVE OF MANY SHALL WAX COLD

Jesus told us that "because iniquity shall abound, the love of many shall wax cold." (Matt. 24:12, JS-M 1:10) We would have to be oblivious not to notice the evils that surround us today. They are increasing. Nephi warned that in the last days all nations will be so wicked that "they will be drunken with iniquity and all manner of abominations." (2 Ne.

27:1) So because of great iniquity which will be rampant in the Last Days, the love of many for each other will wax cold or cease to exist. This could pertain to love in marriages, love of parents for their children and children for their parents. This could also refer to love between neighbors and friends along with friendship between nations. But Christ reminded us immediately in the next verse that those who are not overcome but remain steadfast, and who do not partake of the evil (thereby losing their love) shall be saved. "And because iniquity shall abound, the love of many shall wax cold; But he that remaineth steadfast and is not overcome, the same shall be saved." (JS-M 1:10-11 I.A.)

Mormon forewarned us that there would not only be great wickedness in our day, but also that there shall be great pollutions. "Yea, it shall come in a day when there shall be great pollutions upon the face of the earth; there shall be murders, and robbing, and lying, and deceivings, and whoredoms, and all manner of abominations; when there shall be many who will say, Do this, or do that, and it mattereth not, for the Lord will uphold such at the last day. But wo unto such, for they are in the gall of bitterness and in the bonds of iniquity." (Mormon 8:31 I.A.) This prophesy by Mormon that there would be great pollutions in our day upon the face of the earth and great wickedness has already been fulfilled.

THE RISE OF AN EVIL POWER

Jesus Christ told us in 1831 that in the near future peace would be taken from the earth and that the devil would have power over his own dominion. "And again, verily I say unto you, O inhabitants of the earth: I the Lord am willing to make these things known unto all flesh; For I am no respecter of persons, and will that all men shall know that the day speedily cometh; the hour is not yet, but is nigh at hand, when peace shall be taken from the earth, and the devil shall have power over his own dominion."(D&C 1:35 I.A.)

THE SIGNS OF THE TIMES

After two World Wars, we have seen the rise of atheistic communism. It has spread over the earth leaving many dead and others without true freedom. Many of these people are already rebelling and seeking for freedom. The Lord comforts us by saying He will have power over his saints and reign in their midst and will eventually come down in judgment upon the world. "And also the Lord shall have power over his saints, and shall reign in their midst, and shall come down in judgment upon Idumea, or the world." (D&C 1:36 I.A.)

SECRET COMBINATIONS

Cain was the leader of the first secret combination. (Moses 5:30-31) Organized crime has infiltrated America and many other countries and is growing in strength. It was secret combinations that destroyed both the Jaredite and Nephite civilizations in the Book of Mormon. (Ether 8:18-20) Moroni warned the modern Americas that any nation that upholds secret combinations whose goal is to get power and gain and allows these murderous combinations to spread over the nation, will be destroyed. "And whatsoever nation shall uphold such secret combinations, to get power and gain, until they shall spread over the nation, behold, they shall be destroyed; for the Lord will not suffer that the blood of his saints, which shall be shed by them, shall always cry unto him from the ground for vengeance upon them and yet he avenge them not. Wherefore, O ye Gentiles, it is wisdom in God that these things should be shown unto you, that thereby ye may repent of your sins, and suffer not that these murderous combinations shall get above you, which are built up to get power and gain--and the work, yea, even the work of destruction come upon you, yea, even the sword of the justice of the Eternal God shall fall upon you, to your overthrow and destruction if ye shall suffer these things to be." (Ether 8:22-23 I.A.)

These secret combinations are most abomidable and wicked above all else in the sight of God. (Ether 8:18)

THE JEWS TO BE GATHERED

It was prophesied by the prophet Amos (Amos 9:14) and by the prophet Isaiah (Isa.61:4) that the Jews after their long dispersion among the Gentiles would be gathered to the land of Israel again. Nephi prophesied of their gathering from the four parts of the earth to the land of their inheritance. He even saw that the leaders of the Gentile nations would assist the Jews in their return and establishment as a nation. "And it shall come to pass that they [the Jews] shall be gathered in from their long dispersion, from the isles of the sea, and from the four parts of the earth; and the nations of the Gentiles shall be great in the eyes of me, saith God, in carrying them forth to the lands of their inheritance." (2 Ne. 10:8)

Many Jews have gathered in Israel and they have been established as a nation to the amazement of many. Ezekiel foretold that the Jews would reinhabit and rebuild Israel. (Ezek. 36:10-12, 33-36) He also saw that the barren land of Israel would become highly productive and even fruitful like the Garden of Eden. (Ezek. 36:8, 29-30, 34-35) Ezekiel also prophesied that the land of Israel would be under one nation again. "And I will make them <u>one nation</u> in the land upon the mountains of Israel; and <u>one king</u> shall be king to them all: and they shall be no more two nations, neither shall they be divided into two kingdoms any more at all:" (Ezek. 37:22 I.A.)

Zechariah foretold that Jerusalem would again be the major city of the country of Israel. (Zech. 1:16-17, 2:12, 12:6) The prophets also foresaw that Judah would become a mighty nation in politics and warfare. (Isa. 19:16-17, Zech. 10:3-6) Many of these prophesies about the Jews have already been fulfilled in our day.

MEN SHALL SAY THAT CHRIST DELAYS HIS COMING

Peter warned us that in the last days there would

be people, walking after their own lusts, who would scoff at the prophesies about the Second Coming of Christ. They will contend that since the Bible prophets died, nothing has happened and Christ has not come. They have chosen to ignore the fact that God created the earth and consider the Lord slack in His promises. But Peter reminds us that God is not slack but long-suffering. He wants to give mankind plenty of time to repent so that they will not be burned. Then Peter confirmed that Christ will come a second time. (2 Pet. 3:3-13, JST 2 Pet. 3:3-13) "The Lord is not slack concerning his promise and coming, as some men count slackness; but long-suffering toward us, not willing that any should perish, but that all should come to repentance." (JST 2 Pet. 3:9 I.A.)

Jesus foresaw that His servants in the last days will be in two groups. The faithful and wise servants will heed His warning to watch and always be ready for His coming. But the evil servants will say in their hearts that Jesus will delay His coming. During this supposed delay, the evil servants will disobey His commandments. Jesus will return before the wicked servants expect Him, and they will be judged to be hypocrites and will be cut off. (Matt. 24:44-51, JS-M 1:46-55) "Therefore be ye ready: for in such an hour as ye think not the Son of man cometh."(Matt. 24:44 I.A.)

EARTHQUAKES IN DIVERS PLACES

Jesus predicted that many earthquakes would be felt in different places in our day. (Matt 24:7, Mark 13:8, Luke 21:11) The number of major earthquakes in the world has multiplied dramatically during this century in comparison to the previous centuries where records have been kept. (The World Book Encyclopedia, 1980, 6:19)

WARS AND RUMORS OF WAR, EARTH IN COMMOTION

War is an on-going condition in our present

world. Different factions fight for control of their individual country. Some nations seek world domination. Other nations export revolution and bloodshed. The Lord foresaw these conditions when He inspired Joseph Smith to prophesy in 1832 that war would begin to be poured out beginning at South Carolina with the Civil War. "Verily, thus saith the Lord concerning the wars that will shortly come to pass, beginning at the rebellion of South Carolina, which will eventually terminate in the death and misery of many souls; And the time will come that war will be poured out upon all nations, beginning at this place."(D&C 87:1-2 I.A.)

There will be no end of war until the Prince of Peace returns. Jesus has consoled us by saying that these things must come to pass but not to be troubled or terrified by them. "And when ye shall hear of wars and rumours of wars, be ye not troubled: for such things must needs be; but the end shall not be yet. For nation shall rise against nation, and kingdom against kingdom: and there shall be earthquakes in divers places, and there shall be famines and troubles: these are the beginnings of sorrows." (Mark 13:7-8 I.A., Matt. 24:6-7, Luke 21:9-10)

The Lord has also told us the reason for the wars. "I, the Lord, am angry with the wicked; I am holding my Spirit from the inhabitants of the earth. I have sworn in my wrath, and decreed wars upon the face of the earth, and the wicked shall slay the wicked, and fear shall come upon every man;" (D&C 63:32-33 I.A.)

Unless mankind repents, wars will continue until the Savior returns.

PREPARATORY TRIALS

There will be preparatory trials experienced by the world at large and by the saints before the two events that John the Revelator foresaw in the sixth seal or time period are fulfilled.

THE SAINTS ARE TESTED

During the early history of the Church, the saints were faced with many different trials. The pioneers were driven from their homes in the eastern United States and had to travel 1,400 miles through the treacherous wilderness to reach the haven of the Salt Lake Valley. Then they faced starvation, crickets and primitive living conditions. Through the Lord's help and hard work, they made the wilderness blossom as a rose. The saints of our day will likewise face great trials and tests.

Heber C. Kimball, a counselor in the First Presidency under Brigham Young, made a profound prophecy concerning the saints in the last days. "After a while, the Gentiles will gather to this place by the thousands and Salt Lake City will be classified among the wicked cities of the world. A spirit of speculation and extravagance will take possession of the Saints, and the result will be financial bondage. Persecution comes next and all true Latter-day Saints will be tested to the limit. Many will apostatize and others will be still not knowing what to do. 'Darkness will cover the earth and gross darkness the minds of the people.' Before that day comes, however, the Saints will be put to tests that will try the integrity of the best of them. The pressure will become so great that the more righteous among them will cry unto the Lord day and night until deliverance comes." (Deseret News, Church Dep't, p. 3, May 23, 1931, I.A.)

There have already been problems with speculation, extravagance and financial debt among some of the saints. At this time, the persecution toward the saints is not as severe as Heber C. Kimball foresaw. That will come to pass in the future.

THE TIMES OF THE GENTILES FULFILLED

Anciently, in the early Christian Church, the gospel was first taken to the house of Israel and then later on it was taken to the Gentiles. (Acts 10-11) An angel promised Nephi about 600 B.C. that in the last days the gospel would first be given to the Gentiles and later on to the house of Israel or the Jews. "And the time cometh that he shall manifest himself unto all nations, both unto the Jews and also unto the Gentiles; and after he has manifested himself unto the Jews and also unto the Gentiles, then he shall manifest himself unto the Gentiles and also unto the Jews, and the last shall be first, and the first shall be last." (1 Ne. 13:42, I.A.)

But when the Gentiles shall sin against the gospel that has been taken to them and reject it because of pride and wickedness, then the gospel will be taken from among them. After that, God will remember His covenant with Israel and the gospel will be taken to the House of Israel (which includes the Jews) again. "And thus commandeth the Father that I should say unto you: At that day when the Gentiles shall sin against my gospel...and shall be lifted up in the pride of their hearts above all nations, and above all the people of the whole earth, and shall be filled with all manner of lyings, and of deceits, and of mischiefs, and all manner of hypocrisy, and murder and priestcrafts, and whoredoms, and of secret abominations; and if they shall do all those things, and shall reject the fulness of my gospel, behold, saith the Father, I will bring the fulness of my gospel from among them. And then will I remember my covenant which I have made unto my people, O house of

2

upon the inhabitants of the earth,...And upon my house shall it begin, and from my house shall it go forth, saith the Lord; First among those among you, saith the Lord; who have professed to know my name and have not known me, and have blasphemed against me in the midst of my house, saith the Lord." (D&C 112:24-26, I.A.)

The Lord has not said that vengeance will come upon those who have known Him and have not blasphemed, on the contrary, He has promised the faithful saints that "if ye are prepared ye shall not fear". (D&C 38:30) Someone has committed "blasphemy" when they use contemptuous speech concerning God, his temple, his law or his prophet. If we just go through the motions of participation in the gospel of Jesus Christ and do not become more Christ-like and come to the point where we know God personally, then we might find ourselves among those who "have not known" the Savior.

Those saints who have chosen not to keep the commandments will also find themselves under condemnation. "Nevertheless, Zion shall escape if she observe to do all things whatsoever I have commanded her. But if she observe not to do whatsoever I have commanded her, I will visit her according to all her works, with sore affliction, with pestilence, with plague, with vengeance, with devouring fire." (D&C 97:25-26, I.A.)

Keeping the commandments and not being hypocritical are the keys to avoiding these punishments and calamities.

GOD WILL CHANGE THE TIMES AND THE SEASONS

The Lord has promised that the times and the seasons that we now observe will be altered. "And also that God hath set his hand and seal to change the times and seasons," (D&C 121:12, I.A., Dan. 2:21)

God has given us our time through the movement of the earth. As the earth spins upon its axis, the side that faces the sun has day while the other has night.

This changes as the earth spins. It takes 23 hours, 56 minutes and 4.09 seconds for the earth to spin around once. We get our year from the fact that it takes 365 days, 6 hours, 9 minutes and 9.54 seconds for the earth to go around the sun. Should the Lord change the speed at which the earth spins on its axis or the length of time it takes for the earth to go around the sun, or both, our time would be different than it is now.

Our seasons are caused by the fact that the earth tilts 23½ degrees from the straight up position on its axis. The changing seasons are caused by the changing position of the earth in relation to the direct rays of the sun. If the Lord alterer the 23½ degree tilt of the axis of the earth or turned the earth over, the seasons would be changed or reversed.

Helaman knew that God had the power to control time. "Yea, if he say unto the earth--Thou shalt go back, that it lengthen out the day for hours--it is done; And thus, according to his word the earth goeth back," (Hel. 12:14-15, Joshua 10:12-13)

The Lord has already told us what He is going to do that could easily cause a change in the times and seasons. "For not many days hence and <u>the earth shall tremble and reel to and fro</u> as a drunken man;" (D&C 88:87, I.A.)

This shaking of the earth will cause the worldwide earthquake that John the Revelator saw in the sixth seal when the heavens will also tremble. (See Chapter 3.) "I will not only <u>shake the earth</u>, but the starry <u>heavens shall tremble</u>." (D&C 84:118, I.A.)

When the Lord causes the entire earth to shake and tremble, our times and seasons will most likely be altered.

A RAINBOW NOT SEEN IN A YEAR WILL PRECEDE DESTRUCTION

Those who are watching will receive a forewarning from God of impending destruction. Joseph Smith taught about a special sign that will serve as a warning. "The Lord hath set the bow in the cloud for a sign that while it shall be seen, seed time and harvest, summer and winter shall not fail; but when it shall disappear, woe to that generation, for behold the end cometh quickly." (Teachings, p. 305, I.A.)

The rainbow is a sign given to us from the Lord. When the rainbow is withdrawn, it will be a token that destruction is imminent. "I have asked the Lord concerning His coming; and while asking the Lord, He gave a sign and said, 'In the days of Noah I set a bow in the heavens as a sign and token that in any year that the bow should be seen the Lord would not come; but there should be seed time and harvest during that year: but whenever you see the bow withdrawn, it shall be a token that there will be famine, pestilence, and great distress among the nations, and that the coming of the Messiah is not far distant'." (Teachings, pp. 340-341, I.A.)

It was kind of the Lord to give us the bow as a sign. Rainbows in the sky are caused by the reflection, refraction and scattering of light rays by moisture in the air. When the sun shines through the wet atmosphere (caused by rain, fog, mists, etc.) a rainbow can be seen. The absence of direct sunshine through a disturbed or polluted atmosphere could prevent rainbows from being seen. When the bow is not seen in a year, it will be a warning to us from the Lord.

THE DAY OF WRATH COMES AS A WHIRLWIND

When the day of wrath comes, it will come speedily without much warning to those who are not watching. "For behold, and lo, vengeance cometh speedily upon the ungodly as the whirlwind; and who shall escape it?" (D&C 97:22, I.A.)

A whirlwind is a rotating windstorm. A tornado is an example of a whirlwind. These storms come up suddenly without much warning. The vengeance of the Lord will come upon the wicked, rebellious and unbelieving. "Wherefore, verily I say, let the wicked take heed, and let the rebellious fear and tremble; and let the unbelieving hold their lips, for the day of wrath shall come upon them as a whirlwind, and all flesh shall know that I am God." (D&C 63:6, I.A.)

This vengeance of the Lord will come upon the face or surface of the earth. "Behold, vengeance cometh speedily upon the inhabitants of the earth,... and as a whirlwind it shall come upon the face of the earth, saith the Lord." (D&C 112:24, I.A.)

There will not be time to prepare when the wrath of God comes upon the surface of the earth because it will come speedily and unexpectedly as a windstorm.

A WORLDWIDE EARTHQUAKE DURING THE SIXTH SEAL

(BEFORE A.D. 2000)

During the sixth seal or before the approximate year of 2000 A.D. (if historical records have been kept accurately), John the Revelator prophesied of an event which has not transpired yet. There is to be an earthquake that will be felt by the entire world. (Rev. 6:12-17, D&C 77:6-7, The Ensign, Oct. 1983, pp. 50-53)

Since the sixth seal is the one we are in now and because there are very few years left in the sixth seal, we will focus on this eventful occurrence beginning with Revelation 6:12-14: "And I beheld when he had opened the sixth seal, and, lo, there was an earthquake; and the sun became black as sackcloth of hair, and the moon became as blood; and the stars of heaven fell unto the earth, even as a fig tree casteth her untimely figs, when she is shaken of a mighty wind...and every mountain and island were moved out of their places." (I.A.)

This earthquake is felt worldwide because every mountain and island are moved out of their original places. We are accustomed to earthquakes that occur when the ground trembles and shakes because of the sudden dislocation of material within the earth. Typical earthquakes are felt in a particular location. The natural means that the Lord might use to bring to pass this worldwide earthquake will most likely come from beyond the earth rather than from within it. The gravitational pull from a close encounter with a large heavenly body could cause the entire earth to shake.

It is possible that the dirt that would be thrown

up into the atmosphere as a result of such powerful earthquake will make the sun appear to be black. The refraction of light through a polluted sky can make the moon appear to be red or as blood. The Lord predicted that a veil of darkness will cover the earth which will darken the heavens. "And the day shall come that the earth shall rest, but before that day the heavens shall be darkened, and a veil of darkness shall cover the earth; and the heavens shall shake, and also the earth; and great tribulations shall be among the children of men; but my people will I preserve;" (Moses 7:61, I.A.)

At the same time as the sun becomes black and the moon looks like blood, the scriptures indicate that the stars will fall from heaven. If a real star fell to the earth, it would most likely destroy the entire planet. (Our sun is the closest star to the earth. It is not a large star being classified as a "yellow dwarf" and yet it is one hundred and nine times larger than the earth.) What we usually refer to as "falling stars" are really meteorites entering the earth's atmosphere with great velocity at night. They become incandescent or bright with heat that is generated by resistance to the atmosphere. This causes them to burn brightly as they fall to the earth. They look just like falling stars but are not literally falling stars.

Three specific details are mentioned in regards to this particular earthquake which distinguishes it from all other earthquakes mentioned in the scriptures: (1) The sun becomes black, (2) the moon becomes as blood and (3) the stars of heaven appear to fall to the earth. Whenever these three descriptive details are used to describe an earthquake in scripture, the same earthquake is being discussed. (Sometimes there are minor variations in terms such as "the sun shall refuse to give light" rather than "the sun became black" or "the moon shall not give her light" instead of "the moon shall turn to blood".) These three detailed descriptions are the key words to discovering scriptures that refer to this same earthquake. Revelation 6:12-17 teaches us that the worldwide earthquake takes place during the sixth seal and time period while other scriptures on the same event can give us added insight and more details about what will happen.

GREAT DESTRUCTIONS UPON THE WICKED

In D&C 34:9, the Lord has told us that during this earthquake the stars will refuse to shine and that some will fall and great destructions await the wicked: "But before that great day [the second coming] shall come, the sun shall be darkened, and the moon be turned into blood; and the stars shall refuse their shining, and some will fall and great destructions await the wicked." (I.A.)

THE EARTH TREMBLES AND REELS TO AND FRO, THUNDERINGS, LIGHTNINGS, TEMPESTS, TIDAL WAVES AND FEAR

Another scripture that gives more insight into this worldwide earthquake is D&C 88:87-91. First, we are told why this earthquake will be felt worldwide. Then the Lord gives us added detail about the effects that will be upon nature because of such a massive earthquake: "For not many days hence and the earth shall tremble and reel to and fro as a drunken man; and the sun shall hide his face, and shall refuse to give light; and the moon shall be bathed in blood; and the stars shall become exceedingly angry, and shall cast themselves down as a fig that falleth from off a fig-tree. And after your testimony [the missionaries] cometh wrath and indignation upon the people. For after your testimony cometh the testimony of earthquakes, that shall cause groanings in the midst of her, and men shall fall upon the ground and shall not be able to stand. And also cometh the testimony of the voice of thunderings, and the voice of lightnings, and the voice of tempests, and the voice of waves of the sea heaving themselves beyong their bounds. And all things shall be in commotion; and surely, men's hearts shall fail them; for fear shall come upon all people." (I.A.)

So during this earthquake that takes place in the sixth time period, the earth will tremble and reel to and fro. To "reel" means to sway, stagger or whirl. The worldwide earthquake will be caused by the earth trembling and reeling to and fro. Along with the quaking, there will be thunderings, lightnings, tempests or violent storms, tidal waves and fear upon all people. There are different degrees of fear ranging from being alarmed or frightened to experiencing debilitating panic and terror. While these convulsions in nature may be frightening to the saints, those who are prepared will receive comfort from the Lord. (D&C 38:30) This preparation should include an understanding of the scriptures so that we know what will be happening in the future. By understanding the prophesies, we can eliminate the fear of the unknown and be better prepared emotionally to cope with the challenges. To become spiritually prepared, we need to be trying to live righteously to be worthy to receive the comfort we will need from the Holy Ghost. Being physically prepared will require that we have stored a year's supply of food, clothing and fuel where possible along with some water, garden seeds and tools. The assurance and knowledge that we can take care of our basic needs with help from the Lord regardless of what happens can help alleviate panic and terror.

SIGNS IN HEAVEN AND IN THE EARTH, WEEPING AND WAILING, A HAILSTORM DESTROYS THE CROPS OF THE EARTH

D&C 29:14-16 is another scripture where the Lord forewarns us of this specific earthquake and also adds more details about what will happen on the earth during it: "But, behold, I say unto you that before this great day [the second coming] shall come the sun shall be darkened, and the moon shall be turned into blood, and the stars shall fall from heaven, and there shall be greater signs in heaven above and in the earth beneath; And there shall be weeping and wailing among the hosts of men; And there shall be a great hailstorm sent forth to destroy the crops of the earth." (I.A.)

What did God place in the heavens to give us signs? When the Lord was creating the lights in the heavens which are the sun, moon and stars, he said, "and let them be for signs". (Gen. 1:14, Moses 2:14, Abr. 4:14, I.A.) Needless to say, a worldwide earthquake would certainly cause weeping and wailing among mankind. When the crops of the earth are destroyed by a hailstorm, those who have been faithful in storing a year's supply of food will be very grateful that they did. When speaking of a hailstorm, that does not necessarily mean it will be ice hail. Often in the scriptures, hail refers to meteorite showers or stones as in the following verses: (These scriptures do not refer to this earthquake but are used as examples of meteorites.) "...the Lord sent thunder and hail, and the fire ran along the ground; and the Lord rained hail upon the land of Egypt. So there was hail, and fire mingled with the hail, very grievous," (Ex. 9:23-24, I.A.), "...the Lord cast down great stones from heaven upon them unto Azekah, and they died: they were more which died with hailstones than they whom the children of Israel slew with the sword." (Josh. 10:11, I.A.), "...and I will rain upon him,...an overflowing rain, and great hailstones, fire and brimstone." (Ezek. 38:22, I.A.), "...there followed hail and fire mingled with blood, and they were cast upon the earth: and the third part of the trees was burnt up, and all green grass was burnt up." (Rev. 8:7, I.A.) and finally, "And there fell upon men a great hail out of heaven, every stone about the weight of a talent [about 58 pounds]." (Rev. 16:21, I.A.)

Ice hail does not normally fall mingled with fire, but ignitable gases can accompany meteorites that can cause fire in the atmosphere and on the ground.

BLOOD, FIRE AND VAPORS OF SMOKE

Even more details about this earthquake are given in D&C 45:40-42: "And they shall see signs and wonders, for they shall be shown forth in the heavens above, and in the earth beneath. And they shall behold blood, and fire, and vapors of smoke. And before the day of the Lord come, the sun shall be darkened, and the moon be turned into blood, and the stars fall from heaven." (I.A.) The Lord has said that the signs in the heavens will be in the sun, moon and stars. (Luke 21:25) If red dust accompanies meteorite showers or covers the actual stones, then it can combine with moisture or water and look like blood. Gases can also fall during meteorite showers that can ignite in the atmosphere or on the earth and can start fires that in turn would cause vapors of smoke. These are some of the natural means that the Lord might use to bring to pass these signs. This scripture indicates that fire and smoke are included in the events surrounding this earthquake. So most likely the great hailstorm that destroys the crops of the earth (D&C 29:16) will be meteorites. If the stars falling to the earth are really "falling stars" or meteorites, then they could also be the hailstorm that will destroy the crops of the earth.

THOSE WHO CALL ON THE LORD WILL BE SAVED

Joel also prophesied of this same event. He counseled people to call on the name of the Lord to be delivered. "And I will shew wonders in the heavens and in the earth, blood, fire, and pillars of smoke. The sun shall be turned into darkness, and the moon into blood, before the great and the terrible day of the Lord come. And it shall come to pass, that whosoever shall call on the name of the Lord shall be delivered: for in mount Zion and in Jerusalem shall be deliverance, as the Lord hath said, and in the remnant whom the Lord shall call." (Joel 2:30-32, I.A.)

Peter quoted this prophecy of Joel and made some changes in it: "And I will shew wonders in heaven above, and signs in the earth beneath; blood, and fire, and vapour of smoke: The sun shall be turned into darkness, and the moon into blood, before that great and notable day of the Lord come: And it shall come to pass, that whosoever shall call on the name of the Lord shall be saved." (Acts 2:19-21, I.A.)

Even if some faithful saints die during the judgments that are coming, they will be saved in the kingdom of God. The Lord will deliver those who call on His name in faith.

THE POWERS OF HEAVEN WILL BE SHAKEN

The Lord has warned that at the time of this same event, the powers of heaven will be shaken. "Immediately after the tribulation of those days shall the sun be darkened, and the moon shall not give her light, and the stars shall fall from heaven, and the powers of the heavens shall be shaken:" (JS-M 1:33, I.A., Matt. 24:29) The Savior's words were recorded a little differently in Mark: "But in those days, after that tribulation, the sun shall be darkened, and the moon shall not give her light, And the stars of heaven shall fall, and the powers that are in heaven shall be shaken." (Mark 13:24-25, I.A.)

What are "the powers of heaven"? In Psalms we are told that the Lord created, "The sun to rule by day:...The moon and stars to rule by night:" (Ps. 136:8-9, I.A.) The visible powers of heaven that can be seen from the earth include the sun, moon, stars, planets, comets, meteorites, etc. The Lord will cause not only the earth to shake, but also the heavenly bodies will tremble. "...I will not only shake the earth, but the starry heavens shall tremble. For I, the Lord, have put forth my hand to exert the powers of heaven;" (D&C 84:118-119, I.A.) (See Chapter 5 for a discussion of other possible powers from the heavens that the Lord might exert.)

What will be the response of mankind to the powers of heaven being shaken by the Lord? "Men's hearts failing them for fear, and for looking after those things which are coming on the earth: for the powers of heaven shall be shaken." (Luke 21:26, I.A.)

When Jesus Christ died, there was great destruction in America. The description of what happened is very detailed and is similar to the worldwide earthquake and the accompanying signs that will transpire along with it. In 3 Nephi, Chapter 8, an account is given of tempests, earthquakes, fire, physical upheaval, thunder and lightning. Reading the chapter can enhance a person's understanding of the events that will take place in the sixth seal or time period.

THE SIGN OF THE SON OF MAN

DURING THE SIXTH SEAL

(BEFORE A.D. 2000)

THE HEAVENS ARE OPENED

Joseph Smith gave us an interesting insight into something else that will happen at about the same time as the earthquake when he clarified Revelation 6:14 for us in the Joseph Smith Translation: "And the heavens opened as a scroll is opened when it is rolled together," (I.A.).

So the heavens will be opened around the same time as the worldwide earthquake and heavenly signs take place. (Rev. 6:12-14) What does it mean to have "the heavens opened"? First of all, for the heavens to be opened, it must mean that normally they are closed. A veil is over the true heavens so that we cannot see what the real heavens look like unless they are "opened".

The following scriptures do not refer to the Sign of the Son of Man, but they do prove the existence of a veil. "But the day soon cometh that ye shall see me, and know that I am; for the veil of darkness shall soon be rent, and he that is not purified shall not abide the day." (D&C 38:8, I.A.) And "...immediately after shall the curtain of heaven be unfolded, as a scroll is unfolded after it is rolled up, and the face of the Lord shall be unveiled;" (D&C 88:95, I.A.). "And prepare for the revelation which is to come, when the veil of the covering of my temple, in my tabernacle, which hideth the earth, shall be taken off, and all flesh shall see me together." (D&C 101:23, I.A.)

Joseph Smith and Oliver Cowdery had the experience of having the veil taken from their eyes when they saw the Savior in the Kirtland Temple on April 3, 1836, "The veil was taken from our minds, and the eyes of our understanding were opened." (D&C 110:1, I.A.)

Because of the great faith and knowledge of the brother of Jared, the veil was withdrawn and he saw Jesus, "And because of the knowledge of this man he could not be kept from beholding within the veil;...Wherefore, having this perfect knowledge of God, he could not be kept from within the veil; therefore he saw Jesus; and he did minister unto him." (Ether 3:19-20, I.A.)

There is a veil of darkness over the earth that hides God and his angels from the view of mortals. Therefore, we do not see the heavens as they really are unless they are opened. The scriptures teach us that the heavens are often opened just before people see God, angels and visions. We live in a mortal or physical dimension. God dwells in an immortal or spiritual dimension. As marvelous as our eyes are, they are limited in what they can see. With the aid of a microscope, we can see things that are present but are impossible to view with the naked eye. With the aid of a telescope, we can see heavenly bodies in the sky that are beyond the normal ability of our eyes to see. With special help through the power of God, we can see into the spiritual dimension which is normally not within the range of vision of our mortal eyes. Sometimes, God causes an opening between the two dimensions. When that happens, a person sees an opening in the heavens and is able to view what is really there as the veil of darkness is temporarily rent or unfolded. It is interesting to note that prophets generally gaze "into" heaven during a vision rather than "up" to heaven.

John the Revelator compared what he saw when the heavens opened to looking like a rolled up scroll being opened. The following is an attempt to illustrate his description.

A ROLLED UP SCROLL

(THE HEAVENS ARE CLOSED)

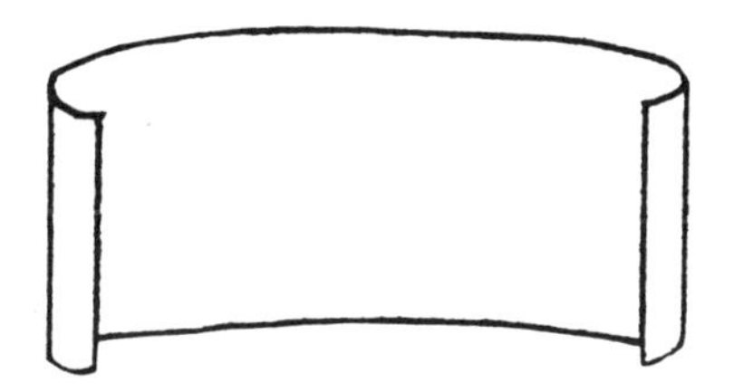

AN OPENED SCROLL

(THE HEAVENS ARE OPENED)

THE SIGNS OF THE LAST DAYS

To gain a better understanding of what happens when the heavens are opened, we will examine other times in the scriptures when this happens. Notice that right after the heavens are opened, a heavenly manifestation from God is seen. In these first three scriptures God is seen or heard when the veil is parted. "And Jesus, when he was baptized, went up straightway out of the water: and, lo, the heavens were opened unto him, and he saw the Spirit of God descending like a dove, and lighting upon him: And lo a voice from heaven saying, This is my beloved Son, in whom I am well pleased." (Matt. 3:16-17, I.A., and Mark 1:10-11, Luke 3:21-22) "Behold, I [Stephen] see the heavens opened, and the Son of Man standing on the right hand of God," (Acts 7:56, I.A.) Lehi "saw the heavens open, and he thought he saw God sitting upon his throne, surrounded with numberless concourses of angels..." (1 Ne. 1:8, I.A.).

In the next four scriptures, angels or visions are seen after the heavens are opened. Jesus said to Nathanael, "Hereafter ye shall see heaven open, and the angels of God ascending and descending upon the Son of Man." (John 1:51, I.A.) Nephi and Lehi "saw the heavens open; and angels came down out of heaven and ministered unto them." (Hel. 5:48, I.A.) Joseph Smith recorded, "The heavens were opened upon us, and I beheld the celestial kingdom of God," (D&C 137:1, I.A.). Peter said he "saw heaven opened" just before he received the vision of the great sheet with unclean animals on it representing the Gentiles. (Acts 10:11)

The armies of God were around the prophet Elisha and he could see them protecting him. When a mortal host of soldiers surrounded the city where Elisha and his servants were, the servant became concerned for their safety. Elisha prayed that his servant would be able to see what Elisha already could see which were the chariots of God around them: "Fear not, for they that be with us are more than they that be with them. And Elisha prayed, and said, Lord I pray thee, open his eyes, that he may see. And the Lord opened the eyes of the young man; and he saw: and, behold, the mountain wa full of horses and chariots of fire round about Elisha." (2 Kgs. 6:16-17, I.A.)

God can remove the veil so that men can see the true heavens whenever he chooses to. The Melchizedek

Priesthood holds the keys to the power to open the heavens, "The power and authority of the higher, or Melchizedek Priesthood, is to hold the keys of all the spiritual blessings of the church--To have the privilege of receiving the mysteries of the kingdom of heaven, to have the heavens opened unto them," (D&C 107:18-19, I.A.).

The heavens will be opened by the Lord near the time of the worldwide earthquake, but this time it will not just be prophets and their servants who will see God and his angels.

THE SIGN OF THE SON OF MAN IS SEEN IN THE HEAVENS

John the Revelator told us what would happen after the worldwide earthquake (Rev. 6:12-14) and after the heavens are opened (Rev. 6:14, JST Rev. 6:14), "And the kings of the earth, and the great men, and the rich men, and the chief captains, and the mighty men, and every bondman, and every free man, hid themselves in the dens and in the rocks of the mountains; And said to the mountains and rocks, Fall on us, and hide us from the face of him that sitteth on the throne, and from the wrath of the Lamb: For the great day of his wrath is come; and who shall be able to stand?" (Rev. 6:15-17, I.A.)

So every description of mankind will try to hide from the face of the Lamb or Jesus Christ, as they see Him sitting on His throne. This event is called the sign of the Son of Man.

In D&C 88:87-91, the Lord told us about the worldwide earthquake which is to take place after the missionaries are called home. Then in D&C 88:92-93, it says an angel will command the people of the earth to go out to see God just before this great sign is seen in heaven, "And angels shall fly through the midst of heaven, crying with a loud voice, sounding the trump of God, saying, Prepare ye, prepare ye, O inhabitants of the earth; for the judgment of our God is come. Behold, and lo, the Bridegroom cometh; go ye out to meet him. And immediately there shall appear a great sign in heaven, and all people shall see it together." (I.A.)

There are two other scriptures besides Revelation 6:12-17 and D&C 88:87-93 that describe the great event of the sun being darkened, the moon turning to blood or not giving her light and the stars appearing to fall from heaven followed by the sign of the Son of Man being seen. These two scriptures are JS-M 1:33-36 and Mark 13:24-26. This is what they teach us about the sign of the Son of Man: "And, as I said before, after the tribulation of those days, and the powers of the heavens shall be shaken, then shall appear the sign of the Son of Man in heaven, and then shall all the tribes of the earth mourn; and they shall see the Son of Man coming in the clouds of heaven, with power and great glory;" (JS-M 1:36, I.A., and Matt. 24:50). "And then shall they see the Son of man coming in the clouds with great power and glory." (Mark 13:26, I.A., and Luke 21:27)

Who is "the Son of Man"? God the Father is also called "Man of Holiness". Jesus Christ is the Son of the "Man of Holiness" and is therefore the Son of Man: "...Man of Holiness is his name, and the name of his Only Begotten is the Son of Man, even Jesus Christ, a righteous Judge," (Moses 6:57, I.A.).

When the heavens are opened, there will appear a great sign. The sign will be that mankind will see Jesus Christ in the clouds of heaven. (For a discussion on the "clouds of heaven", see Chapter 5.) Does that mean that people will see the actual body of Jesus Christ or just the cloud that He is in? When the Lord talked to the brother of Jared, he saw the cloud but not the Lord: "...the Lord came down and talked with the brother of Jared; and he was in a cloud, and the brother of Jared saw him not." (Ether 2:4, I.A.) When Ezekiel saw the Lord, He saw Him in the air sitting on a throne, "...upon the likeness of the throne was the likeness as the appearance of a man above upon it. This was the appearance of the likeness of the glory of the Lord." (Ezek. 1:26, 28, I.A.)

During the sign of the Son of Man, the Lord is seen in the clouds of heaven, and apparently at least His face is visible as He sits on His throne for John saw in his vision that the people will exclaim, "...hide us from the face of him that sitteth on the throne, and from the wrath of the Lamb:" (Rev. 6:16,

I.A.)

President Wilford Woodruff also had a vision of this sign of the Son of Man. He was able to give us insight into something else which will be seen besides the Son of Man in the clouds of heaven: "I became wrapped in vision. I was like Paul; I did not know whether I was in the body or out of the body. A personage appeared to me and showed me the great scenes that should take place in the last days. One scene after another passed before me. I saw the sun darkened; I saw the moon become as blood; I saw the stars fall from heaven: I saw seven golden lamps set in the heavens, representing the various dispensations of God to man--a sign that would appear before the coming of Christ." (J.D. 22:332-333, I.A.)

Chapter 5 will include a discussion on the golden lamps that Ezekiel saw. It is probable that these same golden lamps will be seen when the sign of the Son of Man appears in heaven.

A man in Joseph Smith's day reported that he had seen the sign of the Son of Man as was foretold in the 24th Chapter of Matthew. Joseph Smith's reply was, "...he has not seen the sign of the Son of Man, as foretold by Jesus; neither has any man, nor will any man, until after the sun shall have been darkened and the moon bathed in blood; for the Lord hath not shown me any such sign;" (Teachings, p. 280)

Joseph Smith even knew what the world would have to say to explain away the sign of the Son of Man as a religious occurrence when it is seen in heaven: "There will be wars and rumors of wars, signs in the heavens above and on the earth beneath, the sun turned into darkness and the moon to blood, earthquakes in divers places, the seas heaving beyond their bounds; then will appear one grand sign of the Son of Man in heaven. But what will the world do? They will say it is a planet, a comet, etc. But the Son of Man will come as the sign of the coming of the Son of Man, which will be as the light of the morning cometh out of the east." (Teachings, pp. 286-287, I.A.)

The sign of the Son of Man will be seen coming out of the east. Is it any surprise that much of the world will try to explain away this great religious sign? In ancient America when the great heavenly signs were given of the birth of Jesus Christ, what did many of the people do? And "...the people began to forget those signs and wonders which they had heard, and began to be less and less astonished at a sign or wonder from heaven, insomuch that they began to be hard in their hearts, and blind in their minds, and began to disbelieve all which they had heard and seen--Imagining up some vain thing in their hearts, that it was wrought by men and by the power of the devil," (3 Ne. 2:1-2, I.A.)

Human nature has not changed much in almost two thousand years. Joseph Smith prophesied that many modern men when they see the sign of the Son of Man in heaven will likewise disbelieve that is is from God and try to explain it away.

The sign of the Son of Man is not the second coming of the Lord Jesus Christ. The sign of the Son of Man takes place in the sixth seal (Rev. 6:15-17) while the second coming occurs after a number of judgments and plagues in the beginning of the seventh seal or time period. (Rev. 19:11-16) But many people who do not understand the scriptures will mistakenly think that the worldwide earthquake along with Christ being seen in the heavens is the end of the world (Rev. 6:17, The Ensign, Oct. 1983, p. 52). The sign of the Son of Man is given as a warning to the world that Jesus Christ will come a second time in that generation when the sign is given. This warning is very necessary since the wicked will be burned when the Savior does return.

THE PARABLE OF THE FIG TREE

Immediately after the Savior tells of the sign of

the Son of Man being seen, we are commanded to learn the parable of the fig tree, "Now learn a parable of the fig tree; when his branch is yet tender, and putteth forth leaves, ye know that summer is nigh: So likewise ye, when ye shall see these things, know that it is near, even at the doors. Verily I say unto you, This generation shall not pass, till all things be fulfilled." (Matt. 24:32-34, and JS-M 1:38-39, Mark 13:28-29)

When we see the leaves of the fig tree shoot forth, we know that summer is coming. When we see these signs of the sun being darkened, the moon turning to blood or not giving her light, the stars falling from heaven, the powers of heaven being shaken and when the sign of the Son of Man is seen, we will know that the second coming is near. (Matt. 24:29-30, JS-M 1:33, 36, Mark 13:24-26)

The generation when these signs are given will not pass away before all of the prophesies about the return of the Savior have been fulfilled. (JS-M 1:34) In Luke, we are told that the generation when the times of the Gentiles is fulfilled, or when the missionaries are no longer sent to the Gentiles, will not pass away before all will be fulfilled: "And he spake to them a parable; Behold the fig tree, and all the trees; When they now shoot forth, ye see and know of your own selves that summer is now nigh at hand. So likewise ye, when ye see these things come to pass, know ye that the kingdom of God is nigh at hand. Verily I say unto you, The generation when the times of the Gentiles be fulfilled, shall not pass away till all be fulfilled." (Luke 21:29-32, JST Luke 21:32, I.A.)

The Lord always gives plenty of warning before the wicked are destroyed. This sign of the Son of Man is a warning to the entire world to repent because the Savior will be returning to the earth in that generation when the sign is given and the wicked will be burned.

5

WHAT IS A "CLOUD" FROM HEAVEN?

In the scriptures, prophets described what they saw when God appeared to them with terms from their own experience and time period. If the main mode of travel in their day was a chariot drawn by horses and they saw something traveling in the sky, they might describe it as a heavenly chariot drawn by horses since they would know of no other possible description of locomotion or travel. (For instance, isolated natives today, who know what a car is but have never heard of or seen an airplane, might when they see their first airplane call it "a flying car".) We have done the same thing today. We all know that a "ship" is a large, seagoing vessel. Yet, when someone sees an unknown vehicle in the sky that they cannot describe according to our known modes of travel, he might very well call it a "spaceship". In hearing that term, we would know that it was not really an actual "ship" in space but that "spaceship" describes an object that has the power to navigate in space.

Another way that the prophets could describe what they saw would be to look at the heavenly vehicle and describe it according to what it reminded them of or what it resembled. For instance, what God and angels travel in is variously called in the scriptures: a cloud of heaven, a chariot of fire, chariots like a whirlwind, a pillar of a cloud (by day), a pillar of fire (by night), a wheel within a wheel, a star and a flying roll. That is because it most closely resembled that to the particular prophet or person who saw it and because there are several shapes for these vehicles. Certainly, the prophet knew that a real cloud could not travel or fly, but what he saw resembled a cloud that could fly or navigate. Again, we have done something very similar today. A man saw an unknown vehicle that reminded him of two saucers put together. Therefore, he called it a "flying saucer". We all know that a saucer is a small dish and that a saucer does not have the ability to propel itself through space. Yet, when we hear the term, "flying saucer", we know that it means a space vehicle of unknown origin. In a thousand years, when someone reads our history, they might very well scratch their head and wonder what a "flying saucer" is.

There is a lot of controversy about Unidentified Flying Objects in our society today. Spurious and outlandish stories are circulated about contact with extra-terrestrials that add to the confusion. It is hard to determine the true experiences from the fabricated ones.

Some people might be offended by the thought that God might use a vehicle to travel in. They might think that would lessen the power of God in their minds. Certainly God is all-powerful and can travel however He chooses. Knowing what God travels in is not essential to our exaltation. However, if we gain a better understanding of certain descriptive phrases in the scriptures that have to do with God, then our comprehension of the written word is enhanced. The prophet Ezekiel gave us detailed definitions of such scriptural terms and phrases as: the spirit of the Lord, a cloud, lamps, wheels, cherubims, the voice of the Almighty and the glory of the Lord. Many of these words and phrases are used over again many times in the other books of scripture.

It is always a blessing any time we can gain a better understanding of the scriptures. We should always pursue truth and understanding; even if such discoveries can be shocking and are different from our previous conclusions. Some may prefer not to comprehend these terms. Those who want to understand will enjoy this Chapter.

THE PROPHET EZEKIEL

First, we will study what Ezekiel described as the vehicles that accompanied God when He appeared to him. Fortunately for us, Ezekiel was a stickler for detail. He tried his best in the vocabulary of his day to relate everything he saw when God appeared to him. There might be those who would question whether Ezekiel's writings are authentic and whether he really was a prophet. The Lord himself referred to the words of Ezekiel and called him a prophet. (D&C 29:21)

Ezekiel began by describing what he saw when God was still quite a distance away and was approaching him from the north: "And I looked, and, behold a whirlwind came out of the north, a great cloud, and a fire infolding itself, and a brightness was about it, and out of the midst thereof as the colour of amber, out of the midst of the fire." (Ezek. 1:4, I.A.) What Ezekiel saw resembled a whirlwind, a great cloud and a fire infolding itself. Then within the fire he saw something that was the color of amber which is a golden color.

THE LIKENESS OF CREATURES

As God came closer, Ezekiel saw what appeared to look like "lamps". (Ezek. 1:13) As the "lamps" came very close to him, Ezekiel gave us a detailed description of what were "the likeness of four living creatures". (Ezek. 1:5) All four of them looked alike, "Also out of the midst thereof came the likeness of four living creatures. And this was their appearance; they had the likeness of a man. And every one had four faces, and every one had four wings. And their feet were straight feet; and the sole of their feet was like the sole of a calf's foot: and they sparkled like the colour of burnished brass. And they had the hands of a man under their wings on their four sides; and they four had their faces and their wings. Their wings were joined one to another; they turned not when they went; they went every one straight forward. As for the likeness of their faces, they four had the face of a man, and the face of a lion, on the right side: and they four had the face of an ox on the left side; and they four had the face of an eagle." (Ezekiel 1:5-10, I.A.)

The following drawing is an attempt to recreate what Ezekiel saw according to his very precise description.

THE LIKENESS OF A LIVING CREATURE

(Ezekiel 1:5.)

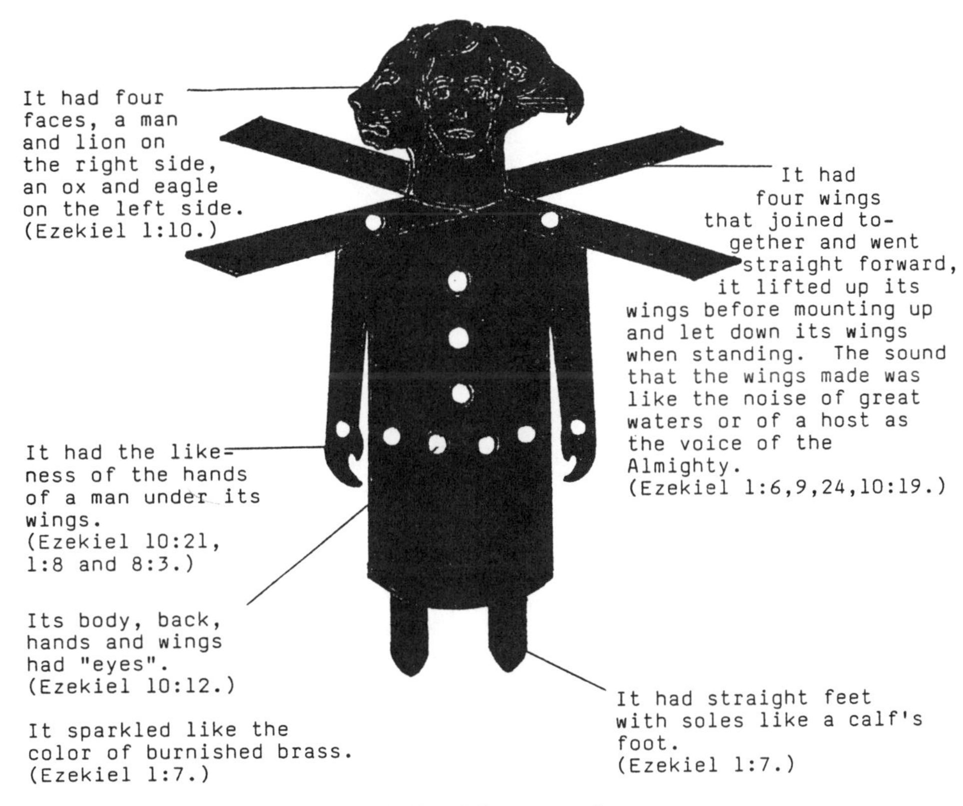

It had the likeness of a man.
(Ezekiel 1:5.)

The four faces of "the likeness of creatures" represented four different classes in the creations of God: a man (a child of God), a lion (the wild animals), an ox (the domestic animals) and an eagle (the birds). Ezekiel also said this about "the likeness of creatures": "And their whole body, and their backs, and their hands, and their wings,...were full of eyes round about," (Ezek. 10:12, I.A.).

Could the eyes that Ezekiel referred to have been round windows with light coming from them? These "creatures" could move, so naturally Ezekiel would think they were living because in his day of 592 B.C. only living things could move since they had no automation or machinery. Could the "creatures" that Ezekiel saw have been robots that resembled a man with four faces?

Joseph Smith made some interesting comments about our present translation of the Bible: "I am going to take exceptions to the present translation of the Bible in relation to these matters. Our latitude and longitude can be determined in the original Hebrew with far greater accuracy than in the English version. There is a grand distinction between the actual meaning of the prophets and the present translation. The prophets do not declare that they saw a beast or beasts, but that they saw the image or figure of a beast...The translation should have been rendered "image" instead of "beast", in every instance where beasts are mentioned by the prophets." (Teachings, pp. 290-291, I.A.) When Ezekiel said he said the likeness of a creature, could he have meant he saw the image or figure of a creature rather than a real, living creature?

A WHEEL WITHIN A WHEEL

Then Ezekiel described four wheels that all looked alike (Ezek. 1:16) that were attached to the four "creatures": "...and their appearance and their work was as it were a wheel in the middle of a wheel...As for their rings, they were so high that they were dreadful; and their rings were full of eyes round about them four." (Ezek. 1:16, 18, I.A.)

The prophet Ezekiel saw four wheels. Each looked like a wheel in the middle of a wheel, and the rings of the wheels were full of what looked like "eyes" all around the rings. The following is a drawing which attempts to represent one of the wheels that Ezekiel described.

THE WHEEL

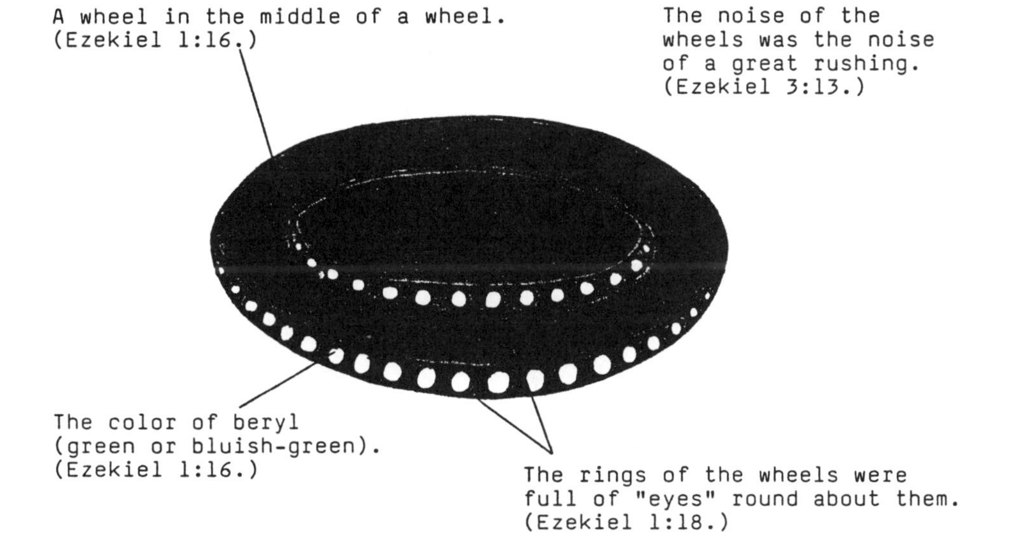
A wheel in the middle of a wheel.
(Ezekiel 1:16.)
The noise of the
wheels was the noise
of a great rushing.
(Ezekiel 3:13.)
The color of beryl
(green or bluish-green).
(Ezekiel 1:16.)
The rings of the wheels were
full of "eyes" round about them.
(Ezekiel 1:18.)

Each of the four wheels were attached to each of the four "creatures": "And when the living creatures went, the wheels went by them: and when the living creatures were lifted up from the earth, the wheels were lifted up." (Ezek. 1:19, I.A.)

The wheels were above the "creatures" because Ezekiel said the rings of the wheels were so high that they were dreadful. (Ezek. 1:18) The wheels were attached to the tops of the "creatures" because Ezekiel referred to them as being "over against them". (Ezek. 3:13) With the wheels attached above the "creatures", they reminded Ezekiel of "lamps": "And the likeness of the living creatures,--their appearance was like burning coals of fire, and like the appearance of lamps:" (Ezek. 1:13, I.A.).

President Wilford Woodruff also saw "lamps": "I saw seven golden lamps set in the heavens, representing the various dispensations of God to man--a sign that would appear before the coming of Christ." (J.D. 22:333, I.A.) It is possible to see how the wheels attached to the "creatures", if seen from a distance, could look like old-fashioned lamps especially if light came out of the "eyes" or windows.

THE CHERUBIMS

Ezekiel called "the likeness of living creatures" the cherubims: "This is the living creature that I saw under the God of Israel by the river of Chebar; and I knew that they were the cherubims." (Ezek. 10:20, I.A.) Cherubims is the plural form of the word cherub. The following drawing is an attempt to recreate what Ezekiel described as "cherubims".

A CHERUB

(Four of these were called the Cherubims.)
(Ezekiel 10:20.)

It appeared to look like a lamp.
(Ekekiel 1:13.)

Ezekiel gave us a description of these cherubims mounting up from the earth: "...and when the cherubims lifted up their wings to mount up from the earth, the same wheels also turned not from beside them." (Ezek. 10:16, I.A.) "And the cherubims lifted up their wings, and mounted up from the earth in my sight: when they went out, the wheels were beside them," (Ezek. 10:19, I.A.).

Cherubims were placed by the garden of Eden to keep Adam and Eve from partaking of the tree of life: "So he drove out the man; and he placed at the east of the garden of Eden Cherubims, and a flaming sword which turned every way, to keep the way of the tree of life." (Gen. 3:24, I.A.)

David wrote a psalm of thanksgiving to the Lord for his mighty and powerful deliverance: "In my distress I called upon the Lord, and cried to my God: and he did hear my voice out of his temple, and my cry did enter his ears. Then the earth shook and trembled; the foundations of heaven moved and shook, because he was wroth. There went up a smoke out of his nostrils, and fire out of his mouth devoured: coals were kindled by it. And he rode upon a cherub, and did fly: and he was seen upon the wings of the wind." (2 Sam. 22:7-9, 11, I.A. and Psalm 18:6-10)

COALS OF FIRE

On one occasion when Ezekiel saw the cherubims, a man in linen was commanded by God to obtain coals of fire from under the cherubims: "And he spake unto the man with linen, and said, Go in between the wheels, even under the cherub, and fill thine hands with coals of fire from between the cherubims, and scatter them over the city. And he went in in my sight. And it came to pass, that when he had commanded the man clothed with linen, saying, Take fire from between the wheels, from between the cherubims; then he went in, and stood beside the wheels. And one cherub stretched forth his hand from between the cherubims unto the fire that was between the cherubims, and took thereof, and put it into the hands of him that was clothed with linen: who took it, and went out." (Ezek. 10:2, 6-7, I.A.)

It is possible that the cherubims generated great heat when they landed and mounted up which caused coals of fire to be underneath them.

THE SPIRIT WAS IN THE WHEELS

It is important in understanding certain scriptures to discover the meaning and definition of particular phrases used by the prophets. "In the spirit" is used a number a times in the scriptures,and Ezekiel explains what that phrase means: "Whithersoever the spirit was to go, they went, thither was their spirit to go, and the wheels were lifted up over against them: for the spirit of the living creatures was in the wheels. When those went, these went; and when those stood, these stood; and when those were ifted up from the earth, the wheels were lifted up over against them: for the spirit of the living creatures was in the wheels." (Ezek. 1:20-21, I.A.)

Certainly, Ezekiel knew that the life or power of the human body comes from the spirit of man inside of it. He could see that the life or power of these "creatures" or cherubims was in the wheels. So later on when Ezekiel reported that "the spirit" took him up, he also meant that the wheels took him up, for the spirit was in the wheels. These five scriptures are about several experiences that Ezekiel had of being taken up in the wheels. "Then the spirit took me up,...So the spirit lifted me up, and took me away, and I went in bitterness, in the heat of my spirit; but the hand of the Lord was strong upon me." (Ezek. 3:12, 14, I.A.) "And he put forth the form of an hand, and took me by a lock of mine head [the cherub did]; and the spirit lifted me up between the earth and the heaven, and brought me in the visions of God to Jerusalem, to the door of the inner gate that looketh toward the north;" (Ezek. 8:3, I.A.). "Moreover the spirit took me up, and brought me unto the last gate" (Ezek. 11:1, I.A.). "Afterwards the spirit took me up, and brought me in a vision by the Spirit of God into Chaldea," (Ezek. 11:24, I.A.). And "...the hand of the Lord was upon me, and brought me thither. In the visions of God brought he me into the land of Israel, and set me upon a very high mountain," (Ezek. 40:1-2, I.A.).

Other prophets have used the same words to describe what happened to them when they were taken up by the spirit. Obadiah said this to the prophet Elijah: "...the Spirit of the Lord shall carry thee whither I know not;" (1 Kgs. 18:12, I.A.). After Elijah was taken into heaven, the mantle of prophet fell upon Elisha. The son of the prophets wanted to make sure Elisha was now the prophet by searching around for Elijah in case the Spirit had returned him to the earth: "...lest peradventure the Spirit of the Lord hath taken him [Elijah] up, and cast him upon some mountain, or into some valley." (2 Kgs. 2:16, I.A.)

During the creation of the earth, "The earth was without form, and void; and darkness was upon the face of the deep. And the Spirit of God moved upon the face of the waters." (Gen. 1:2, I.A., and Moses 2:2, 6:64-65) "And the earth, after it was formed, was empty and desolate,...and darkness reigned upon the face of the deep, and the Spirit of the Gods was brooding upon the face of the waters." (Abr. 4:2, I.A.)

Anciently, Samson was to help free Israel from their bondage to the Philistines. The scriptures record that he received his miraculous strength from the Spirit of the Lord. (Judg. 13:24-25) On three occasions, it was the Spirit of the Lord that strengthened Samson: "And the Spirit of the Lord came mightily upon him [Samson], and he rent him [a young lion]" (Judg. 14:6, I.A.). "And the Spirit of the Lord came upon him [Samson], and he went down to Ashkelon, and slew thirty men" (Judg. 14:19, I.A.). Again "the Spirit of the Lord came mightily upon him [Samson], and the cords that were upon his arms became as flax that was burnt with fire, and his bands loosed from off his hands." (Judg. 15:14, I.A.)

When Jesus was baptized, the voice of Heavenly Father was heard, the Holy Ghost descended in the sign of the dove: "And immediately the Spirit driveth him [Jesus] into the wilderness." (Mark 1:12, I.A.) "And immediately the Spirit took him into the wilderness." (JST Mark 1:10, I.A.) "Then was Jesus led up of the Spirit into the wilderness to be with God." (JST Matt. 4:1, I.A.) So the Spirit drove or took Jesus into the wilderness to be with God. The following are two accounts of the Spirit setting Jesus upon the pinnacle of the temple: "Then Jesus was taken up into the holy city, and the Spirit setteth him on the pinnacle of the temple." (JST Matt. 4:5, I.A.) "And the Spirit brought him to Jerusalem, and set him on a pinnacle of the temple. And the devil came unto him," (JST Luke 4:9, I.A.). Then Jesus was in the Spirit and it took Him to a high mountain where he beheld all the glorious kingdoms of the world. Following are two different accounts of what happened: "And again, Jesus was in the Spirit, and it taketh him up into an exceeding high mountain, and sheweth him all the kingdoms of the world, and the glory of them;" (JST Matt. 4:8, I.A.). "And the Spirit taketh him up into a high mountain, and he beheld all the kingdoms of the world in a moment of time." (JST Luke 4:5, I.A.)

When John the Revelator received his great vision for the seven churches, this is what he records as happening first: "I was in the Spirit on the Lord's day, and heard behind me a great voice, as of a trumpet," (Rev. 1:10, I.A.). During the vision that John received, the Lord referred to Himself as having seven Spirits of God: "These things saith he that hath the seven Spirits of God, and the seven stars;" (Rev. 3:1, I.A. and Rev. 1:20) Another time John saw a door opened in heaven and is then taken into the spirit: "After this I looked, and, behold, a door was opened in heaven: and the first voice which I heard was as it were of a trumpet talking with me; which said, Come up hither, and I will shew thee things which must be hereafter. And immediately I was in the spirit: and, behold, a throne was set in heaven, and one sat on the throne...and there were seven lamps of fire burning before the throne, which are the seven Spirits of God." (Rev. 4:1-2, 5, I.A.) On one occasion, John was taken into the wilderness by the spirit: "So he carried me away in the spirit into the wilderness." (Rev. 17:3, I.A.) Another time the spirit takes John to a high mountain: "And he carried me away in the spirit to a great and high mountain," (Rev. 21:10, I.A.).

When Nephi was desiring to see the things that his father, Lehi, had seen, this happened to him: "...as I sat pondering in my heart I was caught away in the Spirit of the Lord, yea, into an exceeding high mountain, which I never had before seen, and upon which I never had before set my foot." (I Nephi 11:1, I.A.) While Nephi was on the mountain, he saw Mary, the mother of the Lord Jesus Christ: "...I beheld that she was carried away in the Spirit; and after she had been carried away in the Spirit for the space of a time the angel spake unto me, saying: Look! And I looked and beheld the virgin again, bearing a child in her arms. And the angel said unto me: Behold the Lamb of God, yea, even the Son of the Eternal Father!" (1 Ne. 11:19-21, I.A.) Nephi also saw twelve others following the Lamb: "And I also beheld twelve others following him. And it came to pass that they were carried away in the Spirit from before my face, and I saw them not." (1 Ne. 11:29, I.A.) This is what Nephi recorded at the end of his narration of the vision: "And now I make an end of speaking concerning the things which I saw while I was carried away in the spirit;" (1 Ne. 14:30, I.A.). Later, Nephi commented about the experiences he had enjoyed when his body was carried away by the Spirit to high mountains: "And upon the wings of his Spirit hath my body been carried away upon exceedingly high mountains." (2 Ne. 4:25, I.A.)

The following scripture was written about Alma the younger. When he disappeared, the church members felt that the same thing had happened to Alma as happened to Moses. Moses was translated. (Matt. 17:3-4, HC 3:387) About Alma, "the saying went abroad in the church that he was taken up by the Spirit, or buried by the hand of the Lord, even as Moses." (Alma 45:19, I.A.)

When Enoch received his call as a prophet, the Spirit came down from heaven and remained upon him: "And it came to pass that Enoch journeyed in the land, among the people; and as he journeyed, the Spirit of God descended out of heaven, and abode upon him. And he heard a voice from heaven, saying: Enoch, my son," (Moses 6:26-27, I.A.).

Joseph F. Smith recorded that the Spirit of the Lord rested upon him when he saw the hosts of the dead: "As I pondered over these things which are written, the eyes of my understanding were opened, and the Spirit of the Lord rested upon me, and I saw the hosts of the dead, both small and great." (D&C 138:11, I.A.)

From ancient times to our day, prophets have been carried away by the Spirit of the Lord most often to high mountains probably for privacy and seclusion.

THE SPEED OF THE CHERUBIMS

How fast did the cherubims or "the likeness of living creatures" go that were attached to the wheels? Ezekiel likened their speed to a flash of lightning, "And the living creatures ran and returned as the appearance of of a flash of lightning." (Ezek. 1:14,

I.A.) We do not know of any creatures that are alive that can travel as fast as lightning. This scripture lends credence to the supposition that these cherubims were heavenly vehicles and not really living creatures.

THE NOISE OF THEIR WINGS--
AS THE VOICE OF THE ALMIGHTY

We know that God has the voice of a man. At Christ's appearance to the Nephites, they were privileged to hear the voice of Heavenly Father: "...they heard a voice as if it came out of heaven;...it was not a harsh voice, neither was it a loud voice; nevertheless, and notwithstanding it being a small voice it did pierce them that did hear it to the center," (3 Ne. 11:3, I.A.). This scripture plainly teaches us that God's voice has tremendous influence upon the spirits of men but that His voice is not a loud voice.

Ezekiel said that the wings of the cherubims made a noise. Then he likened that noise to the voice of the Almighty because God was present when he heard the noise: "And when they [the cherubims] went, I heard the noise of their wings, like the noise of great waters, as the voice of the Almighty, the voice of speech, as the noise of a host: when they stood, they let down their wings." (Ezek. 1:24, I.A.)

So Ezekiel said that the noise of the cherubims' wings was like the noise of great waters or of a host which was as the voice of the Almighty. He calls the noise of their wings the voice of the Almighty because the great noise was heard when God was above him. The wings of the cherubims made a noise that was similar to the noise made from great waters. That could mean the sound of the ocean or of waterfalls, etc. But the wheels also made a noise: "I heard the noise of the wings of the living creatures that touched one another, and the noise of the wheels over against them, and a noise of a great rushing:" (Ezek. 3:13, I.A.). So the wheels made a great rushing noise. Because of the wheels being attached to the "creatures", the two noises could combine to sound like the rushing of great waters. On April 3, 1836, Joseph Smith and Oliver Cowdery saw the Savior in the Kirtland Temple and described what they heard: "...and his voice was as the sound of the rushing of great waters, even the voice of Jehovah," (D&C 110:3, I.A.).

John the Revelator heard the same noise when he had the vision of the seven churches. He described the Savior and then recorded what he heard: "...and his voice as the sound of many waters." (Rev. 1:15, I.A.) Later on when John was given the vision of the latter-days, he again described what he heard from heaven. He said that it also sounded like great thunder, "And I heard a voice from heaven, as the voice of many waters, and as the voice of a great thunder:" (Rev. 14:2, I.A.). Again John heard this noise and likened it to the sound that a great multitude would make. In the midst of this great noise he heard a proclamation: "And I heard as it were the voice of a great multitude, and as the voice of many waters, and as the voice of mighty thunderings, saying, Alleluia: for the Lord God Omnipotent reigneth." (Rev. 19:6, I.A.)

Those who are present at the second coming of Christ will be privileged to hear the same great noise that many prophets have heard. This sound will be heard by all people and will break down the mountains of the earth. "And he shall utter his voice out of Zion, and he shall speak from Jerusalem, and his voice shall be heard among all people; And it shall be a voice as the voice of many waters, and as the voice of a great thunder, which shall break down the mountains, and the valleys shall not be found." (D&C 133:21-22, I.A.)

THE GLORY OF THE LORD

After writing a thorough description of the cherubims, the prophet Ezekiel described in detail what he saw above these cherubims: "And there was a voice from the firmament that was over their [the cherubims] heads, when they stood, and had let down their wings. And above the firmament that was over their heads was the likeness of a throne, as the appearance of a sapphire stone: and upon the likeness of the throne was the likeness as the appearance of a man above upon it. And I saw the colour of amber, as the appearance of fire round about within it, from the appearance of his loins even upward, and from the appearance of his loins even downward, I saw as it were the appearance of fire, and it had brightness round about. As the appearance of the bow that is in the cloud in the day of rain, so was the appearance of the brightness round about. This was the appearance of the likeness of the glory of the Lord. And when I saw it, I fell on my face, and I heard a voice of one that spake." (Ezek. 1:25-28, I.A.)

Ezekiel related that above the four cherubims in the firmament or sky, he saw what looked similar to a throne which had the appearance of a sapphire stone. A glorious man was on the throne. Within what looked like a sapphire stone was the color of amber like fire all around the man. Round about what looked like a sapphire stone was the appearance of brightness like the colors that are in a rainbow. He called what he saw "the glory of the Lord" and referred to it later on as that and so have many other prophets. Those who do not believe that God has a form like a man must have a difficult time explaining what Ezekiel saw because the prophet is so precise in his description of a glorious man.

The following is an attempt to recreate the description of "the glory of the Lord" given by the prophet Ezekiel.

THE GLORY OF THE LORD
(Ezekiel 1:28.)

It was located in the firmament or sky above the cherubims. (Ezekiel 1:26,10:1.)

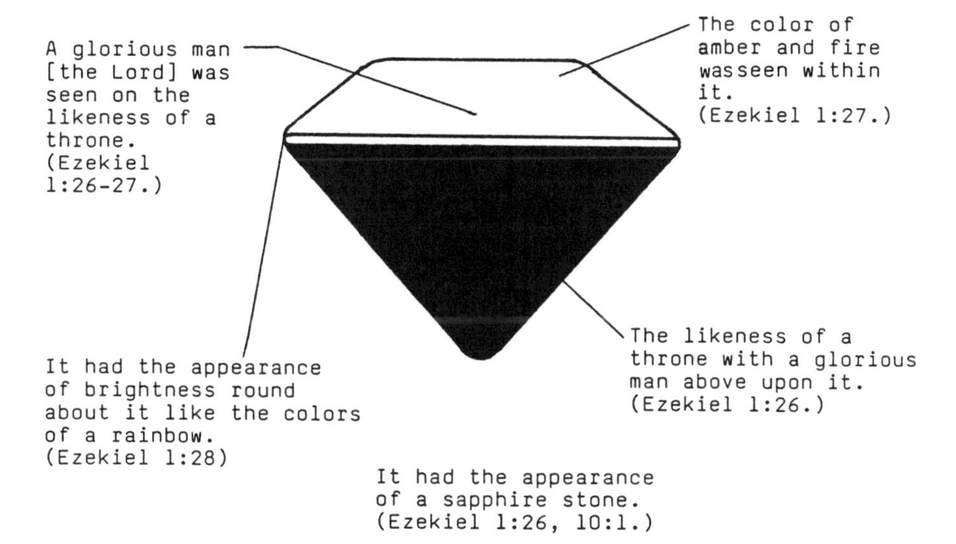

It had the appearance of a sapphire stone. (Ezekiel 1:26, 10:1.)

WHAT IS A "CLOUD" FROM HEAVEN?

It is possible that the Sign of the Son of Man will be seven cherubims set in the heavens with the glory of the Lord above them in the sky. Ezekiel said the cherubims looked like lamps when they were seen from a distance. (Ezek. 1:13) In all probability, the seven golden lamps that President Wilford Woodruff saw in vision that were set in the heavens representing the dispensations of God to man, were seven cherubims. (J.D. 22:333) The glory of the Lord could very well be what mankind will see when they behold the Lamb on the throne. (Rev. 6:16)

Ezekiel saw the glory of the Lord when he went to the plain. It was the same thing that he saw in his first vision by the river of Chebar. "Then I arose, and went forth into the plain: and, behold, the glory of the Lord stood there, as the glory which I saw by the river of Chebar: and I fell on my face." (Ezek. 3:23, I.A.) Again Ezekiel saw it, but this time he called it "the glory of the God of Israel": "...the spirit lifted me up between the earth and the heaven, and brought me in the visions of God to Jerusalem,...And, behold, the glory of the God of Israel was there, according to the vision that I saw in the plain." (Ezek. 8:3-4, I.A.) The glory of the Lord was above the cherub and then it moved to the threshold of the house in Jerusalem: "And the glory of the God of Israel was gone up from the cherub, whereupon he was, to the threshold of the house." (Ezek. 9:3, I.A.)

In the following scripture, Ezekiel called the glory of the Lord a cloud. The cloud must be large because it filled the house. The glory of the Lord left the cherub and went to the house and then went and stood over the cherubims before they mounted up from the earth. "Then I looked, and, behold, in the firmament that was above the head of the cherubims there appeared over them as it were a sapphire stone, as the appearance of the likeness of a throne. Then the glory of the Lord went up from the cherub, and stood over the threshold of the house; and the house was filled with the cloud, and the court was full of the brightness of the Lord's glory. Then the glory of the Lord departed from off the threshold of the house, and stood over the cherubims. And the cherubims lifted up there wings, and mounted up from the earth in my sight:" (Ezek. 10:1, 4, 18-19, I.A. and Ps. 99:1-2).

Another time Ezekiel saw the glory of the Lord go from the midst of the city until it stood upon a mountain to the east of him, "Then did the cherubims lift up their wings, and the wheels beside them; and the glory of the God of Israel was over them above. And the glory of the Lord went up from the midst of the city, and stood upon the mountain which is on the east side of the city." (Ezek. 11:22-23, I.A.) Ezekiel saw the glory of the Lord coming from the east on another occasion. He again heard the noise of many waters. The brightness of the glory of the Lord shown down upon the earth. The glory of the Lord entered the temple through the east gate and filled the house: "And, behold, the glory of the God of Israel came from the way of the east: and his voice was like a noise of many waters: and the earth shined with his glory. And the glory of the Lord came into the house by the way of the gate whose prospect is toward the east. So the spirit took me up, and brought me into the inner court; and, behold, the glory of the Lord filled the house." (Ezek. 43:2, 4-5, I.A.)

There are many other scriptures that refer to "the glory of the Lord". It is spoken of in the Old and New Testaments of the Bible and also in the Book of Mormon, the Doctrine and Covenants and the Pearl of Great Price.

The children of Israel complained to Moses about being hungry, and he promised them that they would see the glory of the Lord in the morning. After they saw the glory of the Lord toward the wilderness, they found quail to eat that evening and the next morning there was manna on the ground (Ex. 16:4-15): "And in the morning, then ye shall see the glory of the Lord;...As Aaron spake unto the whole congregation of the children of Israel, that they looked toward the wilderness, and, behold, the glory of the Lord appeared in the cloud." (Ex. 16:7, 10, I.A.)

Moses also used the phrase "the glory of the Lord" interchangeably with the word "cloud". The cloud was on Mount Sinai for a week. On the seventh day, Moses entered the cloud. The glory of the Lord is like devouring fire as the children of Israel gaze at it: "And Moses went up into the mount, and a cloud covered the mount. And the glory of the Lord abode upon mount Sinai, and the cloud covered if six days: and the seventh day he called Moses out of the midst of the cloud. And the sight of the glory of the Lord was like devouring fire on the top of the mount in the eyes of the children of Israel. And Moses went up into the midst of the cloud," (Ex. 24:15-18, I.A.).

When Moses finished the tabernacle and spread a tent over the top of the pillars, it was filled with the glory of the Lord, "Then a cloud covered the tent of the congregation, and the glory of the Lord filled the tabernacle. And Moses was not able to enter the tent of the congregation, because the cloud abode thereon, and the glory of the Lord filled the tabernacle." (Ex. 40:34-35, I.A.) Moses told Aaron and his sons to prepare an offering because the Lord would appear to them. They prepared the offering. The people could see the glory of the Lord and then fire came out from the glory of the Lord and consumed the offering. This showed the Lord's acceptance of the offering: "And Moses said, This is the thing which the Lord commanded that ye should do: and the glory of the Lord shall appear unto you. And Moses and Aaron went into the tablernacle of the congregation, and came out, and blessed the people; and the glory of the Lord appeared unto all the people. And there came a fire out from before the Lord, and consumed upon the altar the burnt offering and the fat: which when all the people saw, they shouted, and fell on their faces." (Lev. 9:6, 23-24, I.A.)

At the time when the Israelites were murmuring about having to go up against the giants in order to possess the promised land, the glory of the Lord appeared and the Lord told Moses that they would be in the wilderness for forty years, "And the glory of the Lord appeared in the tabernacle of the congregation before all the children of Israel." (Num. 14:10, I.A.)

When Solomon finished the temple, there was a great celebration which culminated in the appearance of the glory of the Lord, "...then the house was filled with a cloud, even the house of the Lord; So that the priests could not stand to minister by reason of the cloud: for the glory of the Lord had filled the house of God." (2 Chr. 5:13-14, I.A.) Solomon made a sacrifice to the Lord and the glory of the Lord appeared and the sacrifice was accepted. The people worshipped: "Now when Solomon had made an end of praying, the fire came down from heaven, and consumed the burnt offering and the sacrifices; and the glory of the Lord filled the house. And the priests could not enter into the house of the Lord, because the glory of the Lord filled the house. And when all the children of Israel saw how fire came down, and the glory of the Lord upon the house, they bowed themselves with their faces to the ground...and worshipped," (2 Chr. 7:1-3, I.A.).

In the last days when the desert will blossom like a rose, the people will be privileged to see the glory of the Lord again, "...the desert shall rejoice, and blossom as the rose...they shall see the glory of the Lord, and the excellency of our God." (Isa. 35:1-2, I.A.)

When the Savior comes again, all people will see the glory of the Lord, "And the glory of the Lord shall be revealed, and all flesh shall see it together: for the mouth of the Lord hath spoken it." (Isa. 40:5, I.A.)

Isaiah prophesied that although there will be gross darkness upon the earth during the last days, the glory of the Lord will be seen, "Arise, shine; for thy light is come, and the glory of the Lord is risen upon thee. For, behold, the darkness shall cover the earth, and gross darkness the people: but the Lord shall arise upon thee, and his glory shall be seen upon thee." (Isa. 60:1-2, I.A.)

The humble shepherds saw the glory of the Lord when Jesus was born, "And, lo, the angel of the Lord came upon them, and the glory of the Lord shone round about them: and they were sore afraid." (Luke 2:9, I.A.)

Just before Stephen was stoned to death, he saw God, "But he, being full of the Holy Ghost, looking up steadfastly into heaven, and saw the glory of God, and Jesus standing on the right hand of God, And said, Behold, I see the heavens opened, and the Son of man standing on the right hand of God." (Acts 7:55-56, I.A.)

When the Lord comes to dwell with his people in the New Jerusalem, the glory of the Lord and the Lamb will be the light of the city: "And the city had no need of the sun, neither of the moon, to shine in it: for the glory of God did lighten it, and the Lamb is the light thereof." (Rev. 21:23, I.A.)

Jesus made this promise to the translated Three Nephites about what would happen to them when He comes a second time: "And ye shall never endure the pains of death; but when I shall come in my glory ye shall be changed in the twinkling of an eye from mortality to immortality;" (3 Ne. 28:8, I.A.).

As Joseph Smith and Sidney Rigdon received the momentous vision of the three degrees of glory, they saw the glory of the Lord with Jesus standing on the right hand of Heavenly Father and also angels worshiping before their throne: "And while we meditated upon these things, the Lord touched the eyes of our understandings and they were opened, and the glory of the Lord shone round about. And we beheld the glory of the Son, on the right hand of the Father, and received of his fulness. And saw the holy angels, and them who are sanctified before his throne, worshiping God, and the Lamb, who worship him forever and ever." (D&C 76:19-21, I.A.)

The Lord referred to what He told His ancient disciples during His earthly ministry in the following scripture. He told them what He would come in when He returns again to the earth, "As ye have asked of me concerning the signs of my coming, in the day when I shall come in my glory in the clouds of heaven," (D&C 45:16, I.A.).

In the last days, when the wicked are fighting among themselves, the glory of the Lord will be at the New Jerusalem which will terrify the wicked and keep them away from Zion: "And the glory of the Lord shall be there, and the terror of the Lord also shall be there, insomuch that the wicked will not come unto it, and it shall be called Zion." (D&C 45:67, I.A.)

Again, the Lord foretold that the glory of the Lord would be in Zion. The righteous will gather to Zion while the wicked will tremble at Zion's terrible ones, "For, behold, I say unto you that Zion shall flourish, and the glory of the Lord shall be upon her; And she shall be an ensign unto the people, and there shall come unto her out of every nation under heaven. And the day shall come when the nations shall tremble because of her, and shall fear because of her terrible ones. The Lord hath spoken it." (D&C 64:41-43, I.A.)

The Lord promised that a cloud would rest upon the temple at the New Jerusalem. He affirmed that the cloud will be the glory of the Lord: "For verily this generation shall not all pass away until an house shall be built unto the Lord, and a cloud shall rest upon it, which cloud shall be even the glory of the Lord, which shall fill the house." (D&C 84:5, I.A.) But the Lord warned that his glory will not rest upon a temple that is defiled, "And inasmuch as my people build a house unto me in the name of the Lord, and do not suffer any unclean thing to come into it, that it be not defiled, my glory shall rest upon it;" (D&C 97:15, I.A.).

On March 27, 1836, in the dedicatory prayer of the Kirtland Temple, Joseph Smith prayed for the same blessings that were given on the day of Pentecost to be given to them: "Let it be fulfilled upon them, as upon those on the day of Pentecost; let the gift of tongues be poured out upon thy people, even cloven tongues as of fire, and the interpretation thereof. And let thy house be filled, as with a rushing mighty wind, with thy glory." (D&C 109:36-37, I.A.) This request by Joseph Smith in the prayer was fulfilled on that same day that he made it: "Brother George A. Smith arose and began to prophesy, when a noise was heard like a rushing mighty wind, which filled the Temple, and all the congregation simultaneously arose, being moved upon by an invisible power; many began to speak in tongues and prophesy; others saw glorious visions; and beheld the Temple was filled with angels, which fact I declared to the congregation. The people of the neighborhood came running together (hearing an unusual sound within and seeing a bright light like a pillar of fire resting upon the Temple), and were astonished at what was taking place." (HC 2:428, I.A.)

When the glory of the Lord was upon Moses, it made it possible for him to endure the glorious person of God face to face: "The words of God, which he spake unto Moses at the time when Moses was caught up into an exceedingly high mountain, And he saw God face to face, and he talked with him, and the glory of God was upon Moses; therefore Moses could endure his presence. And the presence of God withdrew from Moses, that his glory was not upon Moses; and Moses was left unto himself. And as he was left unto himself, he fell unto the earth." (Moses 1:1-2, 9, I.A.)

So the glory of the Lord has been seen by people down through the ages, and it will once again be seen at the New Jerusalem and when the Savior returns again.

A PILLAR OF A CLOUD BY DAY, A PILLAR OF FIRE BY NIGHT

When the Lord was with the Israelites in the wilderness, what he traveled in looked like a pillar of a cloud during the light of day and a pillar of of fire when it was dark at night. We are probably talking about the same pillar, it just looked different at night than it did during the light of day. The following are scriptures about this pillar that accompanied the Israelites.

During the triumphant time when the Israelites were finally allowed to leave the captivity of Egypt, they were led by the pillar which also gave them light at night: "And the Lord went before them by day in a pillar of a cloud, to lead them the way; and by night in a pillar of fire to give them light; to go by day and night:" (Ex. 13:21, I.A.). When the Egyptian armies came to destroy the Israelites by the Red Sea, the pillar moved over between the Egyptians and the Israelites during the night while the Lord caused a strong wind all night that parted the sea and dried the path. The Lord also troubled the Egyptians: (Ex. 14:19-22) "And the angel of God, which went before the camp of Israel, removed and went behind them; and the pillar of the cloud went from before their face and stood behind them. And it came between the camp of the Egyptians and the camp of Israel; and it was a cloud and darkness to the Egyptians, but it gave light by night to the Israelites...And it came to pass, that in the morning watch the Lord looked unto the host of the Egyptians through the pillar of fire and of the cloud, and troubled the host of the Egyptians, And took off [footnote: OR bound] their chariot wheels," (Ex. 14:19, JST Ex. 14:20, Ex. 14:24-25, I.A.).

The Lord promised to come to Moses in a thick cloud, so that the people would know that Moses was a prophet forever. From then on the pillar of a cloud or pillar of fire is often referred to as just a cloud or fire, "And the Lord said unto Moses, Lo, I come unto thee in a thick cloud, that the people may hear when I speak with thee, and believe thee forever." (Ex. 19:9, I.A.) According to His promise, the Lord appeared to Moses in a thick cloud and when He descended on mount Sinai, it caused smoke and great quaking: "...there were thunders and lightnings, and a thick cloud upon the mount,...And mount Sinai was altogether on a smoke, because the Lord descended upon it in fire: and the smoke thereof ascended as the smoke of a furnace, and the whole mount quaked greatly." (Ex. 19:16, 18, I.A.) On one occasion when Moses entered the tabernacle, a cloudy pillar descended and stood at the door of the tabernacle, "And it came to pass, as Moses entered into the tabernacle, the cloudy pillar descended, and stood at the door of the tabernacle, and the Lord talked with Moses." (Ex. 33:9, I.A., and Ex. 34:5-6)

The cloud was seen for years by Israel in their travels in the wilderness, just as it will remain at the New Jerusalem when it is built: "For the cloud of the Lord was upon the tabernacle by day, and fire was on it by night, in the sight of all the house of Israel, throughout all their journeyings." (Ex. 40:38, I.A.) The Israelites learned obedience by resting when the cloud was on the tabernacle and traveling whenever the cloud left it: "And on the day that the tabernacle was reared up the cloud covered the tabernacle,...as it were the appearance of fire,...So it was alway: the cloud covered it by day, and the appearance of fire by night. And when the cloud was taken up from the tabernacle, then after that the children of Israel journeyed: and in the place where the cloud abode, there the children of Israel pitched their tents...as long as the cloud abode upon the tabernacle they rested in their tents. And when the cloud tarried long upon the tabernacle many days, then the children of Israel kept the charge of the Lord, and journeyed not...whether it was by day or by night that the cloud was taken up, they journeyed. Or whether it were two days, or a month, or a year, that the cloud tarried upon the tabernacle, remaining thereon, the children of Israel abode in their tents, and journeyed not:" (Num. 9:15-19, 21-22, I.A.).

The children of Israel marched in their different tribes as they followed the cloud from Sinai to Paran, "And it came to pass...that the cloud was taken up from off the tabernacle of the testimony. And the children of Israel took their journeys out of the wilderness of Sinai; and the cloud rested in the wilderness of Paran. And the cloud of the Lord was upon them by day." (Num. 10:11-12, 34, I.A.)

The Lord told Moses to choose seventy men to help him care for the people. The spirit rested upon them and they prophesied, "And the Lord came down in a cloud, and spake unto him, and took of the spirit that was upon him, and gave it unto the seventy elders: and it came to pass, that, when the spirit rested upon them, they prophesied, and did not cease." (Num. 11:25, I.A.)

Aaron and Miriam complained about Moses marrying an Ethiopian woman. They thought they were prophets like Moses was. The Lord was angry with them and promised to speak to Moses face to face. Miriam became leprous for one week, "And the Lord came down in the pillar of the cloud and stood in the door of the tabernacle, and called Aaron and Miriam: and they both came forth. And the anger of the Lord was kindled against them; and he departed. And the cloud departed from off the tabernacle; and behold, Miriam became leprous, white as snow:" (Num. 12:5, 9-10, I.A.).

The prophet Nehemiah rehersed the blessings that Israel had received from the Lord while they were in the wilderness, "Moreover thou leddest them in the day by a cloudy pillar; and in the night by a pillar of fire, to give them light in the way wherein they should go." (Neh. 9:12, I.A.)

The blessings of being led by the cloud and fire are recounted in this Psalm, "In the daytime also he led them with a cloud, and all night with a light of fire." (Ps. 78:14, I.A.)

Moses and the children of Israel saw the pillar of a cloud by day and the pillar of fire by night for forty years during their journeyings in the wilderness. The prophet Lehi also saw a pillar of fire when he received his first vision, "And it came to pass as he [Lehi] prayed unto the Lord, there came a pillar of fire and dwelt upon a rock before him;" (I

Ne. 1:6, I.A.).

God's pillar has also been seen in our day by Joseph Smith, "...I saw a pillar of light exactly over my head, above the brightness of the sun, which descended gradually until it fell upon me." (JS-H 1:16, I.A.) A pillar of fire was seen resting on the Kirtland Temple on March 27, 1836, the day the Temple was dedicated. (D&C 109) This was reminiscent of the Lord coming down when the Tabernacle was finished by Moses in the wilderness. (Ex. 40:34-35) The Lord also came to Solomon's Temple when it was completed. (1 Kgs. 8:10-11) At the Kirtland Temple, "a noise was heard like the sound of a rushing mighty wind, which filled the temple,...The people of the neighborhood came running together (hearing an unusual sound within and seeing a bright light like a pillar of fire resting upon the Temple), and were astonished at what was taking place." (HC 2:428, I.A.)

In 1877, President John Taylor was given a vision where he saw the foundations of the New Jerusalem being laid. He saw an immense pillar of a cloud hovering over the city as twelve men consecrated the cornerstones: "I saw myriads of angels hovering over them and around them and also an immense pillar of a cloud hover over them...And I saw some come who wore their temple robes to help build the Temple and the city and all the time I saw the great pillar of cloud hovering over the place." (Wilford Woodruff Journals, June 15, 1878, Church Historians Office, and Unpublished, 1:122)

Jesus told the prophet Joseph Smith that His apostles would stand at His right hand in a pillar of fire when He comes again, "...mine apostles, the Twelve which were with me in my ministry at Jerusalem, shall stand at my right hand at the day of the coming in a pillar of fire," (D&C 29:12, I.A.).

CLOUDS

There are many other scriptures that talk about clouds from the Lord. By studying them, we can learn much more about clouds from heaven. The following are scriptures from the Old Testament.

A "chamber" is an enclosed space. Beams from the Lord's chambers are seen in the waters. The Lord makes the clouds His "chariot". A chariot is a vehicle: "O Lord my God, thou art very great; thou art clothed with honor and majesty. Who layeth the beams of his chambers in the waters: who maketh the clouds his chariot; who walketh upon the wings of the wind:" (Ps. 104:1, 3, I.A.

The Lord will defend Zion with clouds over every dwelling place during the Millenium, "And the Lord will create upon every dwelling place of mount Zion, and upon her assemblies, a cloud and smoke by day, and the shining of a flaming fire by night: for upon all the glory shall be a defense." (Isa. 4:5, I.A. and 2 Ne. 14:5)

A psalm was written to the Lord who rides upon the heavens, whose excellency is over Israel and whose strength is in the clouds: "Sing unto God, ye kingdoms of the earth; O sing praises unto the Lord;...To him that rideth upon the heavens of heavens,...Ascribe ye strength unto God: his excellency is over Israel, and his strength is in the clouds. O God, thou art terrible out of thy holy places:" (Ps. 68:32-35, I.A.)

Isaiah warned Egypt that the Lord would ride upon a swift cloud and smite and destroy her, "Behold, the Lord rideth upon a swift cloud, and shall come into Egypt." (Isa. 19:1, I.A.)

Isaiah foresaw that the Gentiles would come to the Lord's temple. It will be asked, "Who are these that fly as a cloud"? "Who are these that fly as a cloud, and as doves to their windows?" (Isa. 60:8, I.A.)

WHAT IS A "CLOUD" FROM HEAVEN?

Jeremiah lamented for the wickedness of Israel and Judah and warned them to repent for the power of the Lord is great (Jer. 4): "Behold, he shall come up as clouds, and his chariots shall be as a whirlwind:" (Jer. 4:13, I.A.).

Daniel had a vision where he saw Jesus who would come in the clouds of heaven to Adam or the Ancient of days: "I saw in the night visions, and behold, one like the Son of Man came with the clouds of heaven, and came to the Ancient of days, and they brought him near before him." (Dan. 7:13, I.A.)

The following scriptures are about clouds being seen and witnessed to in the New Testament.

Jesus prophesied to His ancient disciples that He would come again and it would be said of Him: "Blessed is he who cometh in the name of the Lord, in the clouds of heaven, and all the holy angels with him." (JS-M 1:1, I.A.)

Those who give their lives for the Lord and the gospel will come on the Lord's right hand in a cloud when He returns: "For verily I say unto you, That he shall come; and he that layeth down his life for my sake and the gospel's, shall come with him, and shall be clothed with his glory in the cloud, on the right hand of the Son of Man." (JST Mark 8:43, I.A.)

The following three scriptures are about what happened to Peter, James and John on a high mountain when Jesus was transfigured before them. Moses and Elias appeared: "While he [Peter] yet spake, behold, a bright cloud overshadowed them: and behold a voice out of the cloud, which said, This is my beloved Son, in whom I am well pleased; hear ye him." (Matt. 17:5, I.A.) "And there was a cloud that overshadowed them: and a voice came out of the cloud, saying, This is my beloved Son: hear him." (Mark 9:7, I.A.) "While he [Peter] thus spake, there came a cloud, and overshadowed them: and they feared as they entered into the cloud, And there came a voice out of the cloud, saying, This is my beloved Son: hear him." (Luke 9:34-35, I.A.)

After the worldwide earthquake, the world will see the sign of the Son of man which is recorded in the following three scriptures: "...they shall see the Son of man coming in the clouds of heaven with power and great glory." (Matt. 24:30, I.A. and JS-M 1:36) "And then shall they see the Son of man coming in the clouds with great power and glory." (Mark 13:26, I.A.) Then shall they see the Son of man coming in a cloud with power and great glory." (Luke 21:27, I.A.)

When Jesus was on trial before Caiaphas, He was asked if He was the Son of God. This was His reply: "Hereafter shall ye see the Son of man sitting on the right hand of power, and coming in the clouds of heaven." (Matt. 26:64, I.A., Mark 14:62)

After spending forty days with His apostles after His resurrection, Jesus ascended into heaven when a cloud received Him out of their sight. The apostles were told by two angels that Jesus would come the second time in the same way that He had left: "And when he [the Lord] had spoken these things, while they beheld, he was taken up; and a cloud received him out of their sight. And while they looked stedfastly toward heaven as he went up, behold, two men stood by them in white apparel; Which also said, Ye men of Galilee, why stand ye gazing up into heaven? this same Jesus, which is taken up from you into heaven, shall so come in like manner as ye have seen him go into heaven." (Acts 1:9-11, I.A.)

At the second coming, the righteous who are alive will be caught up together into the clouds with the Lord in the air: "Then they who are alive, shall be caught up together into the clouds with them who remain [the dead], to meet the Lord in the air; and so shall we be ever with the Lord." (JST 1 Thes. 4:17, I.A.)

WHAT IS A "CLOUD" FROM HEAVEN?

John the Revelator spoke of the second coming of the Savior in these words: "For behold, he cometh in the clouds with ten thousand of his saints in the kingdom, clothed with the glory of his Father. And every eye shall see him; and they who pierced him, and all kindreds of the earth shall wail because of him." (JST Rev. 1:7, I.A.)

Just before the end of the world, John saw an angel in vision who he described as follows: "And I saw another mighty angel come down from heaven, clothed with a cloud: and a rainbow was upon his head, and his face was as it were the sun, and his feet as pillars of fire." (Rev. 10:1, I.A.)

John also saw two powerful prophets in his vision. He beheld that after they are killed in Jerusalem, they will resurrect and ascend up to heaven in a cloud: "And they heard a great voice from heaven saying unto them, Come up hither. And they ascended up to heaven in a cloud; and their enemies beheld them." (Rev. 11:12, I.A.)

In vision, John also saw one like the Son of Man sitting on a white cloud as He harvested the earth: "And I looked, and behold a white cloud, and upon the cloud one sat like unto the Son of Man, having on his head a golden crown, and in his hand a sharp sickle. And another angel came out of the temple, crying with a loud voice to him that sat on the cloud, thrust in thy sickle...And he that sat on the cloud thrust in his sickle on the earth; and the earth was reaped." (Rev. 14:14-16, I.A.)

The following scriptures on clouds are taken from the Book of Mormon, Doctrine and Covenants and Pearl of Great Price. They shed even more light on the subject of clouds from heaven. The fact that the experiences with the Lord that are given in our modern scriptures parallel so closely those which are described in the Bible is another powerful witness that Joseph Smith truly was a prophet of God.

The following is the experience that Alma and the sons of Mosiah had when they were rebelling against the Church. An angel descended in a cloud which shook the ground: "And as I said unto you, as they were going about rebelling against God, behold, the angel of the Lord appeared unto them; and he descended as it were in a cloud; and he spake as it were in the voice of thunder, which caused the earth to shake upon which they stood;" (Mosiah 27:11, I.A.).

When He finished teaching the Nephites, Jesus ascended to heaven in a similar manner as to how He did while in Jerusalem: "And it came to pass that when Jesus had touched them all, there came a cloud and overshadowed the multitude that they could not see Jesus. And while they were overshadowed he departed from them, and ascended into heaven." (3 Ne. 18:38-39, I.A.) It is interesting to note that Jesus disappeared into the cloud before ascending to heaven.

While the Jaredites prepared to go to the promised land, the Lord came down in a cloud and talked to the brother of Jared and directed their travels: "...the Lord came down and talked with the brother of Jared; and he was in a cloud, and the brother of Jared saw him not...And it came to pass that the Lord did go before them, and did talk with them as he stood in a cloud, and gave directions whither they should travel." (Ether 2:4-5, I.A.)

The brother of Jared dwelt at Moriancumer for four years and forgot to pray to the Lord and was chastened: "And it came to pass at the end of the four years that the Lord came again unto the brother of Jared, and stood in a cloud and talked with him. And for the space of three hours did the Lord talk with the brother of Jared, and chastened him because he remembered not to call upon the name of the Lord." (Ether 2:14, I.A.)

WHAT IS A "CLOUD" FROM HEAVEN?

Jesus affirmed to all of us that He would return in a glorious cloud: "For behold, verily, verily, I say unto you, the time is soon at hand that I shall come in a cloud with power and great glory." (D&C 34:7:, I.A.)

All of the faithful saints will be taken up in a cloud: "For ye are the church of the Firstborn, and he will take you up in a cloud, and appoint every man his portion. And he that is a faithful and wise steward shall inherit all things." (D&C 34:7, I.A.)

In the dedicatory prayer offered in the Kirtland Temple, Joseph Smith made this inspired plea: "That when the trump shall sound for the dead, we shall be caught up in the cloud to meet thee, that we may ever be with the Lord;" (D&C 109:75, I.A.).

Jesus promised that when He comes in the clouds of heaven that the worthy dead will come and meet Him in the cloud: "And when they shall look for me, and, behold, I will come; and they shall see me in the clouds of heaven, clothed with power and great glory; with all the holy angels, and he that watches not for me shall be cut off...and the saints that have slept shall come forth to meet me in the cloud." (D&C 45:44-45, I.A.)

In the following scripture, the Lord was speaking to those who are worthy of celestial glory: "These are they whom he shall bring with him, when he shall come in the clouds of heaven to reign on the earth over his people." (D&C 76:63, I.A.)

When the Lord spoke about those that would inherit the telestial glory, He said they would not be caught up and received into the cloud: "Last of all, these all are they who will not be gathered with the saints, to be caught up into the church of the Firstborn, and received into the cloud." (D&C 76:102, I.A.)

When John the Baptist came to ordain him to the Aaronic Priesthood, Joseph Smith described him as descending in a cloud: "While we were thus employed, praying and calling upon the Lord, a messenger from heaven descended in a cloud of light, and having laid his hands upon us, ordained us," (JS-H 1:68, I.A.).

The fact that "in the spirit", "the glory of the Lord", "the voice of the Almighty" and "clouds" are repeatedly mentioned in our modern scriptures as well as in the Old and New Testaments of the Bible, is additional evidence that they are true, for the Lord is the same yesterday, today and forever. (Heb. 13:8)

CHARIOTS

A chariot was a vehicle that was used in ancient times. The prophets referred to the glorious vehicles of God as chariots in the scriptural passages that follow.

When Elisha knew that the prophet Elijah was going to be taken into heaven, he accompanied him and saw Elijah taken after a chariot appeared: "And it came to pass, when the Lord would take up Elijah into heaven by a whirlwind, that Elijah went with Elisha from Gilgal. And it came to pass, as they still went on, and talked, that, behold, there appeared a chariot of fire, and horses of fire, and parted them both asunder; and Elijah went up by a whirlwind into heaven. And Elisha saw it, and cried, My father, my father, the chariot of Israel," (2 Kgs. 2:1, 11-12, I.A.).

A great multitude of chariots of the enemy encompassed the city where Elijah and his servants were. The servant feared for his life. The servant of Elijah could not see the chariots of God all around him until the Lord opened his eyes: "And he answered, Fear not: for they that be with us are more than they that be with them. And Elisha prayed, and said, Lord, I pray thee, open his eyes, that he may see. And the Lord opened the eyes of the young man; and he saw: and, behold, the mountain was full of horses and chariots of fire round about Elisha." (2 Kgs. 6:16-17, I.A.)

One might wonder how many chariots the Lord has. In the Old Testament times, David wrote in one of the psalms that God had twenty thousand: "The chariots of God are twenty thousand, even thousands of angels: the Lord is among them, as in Sinai, in the holy place." (Ps. 68:17, I.A.)

Isaiah said that when the Lord returns, His anger at the wicked will be shown in flames of fire: "For, behold, the Lord will come with fire, and with his chariots like a whirlwind, to render his anger with fury, and his rebuke with flames of fire." (Isa. 66:15, I.A.)

The prophet Habakkuk asked if the Lord rode upon his chariots because he was displeased: "Was the Lord displeased...that thou didst ride upon thine horses and they chariots of salvation?" (Hab. 3:8, I.A.)

Zechariah saw four chariots come out from between two mountains that were different colors. He asked the angel what they were. The angel told him that they were the four "spirits" of the heavens from the Lord. The four "spirits" are commanded to go and walk to and fro on the earth: "And I turned, and lifted mine eyes, and looked, And, behold, there came four chariots out from between two mountains;...What are these, my lord? And the angel answered and said unto me, These are the four spirits of the heavens, which go forth from standing before the Lord of all the earth...Get you hence, walk to and fro through the earth. So they walked to and fro through the earth." (Zech. 6:1, 4-5, 7, I.A. and Zech 1:9-11)

In 1838, Joseph Smith wrote a vision he had seen where William Marks was seen being pursued by many enemies. President Smith reported that Brother Marks was saved by entering a chariot of fire and riding off: "I would just say to Brother Marks, that I saw a vision while on the road, that whereas he was closely pursued by an innumerable concourse of enemies, and as they pressed upon him hard, as if they were about to devour him, and had seemingly obtained some degree of advantage over him, but about this time a chariot of fire came, and near the place, even the angel of the Lord put forth his hand unto Brother Marks and said unto him, 'Thou art my son, come here,' and immediately he was caught up in the chariot, and rode away triumphantly out of their midst." (DHC 3:9-11, I.A. and Messages, 1:83.

THE STAR

The wisemen had valuable gifts that would help Joseph, Mary and the young child, Jesus. While the wisemen were traveling to find the newborn King, they inquired of King Herod as to where the young King was. When they left, a "star" guided them to where the young child was: "Now when Jesus was born in Bethlehem of Judea in the days of Herod the king, behold, there came wise men from the east to Jerusalem, Saying, Where is he that is born King of the Jews? for we have seen his star in the east, and are come to worship him. Then Herod, when he had privily called the wise men, enquired of them diligently what time the star appeared. When they had heard the king, they departed; and, lo, the star, which they saw in the east, went before them, till it came and stood over where the young child was. When they saw the star, they rejoiced with exceeding great joy. And when they were come into the house, they saw the young child with Mary his mother, and fell down, and worshipped him:" (Matt. 2:1-2, 7, 9-11, I.A.)

Samuel the Lamanite predicted that a new star would arise when Jesus Christ was born. (Hel. 14:5) A new star was observed in America at the time when the Savior was born. (3 Ne. 1:21) But what is referred to as a "star" by the wisemen that led them to where Jesus was did not behave like a true star. This "star" went before the wisemen until it came and stood over the house where the young child was. Real stars, as they have been studied, do not travel before people and direct them. The nearest star to the earth is the sun (and it is not a large star but is one hundred and nine times larger than the earth). Were the sun to come much closer to the earth, it would burn up the surface of the earth. If the sun came close enough to stand over a house, the whole earth would be burned up. The wisemen were guided to the child, Jesus, by what looked like a star but what did not behave like a real star.

The First Gospel of the Infancy of Jesus Christ, an apocryphal book, said this about the star that guided the wisemen: "And it came to pass, when the Lord Jesus was born at Bethlehem, a city of Judea, in the time of Herod the King; the wise men came from the East to Jerusalem, according to the prophecy of Zoradascht [Zoroaster], and brought with them offerings: namely, gold, frankincense, and myrrh, and worshipped him, and offered to him their gifts. Then the Lady Mary took one of his swaddling clothes in which the infant was wrapped, and gave it to them instead of a blessing, which they received from her as a most noble present. And at the time there appeared to them an angel in the form of that star which had before been their guide in their journey; the light of which they followed till they returned into their own country." (The Lost Books, 3:1-3, I.A.)

The wisemen could very well have seen a chariot of God that had the appearance of a bright star when seen at night from a distance. It could have looked just like the new star that did appear earlier when Jesus was born.

JOSEPH SMITH'S FIRST VISION

Most of us are familiar with the account of Joseph Smith's first vision which is recorded in the Pearl of Great Price: "I saw a pillar of light exactly over my head, above the brightness of the sun, which descended gradually until it fell upon me...When the light rested upon me I saw two Personages, whose brightness and glory defy all description, standing above me in the air." (JS-H 1:16-17, I.A.)

Joseph Smith related his experience of the first vision on several occasions and to a number of people. The following passage is taken from the 1835 account from the "Documentary History of the Church". This account gives us some added detail as it relates that God spoke to him while He was in the midst of the pillar: "I called on the Lord in mighty prayer. A pillar of fire appeared above my head; which presently rested down upon me and filled me with unspeakable joy. A personage appeared in the midst of this pillar of flame, which was spread all around and yet nothing consumed. Another personage soon appeared like unto the first;" (Joshua 1835 Account of the First Vision, end of Book A-1, pp. 120-122, I.A.). So Joseph Smith did not see both personages right at first within the pillar. God the Father appeared first and introduced His beloved Son to Joseph Smith.

Orson Pratt wrote a pamphlet which included an account of the first vision that was much more detailed about what it looked like to Joseph Smith when God and Jesus Christ approached him from a distance and then gradually descended: "And, while thus pouring out his soul, anxiously desiring an answer from God, he, at length saw a very bright and glorious light in the heavens above which, at first seemed to be at a considerable distance. He continued praying, while the light appeared to be gradually descending towards him; and as it drew nearer, it increased in brightness, and magnitude, so that, by the time it reached the tops of the trees, the whole wilderness, for some distance around, was illuminated in a most glorious and brilliant manner. He expected to have seen the leaves and boughs of the trees consumed, as soon as the light came in contact with them; but, perceiving that it did not produce that effect, he was encouraged with the hopes of being able to endure its presence. It continued descending, slowly until it rested upon the earth, and he was enveloped in the midst of it. When it first came upon him, it produced a peculiar sensation throughout his whole system; and, immediately, his mind was caught away, from the natural objects with which he was surrounded; and he was enwrapped in a heavenly vision, and saw two glorious personages, who exactly resembled each other in their features and likeness." (Taken from a pamphlet written by Orson Pratt entitled, "Interestig account of Several Remarkable Visions, and the Late Discovery of Ancient American Records", I.A.) So this light or pillar as it is called in other accounts gradually descended from heaven above until it rested upon the earth. Joseph Smith was enveloped or enclosed in the midst or middle of the pillar.

An undated manuscript of the first vision was found in the Church Historical Department in Salt Lake City. The probable date that it was written was 1833. It also recorded what Joseph Smith saw during the first vision: "...a pillar of light above the brightness of the sun at noon day come down from above and rested upon me and I was filled with the Spirit of god and the Lord opened the heavens upon me and I saw the Lord and he spake unto me...I come quickly as it was written of me in the cloud clothed in the glory of my Father and my soul was filled with love..." (Dean Jessee, "Early Accounts of the First Vision", BYU Studies, vol. 9, no. 3, p. 277, I.A.)

The prophet Joseph Smith used many of the same descriptive words and phrases as Moses, Ezekiel, Stephen and other prophets used when relating the several accounts of his first vision. Some of those phrases were: the Lord opening the heavens, a pillar of light or fire, glorious men seen within the pillar and him being enveloped within the pillar. With the limited education that Joseph Smith received in his youth, it is unlikely that he could have fabricated a vision which parallels so remarkably many other manifestations of God in the Bible. He saw the Lord just as surely as Moses, Ezekiel, Stephen and other ancient prophets did.

OTHER DESCRIPTIONS OF GOD'S CHARIOT

The following passages taken from the Old Testament, can teach us even more about the subject of the heavenly chariots of God and His angels.

Moses compared the care that the Lord gave to His people to an eagle caring for her young. The Lord made Moses ride on the high places of the earth: "As an eagle stirreth up her nest, fluttereth over her young, spreadeth abroad her wings, taketh them, beareth them on her wings: So the Lord alone did lead him, and there was no strange god with him. He made him ride on the high places of the earth," (Deut. 32:11-13, I.A.).

Moses described His God as riding upon the heavens in excellency to his aid: "There is none like unto the God of Jeshurun [footnote: HEB the upright], who rideth upon the heaven in thy help and in his excellency on [footnote: OR majesty through] the sky." (Deut. 33:26, I.A.)

The Lord commanded Elijah to stand on the mountain while the Lord passed by: "And he said, Go forth, and stand upon the mount before the Lord. And, behold, the Lord passed by, and a great and strong wind rent the mountains, and brake in pieces the rocks before the Lord;" (1 Kgs. 19:11, I.A.).

David rejoiced in the following Psalm that when the Lord comes to His temple, He will be sitting on His throne: "For the Lord, when he shall come into his holy temple, sitting upon God's throne in heaven, his eyes shall pierce the wicked." (JST Psalm 11:4, I.A.)

The prophet Isaiah saw the Lord high above him sitting on a throne in the temple: "I saw the Lord sitting upon a throne, high and lifted up, and his train filled the temple." (Isa. 6:1, I.A.) The train that Isaiah saw could mean those who accompanied the Lord who were called "seraphims". The seraphims could fly. (Isa. 6:2-4)

Isaiah reproved Israel for turning to Egypt for help when their Lord possessed such great power and could fly over Jerusalem and deliver and preserve it: "As birds flying [footnote: IE hovering over their young], so will the Lord of hosts defend Jerusalem; defending also he will deliver it; and passing over he will preserve it." (Isa. 31:4-5, I.A.)

The prophet Isaiah promised Israel that if they would keep the Sabbath day holy and do the Lord's will that they would find the Lord a delight and would ride upon the high places of the earth: "If thou...call the sabbath a delight, the holy of the Lord, honourable; and shalt honor him, not doing thine own words: Then shalt thou delight thyself in the Lord; and I will cause thee to ride upon the high places of the earth, and feed thee with the heritage of Jacob thy father: for the mouth of the Lord hath spoken it." (Isa. 58:13-14, I.A.)

The prophet Zechariah lifted up his eyes and saw a flying roll that measured twenty cubits in length and ten cubits in width. By our modern measurements the length of the flying roll would be about thirty feet and the width would be about fifteen feet. The angel told Zechariah that the flying roll is a curse that goes over the face of the earth and "cuts off" the thief and burns down the house of him that swears falsely by the Lord's name: "Then I turned, and lifted up mine eyes, and looked, and behold a flying roll. And he [the angel] said unto me, What seest thou? And I answered, I see a flying roll; the length thereof is twenty cubits [about thirty feet], and the breadth thereof ten cubits [about fifteen feet]. Then said he [the angel] unto me, This is the curse that goeth forth over the face of the whole earth: for every one that stealeth shall be cut off...I will bring it forth, saith the Lord of hosts, and it shall enter into the house of the thief, and into the house of him that sweareth falsely by my name: and it shall remain in the midst of his house, and shall consume it with the timber thereof and the stones thereof." (Zech. 5:1-4, I.A.)

God is all powerful and the creator of everything. The Lord must have excellent reasons for why he chooses to travel in heavenly "chariots". Perhaps He is more comfortable in them than He would be just standing in the air. His appearance is so gloriously bright that it might be necessary for Him, when dealing with mortals, to shield His glorious person from the view of those who are not worthy or prepared to see Him. Apparently the children of Israel could view "the glory of the Lord" without perishing because it was in the distance: "And Moses went up into the mount, and a cloud covered the mount. And the glory of the Lord abode upon mount Sinai, and the cloud covered it six days: and the seventh day he called unto Moses out of the midst of the cloud. And the sight of the glory of the Lord was like devouring fire on the top of the mount in the eyes of the children of Israel." (Ex. 24:15-17, I.A.)

Yet, only those chosen as being worthy by the Lord could go up on mount Sinai and meet God face-to-face without perishing: "And the Lord said unto Moses, Go down, charge the people, lest they break through unto the Lord to gaze, and many of them perish." (Ex. 19:21, I.A.) The Lord has also said, "And no sinful man hath at any time, neither shall there be any sinful man at any time, that shall see my face and live." (JST Ex. 33:20, I.A.)

DESTRUCTION IN AMERICA AND JERUSALEM

After reviewing the scriptures about the worldwide earthquake and what a cataclysmic event it will be it should come as no surprise that there will be great destruction on the earth from it.

NEW YORK, ALBANY AND BOSTON DESTROYED

A warning was issued in 1832 to the people of New York, Albany and Boston through the prophet Joseph Smith that if they did not repent, they would be utterly destroyed: "Nevertheless, let the bishop go unto the city of New York, also to the city of Albany, and also to the city of Boston, and warn the people of those cities with the sound of the gospel, with a loud voice, of the desolation and utter abolishment which await them if they do reject these things. For if they do reject these things the hour of their judgment is nigh, and their house shall be left unto them desolate." (D&C 84:114-115, I.A.)

Wilford Woodruff prophesied of the destruction of these three cities in more detail in a sermon he gave in Logan, Utah, on August 22, 1863. He told them that in a future day they would: "...have a temple and the valley would be full of Latter-day Saints. Then they would remember back when he and President Young visited them and would say,..."that was before New York was destroyed by an earthquake. It was before Boston was swept into the sea, by the sea heaving itself beyond its bounds; it was before Albany was destroyed by fire;...(President Young followed his speech and said: "What Brother Woodruff has said is revelation and will be fulfilled.") (Deseret News 33:678, I.A.)

The Lord always gives plenty of warning before He destroys people, hoping they will use the time to heed the warning and repent.

THE DESTRUCTION OF THE WICKED IN AMERICA

It always seems that calamity and destruction are events that happen to other people and nations. Anciently as prophets foretold of the worldwide flood, the destruction of the Jaredites, the downfall of Israel and the annihilation of the Nephites, the majority of the people had a difficult time believing it could happen to them. They felt that their great and notable cities were immortal. Very few had faith that the words of the prophets were from God and that they would be fulfilled. But regardless of whether we choose to believe it or not, there will be great destruction in America in our day. The Lord was speaking of the Gentiles that would inhabit America in the last days when He said: "Therefore, it shall come to pass that whosoever will not believe in my words, who am Jesus Christ, which the Father shall cause him to bring forth unto the Gentiles [the Book of Mormon],...they shall be <u>cut off</u> from among my people who are of the covenant. Yea, wo unto the Gentiles except they repent; for it shall come to pass in that day, saith the Father, that I will cut off thy horses out of the midst of thee, and <u>I will destroy thy chariots</u>; And <u>I will cut off the cities of thy land</u>, and throw down thy strongholds;...so will I <u>destroy thy cities</u>. For it shall come to pass, saith the Father, that at that day <u>whosoever will not repent and come unto my Beloved Son</u>, them <u>will I cut off from among my people</u>, O house of Israel; And I will execute <u>vengeance</u> and fury upon them, even as upon the heathen, such as they have not heard." (3 Ne. 21:11, 14-15, 18, 20-21, I.A.)

And who will inherit the destroyed cities? The

Lord was speaking to the Lost Tribes of Israel (3 Ne. 21:26-29) when He said: "...thy seed shall inherit the Gentiles and make the desolate cities to be inhabited." (3 Ne. 22:3, I.A.)

The Lord has made an everlasting decree that whoever possesses the land of America must serve Him, the God of the land, or be swept off when they are ripened in iniquity and sin. (Ether 2:7-10) God always keeps His promises.

Joseph Smith made a profound prophesy about destruction which will take place in America that will prepare the way for the return of the Lost Tribes of Israel: "And now I am prepared to say by the authority of Jesus Christ, that not many years shall pass away before the United States shall present such a scene of bloodshed as has not a parallel in the history of our nation; pestilence, hail, famine, and earthquake will sweep the wicked of this generation from off the face of the land, to open and prepare the way for the return of the lost tribes of Israel from the north country." (Teachings, p. 17)

The wicked will be swept off this land just as they were in the days of the Jaredites and Nephites. Joseph Smith made another prophesy about the desolation that awaits the wicked of this generation: "I prophesy, in the name of the Lord God of Israel, anguish and wrath and tribulation and the withdrawing of the Spirit of God from the earth await this generation, until they are visited with utter desolation." (Teachings, p. 328)

The prophet Joseph Smith was not alone in foreseeing disaster coming upon this nation. In 1860, Brigham Young prophesied, "Do you think there is calamity abroad now among the people? Not much...You will hear of magnificent cities, now idolized by the people, sinking in the earth, entombing the inhabitants. The sea will heave itself beyond its bounds, engulphing mighty cities. Famine will spread over the nations," (J.D. 8:123, I.A.)

In 1879, John Taylor added his witness to America as to what lay ahead if wickedness continued to increase in the land: "God will lay his hand upon this nation, and they will feel it more terribly than ever they have done before; there will be more bloodshed, more ruin, more devastation than ever they have seen before." (J.D. 20:318, I.A.)

A warning was given by President Wilford Woodruff in 1880 that this nation would be destroyed just as surely as the Nephite and Jaredite nations perished. He knew this would happen through revelation, visions and the administration of angels: "When I contemplate the condition of our nation, and see that wickedness and abominations are increasing,...I ask myself the question, can the American nation escape? The answer comes, No; its destruction,...is sure; just as sure as the Lord cut off and destroyed the two great and prosperous nations that once inhabited this continent of North and South America, because of their wickedness, so will he them destroy, and sooner or later they will reap the fruits of their own wicked acts, and be numbered among the past...There are changes awaiting us,...I know it by the revelations of Jesus Christ; I know it by the visions of heaven; I know it by the administration of angels, and I know it by the inspiration of heaven," (J. D. 21:301, I.A.).

If President Woodruff thought the nation of America was wicked in 1880, what would he think of the evils of immorality, abortion and crime that permeate our society today? Many of the Lord's latter-day prophets have warned America to repent or destruction awaits the land. Will these warnings fall on deaf ears? Can we repent and prepare ourselves for the future, or will we be numbered among the wicked? The decision is ours and so are the consequences for the choices we make.

In 1836, the prophet Joseph Smith offered this prayer to the Lord for the saints: "...prepare the hearts of thy saints for all those judgments thou art about to send, in thy wrath, upon the inhabitants of the earth, because of their transgressions, that thy people may not faint in the day of trouble." (D&C 109:38, I.A.)

SOME RIGHTEOUS WILL DIE, BUT MOST WILL SURVIVE

Will only the wicked die in the coming destructions? Unfortunately, the judgments that will come upon the sinful will also kill some of the righteous. But the death of the faithful brings them to the peace of paradise on the other side of the veil. So the Lord takes care of His own in life or in death: "...it is a false idea that the Saints will escape all the judgments, whilst the wicked suffer; for all flesh is subject to suffer, and 'the righteous shall hardly escape;' still many of the Saints will escape, for the just shall live by faith; yet many of the righteous shall fall a prey to disease, to pestilence, etc., by reason of the weakness of the flesh, and yet be saved in the Kingdom of God. So that it is an unhallowed principle to say that such and such have transgressed because they have been preyed upon by disease or death, for all flesh is subject to death; and the Savior has said, 'Judge not, lest ye be judged'." (Teachings, p. 162-163)

A PLAGUE OF FLIES

The Lord foretold that after the great day when the sun shall be darkened, the moon turned to blood and the stars fall from heaven (D&C 29:14) and after the hailstorm that destroys the crops of the earth (D&C 29:16), a plague of flies will be sent upon the earth: "And it shall come to pass, because of the wickedness of the world, that I will take vengeance upon the wicked, for they will not repent; for the cup of mine indignation is full; for behold, my blood will not cleanse them if they hear me not. Wherefore, I the Lord will send flies upon the face of the earth, which shall take hold of the inhabitants thereof, and shall eat their flesh, and shall cause maggots to come in upon them; And their tongues shall be stayed that they shall not utter against me; and their flesh shall fall from off their bones, and their eyes from their sockets; And it shall come to pass that the beasts of the forest and the fowls of the air shall devour them up." (D&C 29:17-20, I.A.)

The Lord has told us that the reason this plague of flies will come is because of the wicked who will not repent. The Savior's atoning blood will not cleanse those who refuse to listen and repent. The suffering in hell that awaits the wicked who are unrepentant is far worse than this plague because they will suffer with the devil for a thousand years. The Lord is trying to save the wicked from that condemnation by pleading with them through different plagues to repent before it is too late.

It is possible that the great worldwide earthquake, along with the fires and meteorites that will accompany it, will cause very warm temperatures which are a perfect breeding ground for flies. This might be the natural means that the Lord could use to bring this plague upon the wicked.

A DESOLATING SICKNESS AND AN OVERFLOWING SCOURGE

Unfortunately, even more trials are promised for this wicked generation. If the people reject the testimony of the three witnesses to the Book of Mormon and harden their hearts against the Book that God has caused to go forth, then the Lord's judgment will be a desolating scourge upon the people: "And their testimony shall also go forth unto the condemnation of this generation if they harden their hearts against them; For a desolating scourge shall go forth among the inhabitants of the earth, and shall continue to be poured our from time to time, if they repent not," (D&C 5:18-19, I.A.).

A "scourge" is divine castigation or punishment. This judgment from God will be "desolating" which means it will leave people in forsaken ruin.

In the generation when the times of the Gentiles is fulfilled (or when the missionaries are called home) is when this scourge or sickness will occur: "And in that generation shall the times of the Gentiles be fulfilled. And there shall be men standing in that generation, that shall not pass until they shall see an overflowing scourge; for a desolating sickness shall cover the land. But my disciples shall stand in holy places, and shall not be moved; but among the wicked, men shall lift up their voices and curse God and die." (D&C 45:30-32, I.A.)

Historically, there are several things that happen in the aftermath of great cataclysmic disasters like earthquakes, etc. There is often a breakdown in sanitation facilities and a shortage of food and water because of the broken pipes and ruined highways. Since the worldwide earthquake will effect everyone, there will not be assistance coming in to help from other places. Pollution in the atmosphere and the lack of sanitary conditions may well lead to disease and sickness and could be the natural means used by the Lord to cause this scourge. The Lord could prevent this sickness but will not because the wicked will not repent.

However, the Lord promises that His saints will stand in holy places and will not leave, while the wicked will curse God and die. Even though medical help may not be available, through the power of the Priesthood and faith, the righteous will be taken care of. We need to develop as much spiritual and emotional strength as possible to meet the challenges that lie ahead. This is no time to flirt with sin. Those Church members who are not trying to be righteous will not escape this divine punishment or scourge: "And your minds in times past have been darkened because of unbelief, and because you have treated lightly the things you have received. Which vanity and unbelief have brought the whole church under condemnation. And this condemnation resteth upon the children of Zion, even all. And they shall remain under this condemnation until they repent and remember the new covenant, even the Book of Mormon and the former commandments which I have given them, not only to say, but to do according to that which I have written--That they may bring forth fruit meet for their Father's kingdom; otherwise there remaineth a scourge and judgment to be poured out upon the children of Zion. For shall the children of the kingdom pollute my holy land?" (D&C 84:54-59, I.A.)

Obedience to the commandments contained in the Book of Mormon is the key to avoiding this scourge. We must not only talk about the scriptures but live what they teach.

We are commanded to gather to prepare for tribulation and desolation. (D&C 29:8) We must stand and remain in holy places, "Wherefore, stand ye in holy places, and be not moved until the day of the Lord come; for behold, it cometh quickly, saith the Lord. Amen." (D&C 87:8, I.A.) A place that is holy is set apart for the worship of God. It is hallowed by innocence and virtue. What holy places can we stand in? Our chapels and temples are holy. Our homes can be holy. In fact, we had better do all we can to hallow our homes before this scourge comes.

The warning given is to flee to Zion before the scourge comes: "I declare unto you the warning which the Lord has commanded me to declare unto this generation,...repent ye, and embrace the everlasting covenant, and flee to Zion, before the overflowing scourge overtake you," (Teachings, pp. 17-18, I.A.).

But where do we flee to? Joseph Smith answered that question: "There will be here and there a Stake (of Zion) for the gathering of the Saints. Some may have cried peace, but henceforth. Let this not hinder us from going to the Stakes; for God has told us to flee, not dallying, or we shall be scattered, one here, and another there. There your children shall be blessed, and you in the midst of friends where you may be blessed. The gospel net gathers of every kind. I prophesy, that that man who tarries after he has an opportunity of going, will be afflicted by the devil...The time is soon coming, when no man will have any peace but in Zion and her stakes." (Teachings, pp. 160-161, I.A. and D&C 101:20-21) There are stakes for saints to gather to that they can become a part of all over the world. We can receive strength from each other as well as from the Lord.

THE WICKED WILL KILL EACH OTHER

People become bloodthirsty and seek to kill each other when they have hardened their hearts against God: "And there shall be earthquakes also in divers places, and many desolations; yet men will harden their hearts against me, and they will take up the sword, one against another, and they will kill one another." (D&C 45:33, I.A.)

Rather than repenting during the time of the earthquakes and desolations, many people will turn to the shedding of blood. This is what happened to both the Jaredite and Nephite civilizations when they became ripened in sin and iniquity and refused to repent. (Ether 14-15, Morm. 3-8) Brigham Young foresaw that violence will be rampant: "...and nation will rise up against nation, kingdom against kingdom, and and states against states, in our own country and in foreign lands; and they will destroy each other, caring not for the blood and lives of their neighbors, of their families, or for their own lives. The will be like the Jaredites who preceded the Nephites upon this continent, and will destroy each other" (J.D. 8:123, I.A.).

This warfare will become so widespread that Zion will be the only place where there will be peace, "And it shall come to pass among the wicked, that every man that will not take his sword against his neighbor must flee unto Zion for safety." (D&C 45:68, I.A.)

In 1832, Joseph Smith prophesied about the Civil War and then foretold that bloodshed would spread over the earth, "And it shall come to pass, after many days, slaves shall rise up against their masters, who shall be marshaled and disciplined for war. And thus, with the sword and bloodshed the inhabitants of the earth shall mourn;" (D&C 87:4, 6, I.A.) Slaves are people who have little freedom and are under the control of masters or political leaders. There are millions of people in the world who do not enjoy freedom. Lack of freedom can build resentment and hatred within the slaves toward their masters. When those who are without freedom rise up against their leaders, there will be great bloodshed for they will be very experienced in warfare. A portion of this is already beginning to happen in many of the countries that have been controlled by communism.

When the fulness of His wrath comes, God allows the wicked to punish the wicked, "I have sworn in my wrath, and decreed wars upon the face of the earth and the wicked shall slay the wicked; and fear shall come upon every man;" (D&C 63:33, I.A.).

Even the natural affection of family members will be lost among the wicked. Joseph Smith prophesied of this sad day, and it must have been heart-rending for him to see what would happen in the future: "I saw men hunting the lives of their own sons, and brother murdering brother, women killing their own daughters, and daughters seeking the lives of their mothers...These things are at our doors...I know not how soon these things will take place; but with a view of them, shall I cry peace?" (Teachings, p. 161, I.A.)

Some have felt that this prophesy was fulfilled during the Civil War which was fought between 1861 and 1865. But after the Civil War in 1879, President John Taylor foresaw this fighting within families also. He said it would be so widespread that it would be an affliction to even hear about the warfare: "...but there is yet to come a sound of war, trouble and distress, in which brother will be arrayed against brother, father against son, son against father, a scene of desolation and destruction that will permeate our land until it will be a vexation to hear the report thereof." (J.D. 20:318, I.A.)

There has not been a battle fought on American soil since Pearl Harbor was attacked in 1941. That makes it difficult to imagine this kind of civil violence taking place. However, we must remember what Mormon sadly recounted to his son, Moroni, when the Nephite nation was being annihilated by the Lamanites. After reciting the cruelty and depravity towards their enemies that was practiced by the Nephites, he commented: "O my beloved son, how can a people like this, that are without civilization--(And only a few years have passed away, and they were a civil and a delightsome people) But O my son, how can a people like this, whose delight is in so much abomination--How can we expect that God will stay his hand in judgment against us?" (Moro. 9:11-14, I.A.)

The deterioration of a society into violent bloodshed and savagery can happen in only a few years when they are ripened in iniquity.

THE LAMANITES WILL TREAD DOWN THE GENTILES OF AMERICA

The Lord refers to most of the present population of the Americas as "Gentiles". In the last days, the "remnant of Jacob", or those with Lamanite blood, will go as a young lion among the Gentiles or flocks of sheep and destroy them: "And the remnant of Jacob shall be among the Gentiles in the midst of many people as a lion among the beasts of the forest, as a young lion among the flocks of sheep: who, if he go through, both treadeth down, and teareth in pieces, and none can deliver." (Micah 5:8, I.A.)

Jesus told us exactly who the remnant of Jacob is when He was speaking to the Nephites and Lamanites after His resurrection. Those with Lamanite blood will go through and destroy only the unrepentant Gentiles: "And I say unto you, that if the Gentiles do not repent after the blessing which they shall receive, after they have scattered my people--Then shall ye, who are a remnant of the house of Jacob, go forth among them; and ye shall be in the midst of them who shall be many; and ye shall be among them as a lion among the beasts of the forest, and as a young lion among the flocks of sheep, who, if he goeth through both treadeth down and teareth in pieces, and none can deliver. Thy hand shall be lifted up upon thine adversaries, and all thine enemies shall be cut off." (3 Ne. 20:15-17, I.A., and 3 Ne. 21:12-13)

The Hispanic people and the Indians or native Americans are the "remnant of Jacob". Most of the "Gentiles" in the Americas today are descendants of the people who cruelly scattered and destroyed the Lamanite nations when they first settled in the Americas. If the Gentiles reject or turn away from the restored gospel then the "remnant of Jacob" or the descendants of the Lamanites will cruelly destroy them. Speaking a warning to the American Gentiles, Mormon pleaded: "Therefore, repent ye, and humble yourselves before him, lest he come out in justice against you--lest a remnant of the seed of Jacob shall go forth among you as a lion, and tear you to pieces, and there is none to deliver." (Morm. 5:24, I.A.)

These descendants of the Lamanites will organize themselves in their great anger and grievously afflict the Gentiles of the Americas, "And it shall come to pass also that the remnants who are left of the land will marshal themselves, and shall become exceedingly angry, and shall vex the Gentiles with a sore vexation." (D&C 87:5, I.A.)

The prophesies about how the Lamanites will go among the Gentiles and tread them down and destroy them is very reminiscent of the treatment that the native American Lamanites received from the early colonists and settlers.

THE BANDS OF THE ABOMINABLE CHURCH MADE STRONG

Immediately after the great Sign of the Son of Man is seen in the heavens (D&C 88:93), and angel will make an announcement: "And another angel shall sound his trump, saying: That great church, the mother of abominations, that made all nations drink of the wine of the wrath of her fornication, that persecuteth the saints of God, that shed their blood--she who sitteth upon many waters, and upon the islands of the sea--behold, she is the tares of the earth; she is bound in bundles; her bands are made strong, no man can loose them; therefore, she is ready to be burned. And he shall sound his trump both long and loud, and all nations shall hear it." (D&C 88:94, I.A.)

The "abominable church" is whatever organization which leads men away from the living God and the gospel plan of His authorized Church. The devil is the foundation of it as he is of all falsehoods. This abominable church will rule over people, multitudes, nations and tongues in the last days. (Rev. 17-18)

Tares are poisonous weeds. Young tares are sometimes mistaken for wheat and are therefore counterfeits. The abominable church is a counterfeit for the true Church of God. This deception may be difficult to detect at first but will be apparent when the abominable church reaches its full maturity and is burned.

THE CONSTITUTION WILL HANG BY A THREAD

Joseph Smith prophesied that the constitution of the United States will hang by a thread and if it is saved at all it will be by the people of the Church. Brigham Young quoted this prophesy to the saints in 1868 in the Tabernacle: "How long will it be before the words of the prophet Joseph will be fulfilled? He said if the Constitution of the United States were saved at all it must be done by this people." (J.D. 12:204, I.A.)

The Mormon Elders will be summoned to save the Constitution and will go and do it. For Brigham Young also said, "...when the Constitution of the United States hangs, as it were, upon a single thread, they will have to call for the 'Mormon' Elders to save it from utter destruction; and they will step forth and do it." (J.D. 2:182, I.A.)

President John Taylor amplified what Joseph Smith taught on this subject. He said that the Constitution would be trampled under foot and would be in the grasp of unrighteous men when the Elders of Israel would revive support for the sacred instrument: "Need we be surprised that they should trample under foot the Constitution of the United States? No; Joseph Smith told us that they would do it...the last people that should be found to rally around that sacred instument and save it from the grasp of unrighteous men would be the Elders of Israel!" (J.D. 20:318, I.A.)

John Taylor also taught that the Constitution would be torn to shreds but that the Elders would save it by upholding its principles and by offering freedom to the oppressed of the world: "When the people shall have torn to shreds the Constitution of the United States the Elders of Israel will be found holding it up to the nations of the earth and proclaiming liberty and equal rights to all men, and extending the hand of fellowship to the oppressed of all nations." (J.D. 21:8, I.A.)

All who are blessed with the liberties granted in the sacred Constitution should do all within their power to uphold and defend those rights and privileges for they were granted by God himself.

UNPARALLELED AFFLICTION ON THE JEWS AND JERUSALEM

While the wicked are being destroyed in America and elsewhere, the Savior warned that another tribulation would come: "For then shall be great tribulation, such as was not since the beginning of the world to this time, no, nor ever shall be. And except those days should be shortened, there should no flesh be saved: but for the elect's sake those days shall be shortened." (Matt. 24:21-22, I.A., and Mark 13:19-20)

Tribulation shall come upon what people? Those days will be shortened to save whose flesh? Joseph Smith clarified this scripture in JS-M 1:18-20: "For then, in those days, shall be great tribulation on the Jews, and upon the inhabitants of Jerusalem, such as was not before sent upon Israel, of God, since the beginning of their kingdom until this time; no, nor ever shall be sent again upon Israel. All things which have befallen them are only the beginning of the sorrows which shall come upon them. And except those days should be shortened, there should none of their flesh be saved; but for the elect's sake, according to the covenant, those days shall be shortened." (I.A.)

With the terrible tribulations that the Jews have suffered in the past, this is a frightening prophecy for Jerusalem and the Jews.

One possible way that the Lord might literally shorten the days to save them would be for the earth to spin faster on its axis. (Hel. 12:14-15) On the other hand, it has been prophesied that a veil of darkness will cover the earth. Perhaps that darkness will limit the length of time that the earth will receive daylight. The Lord said that when the veil of darkness will cover the earth and great tribulations will be among men that He will preserve His people, "And the day shall come that the earth shall rest, but before that day the heavens shall be darkened, and a veil of darkness shall cover the earth; and the heavens shall shake, and also the earth; and great tribulations shall be among the children of men; but my people will I preserve;" (Moses 7:61, I.A.).

In his own way, the Lord will shorten the days when this tribulation comes and will save the Jews from certain extinction.

Possibly at the same time as the worldwide earthquake and great destruction upon Jerusalem, the holy temple site on the top of the Temple Mount in Jerusalem will be cleared off. The Moslem Dome of the Rock currently stands on that holy site. The Mosque must be removed so that the Jews can rebuild their prophesied temple in the last days. The site of their ancient temple is the only authorized spot that God has given the Jews to rebuild their temple that was destroyed in 70 A.D.

7

FALSE CHRISTS AND FALSE PROPHETS

GO NOT FORTH TO SEE THEM

The Savior warned us that false Christs and false prophets would perform great miracles in the last days. When will these false Christs and prophets arise? Jesus said they would appear after the tribulation that will come upon Jerusalem: "Behold, these things I have spoken unto you concerning the Jews; and again, after the tribulation of those days which shall come upon Jerusalem, if any man shall say unto you, Lo, here is Christ, or there, believe him not; For in those days there shall arise false Christs, and false prophets, and shall show great signs and wonders, insomuch, that if possible, they shall deceive the very elect, who are the elect according to the covenant." (JS-M 1:21-22, I.A.) "For many shall come in my name, saying--I am Christ--and shall deceive many; And many false prophets shall arise, and shall deceive many; (JS-M 1:6, 9, I.A., and Mark 13:5-6).

After the destruction at Jerusalem, false Christs and false prophets with great power to perform miracles will go forth deceiving many people. Jesus Christ warned almost two thousand years ago as to what to do when this happens: "Wherefore, if they shall say unto you: Behold, he is in the desert; go not forth: Behold, he is in the secret chambers; believe it not; For as the light of the morning cometh out of the east, and shineth even unto the west, and covereth the whole earth, so shall the coming of the Son of Man be." (JS-M 1:25-26, I.A., and Mark 13:21-22) "And again, verily I say unto you, that the Son of Man cometh not in the form of a woman, neither of a man traveling on the earth. Wherefore, be not deceived, but continue in steadfastness." (D&C 49:22-23, I.A.)

We are strongly counseled not to go anywhere to see anyone who claims to be Christ. When the real Jesus Christ returns, He will come from the east and then His coming will cover the entire earth. There will be no need to travel anywhere to see Him.

What a perfect time for false Christs and false prophets to flourish--right after the Sign of the Son of Man is seen in the heavens and many people mistakenly fear that it is the end of the world. (Rev. 6:17) It will be easy for those who have not studied the Book of Revelation and other scriptures to be deceived. The Book of Revelation clearly foretells that the worldwide earthquake will transpire during the sixth seal along with the Lamb being seen on the throne. (Rev. 6:12-17) Then there are many other things that happen after the opening of the seventh seal and before the end of the world. (Rev. 8-9, 11-14, 16-19) Until all of these prophesies are fulfilled, Christ will not return.

Jesus was concerned enough about the power of these false Christs and false prophets that he warned people almost two thousand years ago, "go ye not therefore after them". (Luke 21:8) Regardless of whether we are invited to a public or private meeting to see the supposed Christs and prophets, we are commanded by our Lord to "go not forth". What better way to entice people to go and see the false Christs and false prophets than to show great signs and wonders? Most people would like to see a miracle. But if we go to see these false Christs and prophets, we will pay dearly for the thrill of seeing these signs and wonders. For we may be deceived by Satan through his counterfeit Christs and prophets.

Remember that in Egypt when Moses performed many miracles, the sorcerers and magicians were able to imitate several of the miracles also. (Ex. 7-8)

The second coming of Christ will be seen by the entire world as the rising of the sun is. There will be no need to travel to a special place to see Him. When the true Christ returns, people will either be "taken up" to meet Him or be left to burn with the wicked.

8

FAMINE

If the crops of the earth are going to be destroyed by a hailstorm sent from the Lord at the time of the worldwide earthquake (D&C 29:14-16), then obviously there will be a famine afterwards.

Famines are promised in the last days by the Savior as recorded in Matt. 24:7, Mark 13:8 and Luke 21:11. In our day, Jesus reaffirmed that famines will take place in D&C 43:25 and D&C 87:6.

A YEAR'S SUPPLY AND GARDENS

One of the tribulations of the last days that we can prepare for is famine. Many saints are slack in their preparation even though our modern prophets have repeatedly counseled us to be ready. We have been warned for so many years to have a year's supply of food, clothing and fuel (where possible) and to grow gardens and store seeds, that many "ears are dull of hearing" and many "eyes cannot see afar off".

When the Lord asked Noah to build an ark in preparation for the flood, what if Noah had said to himself, "I have asked the prominent scientists and they say there is not enough water to entirely cover the earth in a flood. There has never been a worldwide flood before, so I cannot imagine one happening now. I do not want to appear to be an alarmist to my friends. My family and I are righteous people, and I know the Lord is too kind to drown us in a flood. Besides, I am not really in to boat building. It sounds like it would be quite a hassle with all those smelly animals. I will keep the other commandments, and we will be alright."

Fortunately for us, Noah believed the Lord and followed His counsel even though it might not have been convenient and easy for him. If we are faithful and have stored what we will need to endure the famine, undoubtedly our future posterity will be very grateful that we did.

EXCUSES FOR DISOBEDIENCE TO COUNSEL

There are many rationalizations among different Church members for not having a year's supply. Some of the better ones are as follows.

"Uncle Joe has had a food supply for over forty years and what good has it done him?" He has been obedient to a commandment of the Lord through His prophets and will be blessed for his faithfulness.

"If there was a shortage of food, the government and the Red Cross would get us food." Taking into consideration the prophesies about civil strife and bloodshed in America and the Constitution hanging by a thread, counting on help from the government may be hazardous to your health.

"Having a year's supply is impractical. People will just steal it when things get bad." If we are obedient, the Lord will bless us regardless of what might happen. Remember that during the drought when the prophet Elijah was sent to get food from a widow woman in Zarephath. She was promised in the name of the Lord that if she gave food to Elijah from the small amount of food that she had left that her barrel of meal and cruse of oil would not be empty until the Lord caused it to rain again. She shared her last food with Elijah and did not lack for meal or oil as was promised. (1 Kgs. 17:8-16) The Lord can multiply a small amount of food into a great quantity. It is recorded that on two separate occasions, Jesus took a few loaves and fishes and miraculously multiplied them to feed thousands of people with many baskets of food left over. (Matt. 14:17-21, 15:34-38) Certainly our Lord still has that same power today to feed His obedient followers. If we are faithful in storing a year's supply of food, etc., we can expect divine intervention if our food storage is depleted because we shared with others or because it was stolen. With the pollutions in the atmosphere after the worldwide earthquake, people may have to stay in their homes to keep from getting sick. Many people would not be interested in wheat anyway.

"I would not want to live if all I had to eat was wheat and beans." When starvation stares us in the face, we may all be somewhat humbled and appreciate even a Sego Lily. Watching our children go hungry would also be a terrible experience.

"We are righteous, God will not allow us to go hungry." If Noah and his family had not obeyed and built the Ark, prepared it and boarded the Ark, they would have drowned with the rest of the people. If we choose not to heed the warning God has given us through His prophets for many years to store and produce food, we can expect no protection from the famine.

"Food storage is a waste of money, I have thrown out so much spoiled food over the years." Keeping the commandments given from God is never a waste of money. It is the best way that we can spend our money. Proper storage of food can help eliminate spoilage. Making the food from our storage a regular part of our daily menus can also help rotate stored food and can prepare us for the day when we will live off of it.

"I am just no good at growing a garden." Noah probably did not know how to build an Ark at first.

However, Noah was willing to learn. We need to practice each summer if at all possible to get expert at growing gardens. Anyone with enough determination can learn how.

DO IT NOW

President Spencer W. Kimball counseled during the days of his Presidency, "We encourage you to grow all the food that you feasibly can on your own property." (Ensign, May 1976, p. 124, I.A.)

This plaintive plea was also made by President Kimball: "We encourage families to have on hand this year's supply; and we say it over and over and repeat over and over the scripture of the Lord where He says, 'Why call ye me, Lord, Lord, and do not the things which I say?'" (Ensign, May 1976, p. 125, I.A.)

President Ezra Taft Benson gave a profound and prophetic sermon on preparedness in the October 1980 General Conference. The following are some excerpts from that talk. "The revelation to produce and store food may be as essential to our temporal welfare today as boarding the ark was to the people in the days of Noah. Make your storage a part of your budget. Store seeds and have sufficient tools on hand to do the job. If you are saving and planning for a second car or a TV set or some item which merely adds to your comfort or pleasure, you may need to change your priorities. We urge you to do this prayerfully and do it now. I speak with a feeling of great urgency. I have seen what the days of tribulation can do to people...Too often we bask in our comfortable complacency and rationalize that the ravages of war, economic disaster, famine, and earthquake cannot happen here. Those who believe this are either not acquainted with the revelations of the Lord or do not believe them. Those who smugly think these calamities will not happen, that they somehow will be set aside because of the righteousness of the Saints, are deceived and will rue the day they harbored such a delusion. The Lord has warned and forewarned us against a day of great tribulation and given us counsel, through His servants, on how we can prepare for these difficult times. Have we heeded His counsel?" (Ensign, Nov. 1980, pp. 32-34, I.A.)

The prophets have spoken plainly and forcefully. Will we heed their counsel and be obedient? Will we believe the prophecies in the scriptures that warn of coming famine and be prepared and live?

Methuselah lived when a sore famine killed many people. (Moses 8:4) There was a grievous famine when Abraham was a young man. (Gen. 12:10, Abr. 1:29-30) Isaac had to move to Gerar because of a famine. (Gen. 26:1-6) Famine was over all of the face of the earth during Jacob or Israel's lifetime. (Gen. 41:56) Israel and his family had to move to Goshen near Egypt to survive it. (Gen. 47:13, 27) King David saw three years of famine when Saul was King. (2 Sam. 21:1) The famine lasted seven years when Elisha was a prophet. (2 Kgs. 8:1) Jeremiah knew days of great famine. (Jer. 14:1, 15, and Lam. 5:10) Thousands died of famine among the Nephites and Lamanites shortly before Christ was born. (Hel. 11:4-6) We will see great desolations by famine in this generation. Joseph Smith was informed of that fact by the angel Moroni in 1823: "...he informed me of great judgments which were coming upon the earth, with great desolations by famine, sword, and pestilence; and that these grievous judgments would come on the earth in this generation." (JS-H 1:45, I.A.)

We have our free agency. We can get a year's supply of food, clothing and fuel (where possible) along with water, seeds and gardening tools, or we can ignore the counsel of the Lord, angels and prophets. The choice is ours. We will live with the consequences of our choices.

THE NEW JERUSALEM

THE SAINTS RETURN TO HELP BUILD THE NEW JERUSALEM

The Lord has already told us that the future New Jerusalem will be built at Indendence, Jackson County, Missouri. The saints will gather to this land of promise which will be called Zion: "...the land of Missouri, which is the land which I have appointed and consecrated for the gathering of the saints. Wherefore, this is the land of promise, and the place for the city of Zion...Behold, the place which is now Independence is the center place;" (D&C 57:1-3, I.A.).

Jackson County, Missouri, is that land set apart by the Lord for the gathering of the saints. The wicked will not be left on that land when the saints go back to build up Zion: "Behold, the destroyer I have sent forth to destroy and lay waste mine enemies; and not many years hence they shall not be left to pollute mine heritage, and to blaspheme my name upon the lands which I have consecrated for the gathering together of my saints." (D&C 105:15, I.A.)

Heber C. Kimball made a prophesy that the western part of the State of Missouri would be swept clean of inhabitants: "The western boundary of the State of Missouri will be swept so clean of its inhabitants that as President Young tells us, when you return to that place, there will not be left so much as a yellow dog to wag his tail." (Deseret News, Church Dep't, May 23, 1931, p. 3, I.A.)

When Joshua and the children of Israel went to inherit the promised land of Canaan, they were commanded to destroy the wicked inhabitants of the land. (Josh. 1-12) It appears that natural causes will prepare the promised land of Jackson County, Missouri, for the return of the saints.

The Lord has said that the converted Gentiles, the Lamanites and the House of Israel will help build the New Jerusalem, "And they [the converted Gentiles] shall assist my people, the remnant of Jacob [the Lamanites], and also many of the house of Israel as shall come, that they may build a city, which shall be called the New Jerusalem. And then shall they assist my people [the Lamanites] that they may be gathered in, who are scattered upon all the face of the land, in unto the New Jerusalem." (3 Ne. 21:23-24, I.A.)

Will all the saints go back to Missouri? Brigham Young answered that question when he said that only a portion of the Priesthood would go back and that not everyone would, "...a portion of the Priesthood will go and redeem and build up the centre Stake of Zion." (J.D. 11:16, I.A.) He also said, "Are we going back to Jackson County? Yes. When? As soon as the way opens up. Are we all going? O no! of course not." (J.D. 18:355, I.A.)

The New Jerusalem will be built especially for those who are descendants of Joseph through his sons, Ephraim and Manasseh, "And that a New Jerusalem should be built up upon this land [America], unto the remnant of the seed of Joseph," (Ether 13:6, I.A. and Ether 13:10).

With the civil strife which will be taking place in America at that time, it will be necessary to have help from the armies of heaven as the saints return to Missouri. Joseph Smith and his scribe saw a vision of these protecting hosts of heaven: "My scribe also received his anointing with us, and saw, in a vision the armies of heaven protecting the Saints in their return to Zion, and many things which I saw." (DHC,

2:381, I.A.)

WHAT WILL THE NEW JERUSALEM BE LIKE?

The Lord has promised that when the time comes to build the city of the New Jerusalem, He will hasten the process and will crown the faithful with joy: "And thus, even as I have said, if ye are faithful ye shall assemble yourselves together to rejoice upon the land of Missouri, which is the land of your inheritance, which is now the land of your enemies. But, behold, I, the Lord, will hasten the city in its time, and will crown the faithful with joy and rejoicing." (D&C 52:42-43, I.A.)

How might the Lord hasten the building of the city of New Jerusalem? He promised that it would come down out of heaven, "And that it [America] was the place of the New Jerusalem, which should come down out of heaven, and the holy sanctuary of the Lord." (Ether 13:3, I.A.)

John the Revelator also prophesied that the New Jerusalem would come down out of heaven from God: "Behold, I come quickly; hold that fast which thou hast, that no man take thy crown. Him that overcometh will I make a pillar in the temple of my God, and he shall go no more out: and I will write upon him the name of the city of my God, which is new Jerusalem, which cometh down out of heaven from my God: and I will write upon him my new name." (Rev. 3:11-12, I.A.)

On December 16, 1877, President John Taylor received a vision about the foundation of the New Jerusalem. He saw in more detail just how the heavenly hosts would come down from heaven and establish the New Jerusalem: "I saw the whole states of Missouri and Illinois and part of Iowa were a complete wilderness with no living human being in them...I saw myriads of angels hovering over them and around about them and also an immense pillar of a cloud hover over them. And I saw some come who wore their temple robes to help build the Temple and the city and all the time I saw the great pillar of a cloud hovering over the place." (Wilford Woodruff Journals, June 15, 1878, Church Historians Office, and Unpublished, 1:122)

The Lord told Enoch that the elect of God would gather from all over the world to the New Jerusalem before the second coming of the Lord, "And righteousness will I send down out of heaven; and truth will I send forth out of the earth,...to gather out mine elect from the four quarters of the earth, unto a place which I shall prepare, an Holy City, that my people may gird up their loins, and be looking forth for the time of my coming; for there shall be my tabernacle, and it shall be called Zion, a New Jerusalem." (Moses 7:62, I.A. and D&C 84:2-5)

A beautiful temple will be constructed at the New Jerusalem upon the temple lot that the Lord has chosen: "Which city shall be built, beginning at the temple lot, which is appointed by the finger of the Lord, in the western boundaries of the State of Missouri, and dedicated by the hand of Joseph Smith, Jun., and others with whom the Lord was well pleased. Verily this is the word of the Lord, that the city New Jerusalem shall be built by the gathering of the saints, beginning at this place, even the place of the temple, which temple shall be reared in this generation." (D&C 84:3-4, I.A., and D&C 57:3)

President Wilford Woodruff taught that the United Order will be lived at the New Jerusalem: "It has been promised that the New Jerusalem will be built up in our day and generation, and it will have to be done by the United Order of Zion and according to celestial law." (J.D. 17:250, I.A.)

Zion or the New Jerusalem will also be a place of peace, refuge and safety amidst the wickedness and bloodshed that will be rampant elsewhere, "And it shall be called the New Jerusalem, a land of peace, a city of refuge, a place of safety for the saints of the Most High God." (D&C 45:66, I.A., and D&C 45:71, Isa. 35:10)

Those who dwell in the New Jerusalem will be blessed and made righteous through the atonement of Jesus Christ: "And then cometh the New Jerusalem; and blessed are they who dwell therein, for it is they whose garments are white through the blood of the Lamb;" (Ether 13:10, I.A.).

JESUS CHRIST WILL BE SEEN IN THE MIDST OF THE NEW JERUSALEM

The crowning blessing which the inhabitants of the New Jerusalem will receive will be the presence of Jesus Christ and the powers of heaven. This will happen as has been promised by the Lord: "...it shall be a New Jerusalem. And the powers of heaven shall be in the midst of this people; yea, even I will be in the midst of you." (3 Ne. 20:22, I.A., 3 Ne. 21:25)

As the devil will exercise power over his kingdom in the last days, the Lord will have power over His Saints: "...the devil shall have power over his dominion. And also the Lord shall have power over his saints, and shall reign in their midst," (D&C 1:35-36, I.A.).

When the wicked see the glory of the Lord and the powers of heaven or immense pillar of a cloud over the New Jerusalem, they will be terrified and will not come to it, "And it shall be called the New Jerusalem,..And the glory of the Lord shall be there and the terror of the Lord also shall be there, insomuch that the wicked will not come unto it, and it shall be called Zion." (D&C 45:45:66-67, I.A.)

Another word for "the glory of the Lord" is a cloud which will rest upon the temple and fill the house as in the days of Solomon's temple (1 Kgs. 8:10-11): "Verily this is the word of the Lord, that the city New Jerusalem shall be built...For verily this generation shall not all pass away until an house shall be built unto the Lord, and a cloud shall rest upon it, which cloud shall be even the glory of the Lord, which shall fill the house." (D&C 84:4-5, I.A.)

What a blessing it will be for those saints who are privileged to live in the New Jerusalem. They will enjoy the presence of the Savior, peace, joy and the united order of Zion.

THE CALLING OF THE 144,000 DURING THE SIXTH SEAL

(BEFORE A.D. 2000)

AFTER THE RETURN OF THE TEN LOST TRIBES

144,000 ARE SEALED

During the sixth seal or before the approximate year of 2000 A.D. (D&C 77:9-11, Ensign, Oct. 1983, p.52), 144,000 high priests from the twelve tribes of Israel will be called and sealed: "And I saw another angel...and he cried with a loud voice to the four angels,...Saying, Hurt not the earth, neither the sea, nor the trees, till we have sealed the servants of our God in their foreheads. And I heard the number of them which were sealed: and there were sealed an hundred and forty and four thousand of all the tribes of the children of Israel. Of the tribe of Juda were sealed twelve thousand. Of the tribe of Reuben were sealed twelve thousand. Of the tribe of Gad were sealed twelve thousand. Of the tribe of Aser were sealed twelve thousand. Of the tribe of Nephthalim were sealed twelve thousand. Of the tribe of Manasses were sealed twelve thousand. Of the tribe of Simeon were sealed twelve thousand. Of the tribe of Levi were sealed twelve thousand. Of the tribe of Issachar were sealed twelve thousand. Of the tribe of Zabulon were sealed twelve thousand. Of the tribe of Joseph were sealed twelve thousand. Of the tribe of Benjamin were sealed twelve thousand." (Rev. 7:2-8, I.A.)

These one hundred and forty and four thousand will be sealed by the angel who cried to the four angels. John the Revelator also told us that these very special servants will be virgin men who will be redeemed from among men: "And I looked, and, lo, a Lamb stood on the mount Sion, and with him an hundred forty and four thousand, having his Father's name written in their foreheads. And they sung as it were a new song before the throne, and no man could learn that song but the hundred and forty and four thousand, which were redeemed from the earth. Thee are they which were not defiled with women; for they are virgins. These are they which follow the Lamb whithersoever he goeth. These were redeemed from among men, being the firstfruits unto God and to the Lamb." (Rev. 14:1, 3-4, I.A., and D&C 133:18)

When the prophet Joseph Smith clarified some of the scriptures in the Book of Revelation, he said these men would be high priests. These special missionaries will be ordained by the angels who have power over the nations: "Q. What are we to understand by sealing the one hundred and forty-four thousand, out of all the tribes of Israel--twelve thousand out of every tribe? A. We are to understand that those who are sealed are high priests, ordained unto the holy order of God, to administer the everlasting gospel; for they are they who are ordained out of every nation, kindred, tongue, and people, by the angels to whom is given power over the nations of the earth, to bring as many as will come to the church of the Firstborn." (D&C 77:11, I.A.)

President Joseph Fielding Smith shared his insight into the sealing of the 144,000 when he compared their calling to that of the apostle John and the Three Nephite Disciples: "This certainly is a great honor to be one of the 144 thousand who are specially called by the power of 'the angels to whom is given power over the nations of the earth' to bring souls unto Christ. John the Apostle, had the great desire to bring souls to Christ. The Three Nephite Disciples likewise sought this great honor and it was granted to them. It is one of the noblest desires that a man can have. It will be a wonderful blessing to those who are called in this great group." (Church History, 2:71-72, I.A.)

President Joseph Fielding Smith felt that the specially called 144,000 will have similar missions to John the Apostle and the Three Nephite Disciples, who were translated by the Lord. (3 Ne. 28:36-38, D&C 7:1-3)

Joseph Smith taught that the 144,000 would receive divine help by being sealed up against plagues and pestilence. (HC 2:260) This would mean that they could carry on their missionary work without being affected by the plagues and pestilences which will be poured out at times during their ministry.

It is possible that what is meant by the 144,000 being sealed will be that they will be translated before they begin their missionary work. This is what happened to the Three Nephites who received a special mission and were translated: "And now behold, as I spake concerning those whom the Lord hath chosen, yea, even <u>three</u> who were caught up into the heavens, Therefore, that they might not taste of death there was a change wrought upon their bodies, that <u>they might not suffer pain</u> nor sorrow save it were for the sins of the world." (3 Ne. 28:36, 38, I.A.)

JOHN SEES THE FAITHFUL IN HEAVEN

John's vision of what will take place in the last days on the earth is briefly interrupted after the sealing of the 144,000. He foresaw a multitude of faithful followers of Christ dressed in white robes in heaven: "These are <u>they which came out of great tribulation</u>, and have washed their robes, and made them <u>white</u> in the blood of the Lamb." (Rev. 7:14, I.A.)

The fortunate saints who John saw will dwell with God and will not suffer any more from hunger, thirst or heat: "For the Lamb which is in the midst of the throne shall feed them, and shall lead them into living fountains of waters: and God shall wipe away all tears from their eyes." (Rev. 7:17, I.A.)

While the Lord was revealing the great tribulations that will be coming in the last days to John, He chose to comfort His saints by showing that those who suffer or die in these trials will experience great joy. Their death will really be a victory and their blissful reunion with God will be a triumph because of their faithful endurance and their happy state.

THE TEN TRIBES TO RETURN

There are several reasons to believe that the Ten Tribes will return before the 144,000 can be called and sealed during the sixth seal.

First of all, in the Church today most of the members come from the tribe of Joseph through either Ephraim or Manasseh, his sons. There are some from the tribe of Judah, although not many. The other tribes have little representation in the Church. To have 12,000 virgin men called from each of the twelve tribes of Israel would most likely require the return of the Ten Tribes.

Secondly, Joseph Smith said that the destruction in America would prepare the way for the return of the lost tribes of Israel: "And now I am prepared to say by the authority of Jesus Christ, that not many years shall pass away before the United States shall present such a scene of bloodshed as has not a parallel in the history of our nation; pestilence, hail, famine, and earthquake will sweep the wicked of this generation from off the face of the land, to open and prepare the way for the return of the lost tribes of Israel from the north country." (Teachings, p. 17, I.A.)

Jesus was speaking to the Nephites and Lamanites when He taught that in this day when the gospel is preached to the Lamanites, the work would be commenced in gathering the lost tribes. They would inhabit the desolate cities of the Gentiles: "And then shall the work of the Father commence at that day, even when the gospel shall be preached among the remnant of this people [the Lamanites]. Verily, I say unto you, at that day shall the work of the Father commence among all the dispersed of my people, yea, even the tribes which have been lost, which the Father hath led away out of Jerusalem...whereby his people may be gathered home to the land of their inheritance. For thou shalt break forth on the right hand and on the left, and thy seed shall inherit the Gentiles and make the desolate cities to be inhabited." (3 Ne. 21:26, 28, 3 Ne. 22:3, I.A.)

Thirdly, Joseph Smith helped in our understanding of the Book of Revelation immeasurably when he gave us the revelation of D&C 77 from the Lord. In that section, we are taught that Elias was to gather the tribes of Israel and restore all things in the sixth seal: "Q. What are we to understand by the angel ascending from the east, Revelation 7th chapter and 2nd verse? A. We are to understand that the angel ascending from the east is he to whom is given the seal of the living God over the twelve tribes of Israel; wherefore, he crieth unto the four angels having the everlasting gospel, saying: Hurt not the earth, neither the sea, nor the trees, till we have sealed the servants of our God in their foreheads [the 144,000]. And if you will receive it, this is Elias which was to come to gather together the tribes of Israel and restore all things. Q. What time are the things spoken of in this chapter to be accomplished? A. They are to be accomplished in the sixth thousand years, or the opening of the sixth seal." (D&C 77:9-10, I.A.)

According to that revelation then, the major gathering of the twelve tribes of the House of Israel takes place during the sixth thousand year period or during the sixth seal. That would require the return of the Ten Lost Tribes before the approximate year of 2000 A.D.

Who is the Elias spoken of in D&C 77:9? John the Revelator was given the mission to gather the tribes of Israel, and he is this Elias: "Q. What are we to understand by the little book which was eaten by John, as mentioned in the 10th chapter of Revelation? A. We are to understand that it was a mission, and an ordinance, for his [John the Revelator] to gather the tribes of Israel; behold, this is Elias, who, as it is written, must come and restore all things." (D&C 77:14, I.A.)

Joseph Smith said during the Conference of June 2-6, in 1831, that John the Revelator was at that time laboring among the Lost Ten Tribes. (HC 1:176)

In Rev. 7:1, we are told that first the four angels restore the gospel. (D&C 77:8) Then second in Rev. 7:2, we are informed about the angel that gathers the tribes of Israel. (D&C 77:9, 14) Then third in Rev. 7:4-8, we are told of the sealing of the 144,000. The gospel has already been restored. Next the Ten Tribes will be gathered and then the 144,000 will be sealed.

BACKGROUND INFORMATION ON THE LOST TRIBES

The Ten Tribes were led away out of the land about 700 B.C. The only account we have of them being led away is in the Aprocrypha in 2 Esdras 13:39-47: "And whereas thou sawest that he gathered another peaceable multitude unto him; those are the Ten Tribes which were carried away prisoners out of their own land in the time of Osea the king, whom Salmanasar, the King of Assyria, led away captive, and he carried them over the waters and so they came into another land. But they took counsel among themselves, that they would leave the multitude of the heathen, and go forth into a further country, where never mankind dwelt, that they might there keep their statutes, which they never kept in their own land. And they entered Euphrates by the narrow passages of the river, for the Most High then showed signs for them, and held still the floods till they were passed over. For through that country there was a great way to go, viz., of a year and a half; and the same region is called Arsareth. Then dwelt they there until the latter time; and now when they shall begin to come, the Highest shall stay the springs of the streams again, that they may go through;" (Mormon Doctrine, p. 456, 3 Ne. 15:15).

Since it took them so long to get to Arsareth, a year and a half, surely some would have stopped along the way and settled down most likely in Europe and Scandinavia. So some of the blood of the tribes of Israel has been scattered throughout the world.

However, the majority of them were led to Arsareth where mankind had never dwelt before through the power and direction of the Lord. Nephi recorded this about them in around 580 B.C., "...the house of Israel, sooner or later, will be scattered upon all the face of the earth and also among all nations. And behold, there are many who are already lost from the knowledge of those who are at Jerusalem. Yea, the more part have been led away;" (1 Ne. 22:4, I.A.).

The land of Arsareth is often referred to in the scriptures as the land of the north or the north country or countries. After being led away by the Lord, the Ten Tribes became lost to the knowledge of other people. (3 Ne. 15:15, 16:1)

Why have the Ten Tribes been lost to the knowledge of other people? Jesus gave us the answer when He was speaking to the Nephites about the Jews when He said: "And verily, I say unto you again that the other tribes [the Ten Tribes] hath the Father separated from them; and it is because of their iniquity that they know not of them." (3 Ne. 15:20, I.A.)

Perhaps if the Jews had been righteous, they would have known all about the Ten Tribes and where they were taken.

After visiting the Nephites and the Lamanites, Jesus Christ showed himself to the Lost Ten Tribes: "But now I go unto the Father, and also to show myself unto the lost tribes of Israel, for they are not lost unto the Father, for he knoweth whither he hath taken them." (3 Ne. 17:4, I.A.) So Jesus said that the Father knew where the lost tribes were at that time because He had taken them there.

In 1836, in the Kirtland Temple, the priesthood keys were given by Moses for the leading of the Ten Tribes back from the land of the north: "After this vision closed, the heavens were again opened unto us; and Moses appeared before us, and committed unto us the keys of the gathering of Israel from the four parts of the earth, and the leading of the ten tribes from the land of the north." (D&C 110:11, I.A., and D&C 35:25)

GOD WILL BRING THE TEN TRIBES BACK

The Lord led the Ten Tribes out of the land, and we have been promised that He will bring the Ten Tribes back from the land of the north. Speaking of these tribes of Israel, the Lord will command them: "...come forth, and flee from the land of the north, saith the Lord:" (Zech. 2:6, I.A., and Jer. 31:8, Deut. 30:1-3, Isa. 43:6).

When the Ten Tribes return, it will be such a miraculous event wrought by the Lord that it will overshadow when Israel was delivered from bondage in Egypt: "Therefore, behold, the days come, saith the Lord, that it shall no more be said, The Lord liveth, that brought up the children of Israel out of the land of Egypt; But, the Lord liveth, that brought up the children of Israel from the land of the north, and from all the lands whither he had driven them:" (Jer. 16:14-15, I.A., and Jer. 23:7-8).

THE TEN TRIBES COME TO AMERICA AND ZION

The Lord has told us that the Ten Tribes will return through the power and miracles of the priesthood. These miracles will cause a highway to appear in the ocean: "And they who are in the north countries shall come in remembrance before the Lord; and their prophets shall hear his voice, and shall no longer stay themselves; and they shall smite the rocks, and the ice shall flow down at their presence. And an highway shall be cast up in the midst of the great deep." D&C 133:26-27, I.A., Isa. 51:10-11,2 Ne. 8:10-11)

Through the power of God, a highway or road will come up out of the middle of the ocean to facilitate the return of the Ten Tribes from the north country where they are. We know that they will come from the extreme north since ice will flow down before them.

The wicked may want to walk along that highway and go into the land of the north, but the Lord will prevent this from happening: "And an highway shall be there, and a way, and it shall be called The way of holiness; the unclean shall not pass over it; but it shall be for those: the wayfaring men,...but the redeemed shall walk there: And the ransomed of the Lord shall return, and come to Zion with songs and everlasting joy upon their heads: they shall obtain joy and gladness, and sorrow and sighing shall flee away." (Isa. 35:8-10, I.A.)

After the Israelites crossed the Red Sea on dry

ground, the armies of Egypt attempted to follow them across. The Egyptians were drowned in the Sea when the Lord through Moses caused the water to go back and cover their pathway. (Ex. 14:26-28) Perhaps that is how the Lord will prevent the enemies of the Ten Tribes from following the highway back into the land of the north. For it says, "Their enemies shall become a prey unto them," (D&C 133:28, I.A.).

Although the Ten Tribes will have to pass through barren deserts, they will be blessed with water: "And in the barren deserts there shall come forth pools of living water; and the parched ground shall no longer be a thirsty land." (D&C 133:29, I.A., and Isa. 35:6-7)

We are told in Esdras 13:39 in the Apocrypha that the Ten Tribes as a "peaceable" people. If they have not devoted a large part of their resources for weapons, armaments and warfare (as many of our nations have), you can imagine what technological treasures they might have. They will bring their rich treasures to those at the New Jerusalem: "And they shall bring forth their rich treasures unto the children of Ephraim, my servants." (D&C 133:30, I.A.)

Wilford Woodruff taught that the Ten Tribes would receive their endowments in Zion: "...the ten tribes of Israel...will come to Zion, receive their endowments, and be crowned under the hands of the children of Ephraim," (J.D. 4:231-232, I.A.).

When they come down to Zion from the land of the north, the hills will tremble: "And the boundaries of the everlasting hills shall tremble at their presence." And there shall they fall down and be crowned with glory, even in Zion, by the hands of the servants of the Lord, even the children of Ephraim. And they shall be filled with songs of everlasting joy." (D&C 133:31-33, I.A.)

THE SONS OF LEVI MAKE A RIGHTEOUS OFFERING

Among the Ten Tribes who return will be those from the tribe of Levi, who are also descendants of Aaron who was a Levite. These sons of Levi will make an offering to the Lord in righteousness: "...he shall purify the sons of Levi, and purge them as gold and silver, that they may offer unto the Lord an offering in righteousness." (3 Ne. 24:3, I.A., and Mal. 3:3, D&C 13:1)

This offering in righteousness by the descendants of Levi and Aaron will be a sacrificial offering in the temple at the New Jerusalem: "...the sons of Aaron shall offer an acceptable offering and sacrifice in the house of the Lord, which house shall be built unto the Lord in this generation, upon the consecrated spot as I have appointed--" (D&C 84:31, I.A.). The consecrated spot for the house or temple of the Lord was Independence, Missouri, or the center spot for the New Jerusalem. (D&C 57:1-3)

In case we might wonder why the law of sacrifice will be reinstated, the prophet Joseph Smith explained it: "...the offering of sacrifice, which also shall be continued at the last time; for all the ordinances and duties that ever have been required by the Priesthood, under the directions and commandments of the Almighty in any of the dispensations, shall all be had in the last dispensation,...bringing to pass the restoration spoken of by the mouth of all the Holy Prophets; then shall the sons of Levi offer an acceptable offering to the Lord." (Teachings, p. 171-172, I.A.) The law of sacrifice which was given anciently to Adam and his posterity will be practiced again after the return of the Ten Tribes and in the New Jerusalem as part of the restoration of all things in the last days.

THE SCRIPTURES OF THE LOST TRIBES

When the Ten Tribes return, they will bring with them their scriptures and history. What a glorious blessing it will be to read their record which will cover about two thousand and seven hundred years of their history. They were led away about 700 B.C. "I shall also speak unto the other tribes of the house of Israel, which I have led away, and they shall write it;...And it shall come to pass that the Jews shall have the words of the Nephites, and the Nephites shall have the words of Jews, and the Nephites and the Jews shall have the words of the lost tribes of Israel; and the lost tribes of Israel shall have the words of the Nephites and the Jews." (2 Ne. 29:12-13, I.A.)

When we have the Bible, the Book of Mormon and the record of the Ten Tribes of Israel, three civilizations will have given their witness that Jesus is the Christ.

THE TEN TRIBES RETURN TO ISRAEL

When the Ten Tribes return, they will first inhabit the cities that are left desolate by the Gentiles. (3 Ne. 21:14-28, 22:3) Then they will receive their temple blessings from the temples of Zion. (D&C 133:31-33)

Some time after that, at least some of the Ten Tribes will return to Israel to receive their inheritance there: "In those days the house of Judah shall walk with the house of Israel, and they shall come together out of the land of the north to the land that I have given for an inheritance unto your fathers." (Jer. 3:18, I.A.)

Anciently, Judah and Israel were divided into two kingdoms. But in the last days, they will be united under one king, "Thus saith the Lord God; Behold, I will take the children of Israel from among the heathen, whither they be gone, and will gather them on every side, and bring them into their own land. And I will make them one nation in the land upon the mountains of Israel; and one king shall be king to them all: and they shall be no more two nations, neither shall they be divided into two kingdoms any more at all:" (Ezek. 37:21-22, I.A., and Jer. 16:15, Zech. 10:3-10).

Thus the Ten Tribes will be joined by the rest of Israel that has been gathered, and they will inhabit the land promised to the posterity of Abraham: "And then also cometh the Jerusalem of old; and the inhabitants thereof, blessed are they, for they have been washed in the blood of the Lamb; and they are they who were scattered and gathered in from the four quarters of the earth, and from the north countries, and are partakers of the fulfilling of the covenant which God made with their father, Abraham." (Ether 13:11, I.A.)

Joseph Smith taught that because of the transgression of ancient King David, his throne will be given to another latter-day King David: "...the throne and kingdom of David is to be taken from him and given to another by the name of David in the last days, raised up out of his lineage." (HC 6:253, I.A.)

Because of their wickedness in ancient times, the children of Israel were scattered throughout the world, and the Ten Tribes chose to leave the land of their fathers. In the last days, the descendants of Israel will be gathered in again when the tribes of Israel will inhabit the Holy Land in righteousness. Thus the ancient promises to Abraham, Isaac and Jacob about their posterity will be fulfilled.

11

ARE THE TEN LOST TRIBES UNDER THE EARTH?

ARE THEY IN THE NORTH COUNTRIES?

The Ten Tribes have been lost for approximately two thousand and seven hundred years. During that length of time, their population must have multiplied until it is at least into the millions of people by now. There are really only two theories as to where they could be which would allow for enough land mass to accommodate that large of a population.

One theory is that the Ten Tribes were led north and then God broke off a piece of land in the north and took them into space or transported them to another planet. (Similar to what happened to the City of Enoch.) Then, the theory goes, God will bring them back to the north, and they will come back. Since the City of Enoch left, we have been given ample evidence in the scriptures and other ancient writings that they were translated and taken into heaven. (Gen. 5:24, D&C 107:49, Moses 7:21, 23-24) We also have several scriptures which indicate that the City of Enoch will be brought back to the earth. (Moses 7:62-63, D&C 45:11-12) If the Lost Tribes were taken to heaven, why are there no scriptures to confirm it as we have concerning the City of Enoch? There is no mention in the scriptures of the Ten Tribes being brought back to the earth either as has been prophesied regarding the return of the City of Enoch. To the contrary, the scriptures refer to the Ten Tribes as being in the north countries right now: "And <u>they who are in the north countries</u> shall come in remembrance before the Lord;" (D&C 133:26, I.A.).

When speaking of the location of the Lost Tribes, Esdras said in the Apocrypha that it took one and a half years to travel to Arsareth where men had never dwelt before and, "Then dwelt they there until the latter time" (2 Esdras 13:46, I.A.).

The angel Moroni told Joseph Smith in one of their visits together that the Ten Tribes had been in the land of the north for a long time: "...the ten tribes of Israel will be revealed in the north country, whither they have been for a long season;" (Letter by Oliver Cowdery, published in the "Latter Day Saints' Messenger and Advocate", I.A.).

These statements leave little doubt that the Ten Tribes went into the north country and that they will remain there until the Lord brings them back in the latter-days.

The City of Enoch also went through a special process called translation when they were taken into heaven. (Heb. 11:5, D&C 107:49, 45:12, Moses 7:69) There is nowhere in the scriptures that it says that the Ten Tribes were translated.

We need to discover where Arsareth is which is called in the scriptures the land of the north or the north country or countries.

THE HOLLOW EARTH THEORY

The other theory as to where the Ten Tribes have been taken is called "the hollow earth" theory. This theory purports that there are openings in the earth at the poles, which openings lead into the interior of the earth where there is an inner sun and continents along with oceans. The following diagram is an attempt to represent the possible dimensions of this theory.

THE HOLLOW EARTH

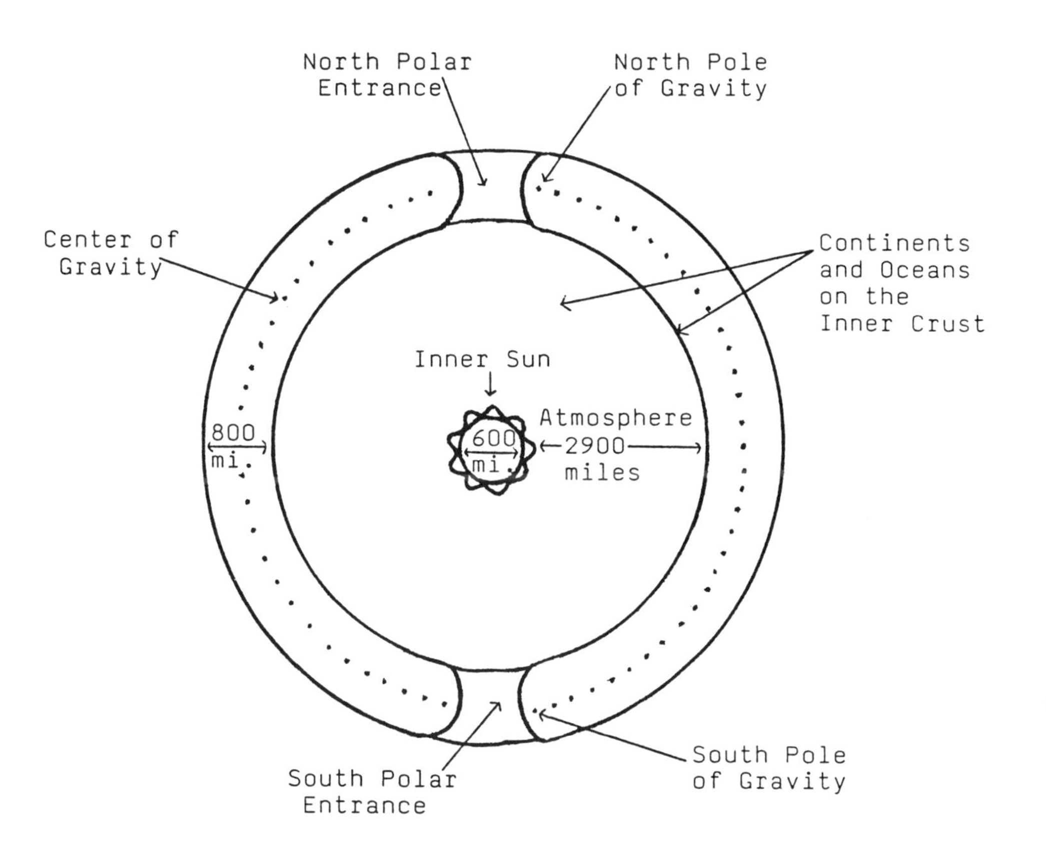

(See The Hollow Earth, by Dr. Raymond Bernard.)

SCRIPTURAL EVIDENCE

Certainly if there were men dwelling inside the earth, or in other words "under the earth" upon which we live, then the scriptures would mention it for: "Surely the Lord God will do nothing, but he revealeth his secret unto his servants the prophets." (Amos 3:7, I.A.)

We will now examine the scriptures that suggest that there are men living "under the earth". John the Revelator received the greatest revelation on the last days that we have, which is the Book of Revelation. John was also given the mission of gathering the tribes of Israel. (D&C 77:9, 14) Nephi saw in a vision the event of the last days but was forbidden to write all of what he saw: "But the things which thou shalt see hereafter thou shalt not write; for the Lord hath ordained the apostle of the Lamb of God [John the Revelator] that he should write them." (1 Ne. 14:25, I.A.) With both of those special callings, surely John the Revelator would have known if there were men under the earth. John was given a book with seven seals. The angel asked, "Who is worthy to open the book, and to loose the seals thereof? And no man in heaven, nor in earth, neither under the earth, was able to open the book, neither to look thereon." (Rev. 5:3, I.A.)

John saw that no man in heaven or earth or under the earth was worthy to open the book. Fortunately, Jesus was worthy to open it. (Rev. 5:5-8)

A vision of that great day at the second coming when every knee shall bow and every tongue confess that Jesus is the Christ was also shown to John: "And every creature which is in heaven, and on the earth, and under the earth, and such as are in the sea, and all that are in them, heard I saying, Blessing, honour, and glory, and power, be unto him that sitteth upon the throne, and unto the Lamb for ever and ever."

Those who John saw praising the Lord in the vision were located in heaven, on the earth, under the earth and in the sea. We have two other scriptures which testify of this same event that also include the people "under the earth" bowing their knees to the Savior: "And this shall be the sound of his trump, saying to all people, both in heaven and in earth, and that are under the earth--for every ear shall hear it, and every knee shall bow, and every tongue shall confess," (D&C 88:104, I.A.). "That at the name of Jesus every knee should bow, of things in heaven, and in earth, and things under the earth; And that every tongue should confess that Jesus Christ is Lord, to the glory of God the Father." (Philip. 2:10-11, I.A.)

If there were not people living under the earth, they could not bow their knees and confess to Jesus Christ when He returns.

According to many of our modern textbooks, the earth has a molten core which would make living "under the earth" impossible. The fact is that scientists have not been able to probe deeply enough into the earth to definitely prove their theory that the earth is solid.

The fact that our modern scriptures refer to people "under the earth" just as the Bible does, is further evidence that there are men living "under the earth".

The Lord has even commanded us to learn about things that are under the earth: "Teach ye diligently...Of things both in heaven and in the earth and under the earth; things which have been, things which are, things which must shortly come to pass;" (D&C 88:78-79, I.A.). Would Jesus command us to study things which are under the earth, if the earth had a molten core? At this time, we know very little about "under the earth".

At the Second Coming, Jesus will reveal

everything that has been kept secret from the world. Hidden mysteries that are in the earth as well as upon the earth will be included in what will be revealed: "Yea, verily I say unto you, in that day when the Lord shall come, he shall reveal all things--Things which have passed, and hidden things which no man knew, things of the earth, by which it was made, and the purpose and the end thereof--Things most precious, things that are above, and things that are beneath, things that are in the earth, and upon the earth, and in heaven." (D&C 101:32-34, I.A.)

Jesus gave a detailed description to Adam of all His creations that bear record of Him, "...all things are created and made to bear record of me,...things which are in the heavens above, and things which are on the earth, and things which are in the earth, and things which are under the earth, both above and beneath: all things bear record of me." (Moses 6:63, I.A.) Jesus knows this earth better than anyone else because He created it. If there was not an area "under the earth" which is different than "in the earth", why would the Lord so clearly delineate between the heavens, on the earth, in the earth and under the earth?

The Lord was speaking to the Nephites in America when he proclaimed to them that He rules in the heavens above them and in the earth beneath them: "Know ye not that there are more nations than one? Know ye not that I, the Lord your God, have created all men, and that I remember those who are upon the isles of the sea; and that I rule in the heavens above and in the earth beneath;" (2 Ne. 29:7, I.A.).

When all men shall be filled with the knowledge of God during the millenium, they will sing a new song. (D&C 84:98) There will be rejoicing in this song about Zion being established again, about being redeemed by the Lord and about Satan being bound. (D&C 84:99-100) Then there will be rejoicing in the song about the gathering of Israel and the restoration of all things: "The Lord hath gathered all things in one. The Lord hath brought down Zion from above. The Lord hath brought up Zion from beneath." (D&C 84:100, I.A.) Obviously, the Zion that is brought down from above is the return of the City of Enoch. But we are also told that the Lord will bring up Zion "from beneath". Could that refer to the return of the Lost Tribes of Israel?

Then the song includes some beautiful poetry: "The earth hath travailed and brought forth her strength; and truth is established in her bowels;" (D&C 84:101, I.A.). The word "travail" is often used in the scriptures in reference to suffering the pangs of being in labor and of childbirth. (Rev. 12:2) This scripture reveals that the earth will travail and then will bring forth her strength. The travail or labor could symbolize or represent the worldwide earthquake, etc. The birth or bringing forth of the earth's strength could figuratively describe the Ten Tribes leaving the inside of the earth and being brought to the outside of the earth.

Then the song adds that truth will be established "in her bowels". We all know that bowels are located within a person. The bowels of the earth could also have reference to the inside of the earth. Certainly not all of the people living inside the earth will return to the surface. Therefore, truth could still be established in the bowels of the earth after the Lost Tribes leave.

During the time of the worldwide earthquake, the Lord made it clear that there would be signs in the heavens above and in the earth beneath: "But, behold, I say unto you that before this great day [the second coming] shall come the sun shall be darkened, and the moon shall be turned into blood, and the stars shall fall from heaven, and there shall be greater signs in heaven above and in the earth beneath;" (D&C 29:14, I.A.). "And they shall see signs and wonders, for they shall be shown forth in the heavens above, and in the earth beneath." (D&C 45:40, I.A.)

The signs in the heavens would be visible to people on the face or surface of the earth, but who would the signs in the earth beneath be seen by? The Ten Tribes were shown signs when they went into the land of the north. (2 Esdras 13:39-47) Perhaps the Lord will show signs under the earth to the Ten Tribes so that they will know that the time has come for them to return to the surface of the earth and to the land of their fathers. If it took them one and a half years to go to Arsareth, it will most likely take them about one and a half years to return.

It is also very interesting to note that during the creation of the earth, God created "the light" (note that this light is singular) and divided it from the darkness on the first day of creation. (Moses 2:3-5, Abr. 4:3-5, Gen. 1:3-5) Then later on during the fourth day, He created "the lights" (note that they are plural) which are then identified as the sun, moon and stars. (Moses 2:14-19, Abr. 4:14-19, Gen. 1:14-19) If the Lord created all the lights that are visible from the surface of the earth (the sun, moon and stars) on the fourth day, then what was the light that he created on the first day? Could it have been the sun inside the earth?

The following scripture describes the Ten Tribes as being in more than one north country as they are in "the north countries". It also illustrates that the location of the Ten Tribes is somewhere that will require them to pass through "ice" that will flow down and to pass over "an ocean" requiring a highway to be cast up through the power of the Lord. That limits them to coming from the region of the North Pole: "And they who are in the north countries shall come in remembrance before the Lord; and their prophets shall hear his voice, and shall no longer stay themselves; and they shall smite the rocks, and the ice shall flow down at their presence. And an highway shall be cast up in the midst of the great deep." (D&C 133:26-27, I.A.)

Why would the present location of the Ten Tribes be kept from the general knowledge of the people on the face or surface of the earth? The Lord said that the Jews did not know where the tribes had been taken because of their wickedness: "And verily, I say unto you again that the other tribes hath the Father separated from them [the Jews]; and it is because of their iniquity that they know not of them." (3 Ne. 15:20, I.A.)

Most likely, the inhabitants on the surface of the earth do not know about the Ten Lost Tribes because of their general iniquity. Many would just attempt to gain dominion over the "peaceable" Ten Tribes through aggression and violence. This might lead to unnecessary bloodshed. There is also the possibility that our people might contaminate their civilization with pornography, immorality and depravity. These evils of our world are the very reason that the Ten Tribes wanted to go to a land where no man had lived before that was separate, so that they would not be influenced by the wicked world around them.

Apparently Wilford Woodruff knew where the Ten Lost Tribes have been hidden. He said they are on a portion of the earth that is separate from the main land: "The ten tribes of Israel are on a portion of the earth--a portion separate from the main land." (Wilford Woodruff, by Cowley, p. 448) Certainly the inside of the earth is separate from the outside or face of the earth.

There must be a power beneath the earth for Wilford Woodruff also said that there was no power on the earth nor beneath the earth that could stop the wars that are prophesied: "There is no power on earth, nor beneath the earth, nor anywhere else, that can stay the fulfillment of these things [wars]. And they are at our doors." (Conference Report, April 1898, p. 32)

This situation could be very similar to when the ancient inhabitants of Europe thought that the world was flat, and they ridiculed anyone that said it was not flat. This erroneous theory kept their explorers from discovering North and South America for hundreds of years. When the Lord wanted the Europeans to know about the Americas, he inspired Christopher Columbus to sail across the ocean and the New World was discovered. That scientific theory was certainly proven wrong.

PHYSICAL EVIDENCES

There are several physical evidences that support the "hollow earth" theory. In the general area of the North and South Poles, there are famous streaming lights that illuminate the sky. These lights from the North Pole are called the Aurora Borealis or the Northern Lights. These lights from the South Pole are called the Southern Lights. Could these well-known lights be caused by the rays of light from the inner sun shining through the holes at the poles and then reflecting off of the atmosphere and clouds?

Most people have heard about the Northern and Southern Lights, but there are other evidences that are only seen and written about by explorers and visitors to the polar regions. Since few of us take our vacations at the poles, these evidences are difficult to verify. It is reported that in the extreme north during certain times of the year, red, pink, yellow and blue pollen can be seen on the snow and ice. Since there is only ice in that area and no vegetation, where the pollen comes from is a mystery. Perhaps the pollen is carried by streams of water from the inside of the earth. Also seeds of tropical plants have been found drifting down in currents from the area of the North Pole. Polar explorers have discovered that millions of birds and animals, like the musk-ox, are seen migrating further north in the winter toward the North Pole and further South in the winter toward the South Pole. Why would they do that if it gets colder the closer you get to the poles, unless there was some place near the poles for them to survive during the winter? Some arctic explorers have reported that the further north you go after the 82 degree latitude, the milder it gets with warm northerly winds and an open sea for hundreds of miles. (The Hollow Earth, p. 121-134) (When the warm air from inside the earth meets the cold air at the poles, it produces a great deal of fog and cloud cover in the polar regions.)

Rear Admiral Richard E. Byrd was a famous American explorer. In February of 1947, he said the following just before his seven-hour flight that went 1,700 miles beyond the North Pole: "I'd like to see that land beyond the Pole. That area beyond the pole is the center of the Great Unknown." Admiral Byrd also said, "This is the most important expedition in the history of the World" just before he departed to explore the land beyond the South Pole.

In January of 1956, Admiral Byrd reported: "On January 13th, members of the United States expedition accomplished a flight of 2,700 miles from the base at McMurdo Sound, which is 400 miles west of the South Pole, and penetrated a land extent of 2,300 miles beyond the Pole." The radio announcement from Byrd's Antarctic expedition was confirmed by the American Press on February 5, 1956.

On March 13, 1956, Admiral Byrd said, "The present expedition has opened up a vast new territory", when he returned from the expedition to the region of the South Pole. (The Hollow Earth, p.

19-20, I.A.)

What was Admiral Byrd referring to when he spoke of a land beyond the pole which he referred to as the center of the great unknown? What vast new territory did his expedition open up? Could it be that Admiral Byrd actually went into the earth through the polar openings, and that the land beyond the poles is really inside the earth?

The theory that the earth has a molten core probably uses as evidence that the earth gets warmer the deeper you go into its surface. But unless someone were to drill a hole clear to the center of the earth, there is no concrete proof for this theory.

PICTORIAL EVIDENCE FROM OTHER PLANETS, SUNS AND MOONS

If the earth is really hollow with an inner sun and holes at the poles, then it may follow that other planets, suns and perhaps even some moons could be hollow with holes at the poles and an inner sun.

There is pictorial evidence available that indicates the possibility that other heavenly bodies might be hollow. Some people may question whether an inner sun within a hollow planet would remain stationary. Pictures of Saturn are a good example of this principle of centrifugal force. The distance between Saturn and its innermost ring is 7,000 miles. In spite of this, Saturn remains in a stationary position within its rings.

Pictures have been taken of new suns being formed in our galaxy. They very clearly show a small inner star or sun with massive swirls of matter gathering around and encompassing the small star in the formation of new suns. (National Geographic, May 1974, Mayall telescope, Kitt Peak National Observatory, Tucson, Arizona)

Through the modern technology of sounding rockets, pictures of the solar atmosphere of our sun have been taken. These images reveal dark areas at both polar regions. It is explained that, "dark areas mark holes in the polar regions". (1976, John Davis, American Science and Engineering, Inc., Cambridge, Massachusetts)

We are told that the lighted areas at both poles on the planet Mars are caused by ice. If the bright lights at both poles were really ice, then why would the light from them extend out into the atmosphere of Mars as it does in many pictures? (E. C. Slipher, Lowell Observatory, Flagstaff, Arizona; Mariner 6, July 1969; Mariner 7, August 1969; infrared photographs of Mars from Mount Wilson and Palomar Observatories) If the lights were caused by the rays of an inner sun shining out through the poles, then naturally the light would reflect off the atmosphere and extend out beyond the surface of Mars.

The topography of Venus has been a mystery in the past because of the heavy clouds that surround it. On December 4, 1978, the Pioneer Venus Orbiter through the advanced technology of special radar instruments was able to penetrate the thick clouds and reveal the surface topography of Venus. However, when the government released the pictures to the public, information on large areas at the poles of Venus was not given. The poles were simply blocked out while the surface of the rest of the planet was revealed. No explanation was given as to why the topography of the poles was not released except that, "The data cover all of the planet except for small regions near each pole".

In February of 1979, the Voyager 1 was able to make a close-up computer-generated mosaic of Jupiter's poles. The pictures of Jupiter were very detailed except for both poles. It appears that black paper was placed over the north and south poles with no reason given for the blackout except, "The black area at the pole results from missing information". This was written on the pictures of both the north and south poles of Jupiter. The Voyager 1 report does point out however that grand-scale auroras (like the Northern and Southern Lights) were seen around both of Jupiter's poles.

What could be the reason for blocking out information on the poles unless something is being withheld from the public?

Voyager 1 also took pictures of Io, a moon that circles Jupiter. A bright hole of light is visible at the top of this moon. The explanation given for this brilliant hole is that it is an active volcano. Pictures of another one of Jupiter's moons, Amalthea, also reveal a bright round hole at the top of the moon.

There is pictorial evidence available which indicates that perhaps planets, suns and some moons may have holes in the areas of their north and south poles although conclusive evidence has been withheld.

12

THE FUTURE OF THE LAMANITES

Great blessings are promised to the Lamanites (who are also called the remnant of Jacob) in the last days. The Lamanites are the native Americans who live from northern Canada down to the southern most part of South America and in the Pacific Islands. Columbus called them "Indians" because at first he thought he had landed in India when he discovered America.

THEY WILL HAVE THE GOSPEL PREACHED TO THEM

Jesus prophesied to the Nephites and the Lamanites when He visited them after His resurrection, and he promised that their descendants in the last days would have the gospel preached to them: "And then shall the work of the Father commence at that day [the last days], even when <u>this gospel shall be preached among the remnant of this people</u>...to prepare the way whereby <u>they may come unto me</u>, that they may call on the Father in my name." (3 Ne. 21:26-27, I.A., and Hel. 15:11, D&C 30:6, 109:65)

We are seeing phenomenal numbers of the children of Lehi accept the gospel and join the Church. There are now more members of the Church who speak Spanish than English because of this tremendous growth.

THEY SHALL BLOSSOM AS THE ROSE

The Lord knew that before the great day of His second coming, the Lamanites would blossom into a choice people: "But before the great day of the Lord shall come, Jacob shall flourish in the wilderness, and the Lamanites shall blossom as the rose." (D&C 49:24, I.A.)

This is happening before our very eyes in a marvelous manner. Nephi said this about his posterity in the last days: "And then shall the remnant of our seed know concerning us, how that we came out from Jerusalem, and that they are descendants of the Jews. And the gospel of Jesus Christ shall be declared among them; wherefore, they shall be restored unto the knowledge of their fathers, and also to the knowledge of Jesus Christ, which was had among their fathers. And then shall they rejoice; for they shall know that it is a blessing unto them from the hand of God; and their scales of darkness shall begin to fall from their eyes; and many generations shall not pass away among them, save they shall be a pure and delightsome people." (2 Ne. 30:4-6, I.A.)

The prayers of Mormon (W of M 1:8) and many other righteous Nephites will be answered when the Lamanites once again become a pure and delightful people.

What a joy it must be to the Lamanite people to learn of the choice ancestors that they have as they read the Book of Mormon. They are related to great prophets like Lehi, Nephi, Jacob, Mosiah, Alma and Helaman. Spiritual giants like Mormon and Moroni, who have helped greatly in the restoration of the gospel and the Nephite record, share their ancestry. Their progenitors are some of the choicest people who have ever lived, and they have a right to be proud of them. The Lamanites have received terrible treatment in the past (as have the Jews), but they are the covenant people of the Lord and will be blessed abundantly according to their righteousness.

THEY SHALL BECOME A RIGHTEOUS BRANCH

Nephi found great joy and satisfaction in the remnant of his posterity in our day. He saw that they would once again become a righteous people: "And behold how great the covenants of the Lord, and how great his condescensions unto the children of men; and because of his greatness, and his grace and mercy, <u>he has promised unto us that our seed shall not utterly be destroyed</u>, according to the flesh, but that he would preserve them; and in future generations <u>they shall become a righteous branch unto the house of Israel</u>." (2 Ne. 9:53, I.A.)

The future looks bright for those of the Lamanite people who are faithful. Many will accept the gospel of Jesus Christ and the record of their fathers, the Book of Mormon, and thus become a righteous and choice people.

13

THE SEVENTH SEAL

THE GATHERING OF THE RIGHTEOUS

SILENCE IN HEAVEN

When the seventh seal is opened, which contains the events for the seventh thousand years or for the approximate time period between 2000 A.D. and 3000 A.D., this is what John observed: "And when he had opened the seventh seal, there was <u>silence in heaven</u> about the space of half an hour." (Rev. 8:1, I.A.)

Just previous to this, at the end of the sixth seal, there was noise made in heaven by the trumpets of the angels: "And angels shall fly through the midst of <u>heaven</u>, crying as with a loud voice, <u>sounding the trump of God</u>," (D&C 88:92, I.A.).

And then the heavens will be opened and the Sign of the Son of Man is seen by the world. (D&C 88:93) Then another angel will sound his trump and will denounce the abominable church. (D&C 88:94) In the very next verse, after the trumpet sounds, we are told, "...there shall be <u>silence in heaven</u> for the space of half an hour;" (D&C 88:95, I.A.).

Anciently, trumpets were used for several reasons. One purpose for the blowing of trumpets was <u>to sound an alarm</u>. Another reason they were used was as <u>a signal for battle</u>. Trumpets were also blown <u>to announce the arrival of royalty</u>. Sounds of trumpets will be heard throughout the events of the last days. Each time they are used, it will be for one of these three reasons. The royalty they announce will be Jesus Christ, the King of Kings.

Apparently, after the trumpets and sign at the end of the sixth seal which will cause noise in heaven, the beginning of the seventh seal will be marked by "silence in heaven".

The silence was not on the earth but "there was silence in heaven about the space of half an hour". (Rev. 8:1, I.A., and D&C 88:95) God's time in heaven is different than man's time on this earth: "And the Lord said unto me, by the Urim and Thummim, that Kolob was after the manner of the Lord, according to its times and seasons in the revolutions thereof; that one revolution was a day unto the Lord, after his manner of reckoning, it being one thousand years according to the time appointed unto that whereon thou standest. This is the reckoning of the Lord's time, according to the reckoning of Kolob." (Abr. 3:4, I.A.) Peter said that, "...one day is with the Lord as a thousand years, and a thousand years as one day." (2 Pet. 3:8, I.A.)

Therefore, one day to the Lord is equal to a thousand years on the earth because of the difference in the speed of revolution between Kolob (which is the same as the Lord's time) and the earth. With twenty-four hours in a day compared to one thousand years on the earth, a half hour of the Lord's time in heaven is probably almost twenty-one (20.83) years of our time. This absence of noise and trumpets in heaven will most likely last almost twenty-one years on the earth.

Immediately after the silence in heaven, a great sign will be seen in heaven: "And there shall be silence in heaven for the space of half an hour; and immediately after shall the curtain of heaven be unfolded, as a scroll is unfolded after it is rolled up, and the face of the Lord shall be unveiled;" (D&C 88:95, I.A.)

This scripture states that "immediately" after the the silence in heaven, the Lord will appear. We have to remember that this is according to the Lord's time of a thousand years being one day to Him. He will appear soon after the silence in heaven is broken by the trumpets of angels. But it will be "immediately" according to the Lord's time and not ours. For there are seven angels who must first break the heavenly silence by heralding seven judgments with their trumpets. Seven angels must also pour out seven plagues upon the earth. During this time, two prophets will prophesy in Jerusalem for almost three and a half years which will culminate in the Battle of Armageddon. All of these will take place after the trumpets break the silence in heaven and before the Savior returns.

A trumpet will also announce the return of Jesus Christ when He comes: "For the Lord himself shall descend from heaven with <u>a shout</u>, with the voice of the archangel, and with <u>the trump of God</u>:" (1 Thes. 4:16, I.A.).

What could be the reason for the one-half hour of silence in heaven? Perhaps silence will reign as the heavenly hosts view the wickedness that will be on the earth: "For all flesh is corrupted before me; and <u>the powers of darkness prevail</u> upon the earth, among the children of men, in the presence of the hosts of heaven--<u>Which causeth silence to reign</u>, and all eternity is pained, and the angels are waiting the great command to reap down the earth, to gather the tares that they may be burned; and, behold, the enemy is combined." (D&C 38:11-12, I.A.)

Apparently, during this time period before the Lord comes, the wicked will combine, perhaps this means politically. Also, each person will be given a chance to choose righteousness or wickedness before the second coming when the wicked are burned.

A TEMPLE BUILT AT JERUSALEM

Sometime after the destruction during the sixth seal, the Jews will build their temple on the ancient temple sight which is now occupied by the Moslem Dome of the Rock.

During the seventh seal, there will be two mighty prophets raised up to the Jewish people in Jerusalem. Just before these two witnesses will begin their prophesying in Jerusalem, John is requested during the vision to measure the temple of God in Jerusalem. (Rev. 11:1-2) So some time before the ministry of the two Jewish prophets, the temple will be built by the Jews in Jerusalem. Joseph Smith said that the Jews will build their temple before the second coming. (Teachings, p. 286)

The prophet Ezekiel saw the latter-day temple in Jerusalem in vision. He saw that water would come out from under the temple. This water will form a river that will flow to the Dead Sea. This will heal the water of that sea so that it will support foliage around it and fish within it. (Ezek. 47:1-12)

Zechariah also prophesied that the Lord's house would be built in Jerusalem in our day. (Zech. 1:16) He foretold that living waters would form a new river that would flow westward out from Jerusalem toward the Mediterranean Sea and also eastward to the Dead Sea. (Zech. 14:8) Zechariah said that the water will come out from under the temple when Christ appears on the Mount of Olives and saves the Jews. (Zech. 14:4-8)

The prophet Joel foretold that: "Judah shall flow with waters, and a fountain shall come forth of the house of the Lord, and shall water the Valley of Shittim." (Joel 3:18, I.A.) Shittim is located east of Jordan and just opposite of Jericho.

The Jews have waited almost two thousand years to reconstruct their temple. The day that their temple is finally completed will be a glorious and long-awaited day for the Jewish people.

THE GOSPEL PREACHED IN ALL THE WORLD

Through the missionary efforts of the Church and the 144,000 special ministers of Israel, the gospel will be preached in all the world: "And again, this Gospel of the Kingdom shall be preached in all the world, for a witness unto all nations, and then shall the end come, or the destruction of the wicked;" (JS-M 1:31, I.A., and Matt. 24:14, Mark 13:10, D&C 133:37).

God has given the commandment for his missionaries to preach the gospel to every person: "And if they desire to take upon them my name with full purpose of heart, they are called to go into all the world to preach my gospel unto every creature." (D&C 18:28, I.A., and D&C 112:28, Teachings, p. 364)

THE GATHERING OF ISRAEL AND THE SAINTS

Previous to this time, many of the House of Israel will have been gathered into the Church. But during the seventh seal, Israel and the righteous will be gathered to certain locations.

The 144,000 high priests, who will be called from the twelve tribes of Israel, will be special missionaries ordained by the Lord to warn the people before the end of the world. (Rev. 14:1-5) Everyone will be commanded to gather to the lands of their inheritance. The worldwide gathering will take place after the Lost Tribes return. (3 Ne. 21:26-29) After the Lord commences His work to gather the Lost Tribes, He will command people everywhere to gather through His missionaries: "Yea, and then shall the work commence, with the Father among all nations in preparing the way whereby his people may be gathered home to the land of their inheritance. And they shall go out from all nations; and they shall not go out in haste, nor by flight, for I will go before them, saith the Father, and I will be their rearward." (3 Ne. 21:28-29, I.A., and Isa. 52:11-12)

So this gathering will not be in haste, but there will be time to accomplish it. Who has the Lord put in charge of the gathering of Israel? John the Revelator was given this special mission. (D&C 77:14, Rev. 10:8-11)

Where will the people be gathered to? The Jews and the Ten Tribes will be gathered to Jerusalem and Palestine. The rest Israel will be gathered to the Americas: "And then cometh the New Jerusalem;...and they are they who are numbered among the remnant of the seed of Joseph, who were of the house of Israel. And then also cometh the Jerusalem of old; and the inhabitants thereof,...and they are they who were scattered and gathered in from the four quarters of the earth, and from the north countries, and are partakers of the fulfilling of the covenant which God made with their father, Abraham." (Ether 13:10-11, I.A.)

Is Zion only the area of the New Jerusalem? No, it includes all of North and South America according to Brigham Young: "The land of Joseph is the land of Zion; and it takes North and South America to make the land of Joseph." (J.D. 6:296, I.A., and DHC 6:318-319)

The reason that people will be commanded to flee out from all nations will be because of wickedness, "Let them, therefore, who are among the Gentiles flee unto Zion [the Americas]. And let them who be of Judah flee unto Jerusalem, unto the mountains of the Lord's house. Go ye out from among the nations, even from Babylon, from the midst of wickedness, which is spiritual Babylon." (D&C 133:12-14, I.A., D&C 57:1-3, Brigham Young, J.D. 12:38)

Those who are among the elect of God will heed

the warning to gather to prepare for the tribulations which will be sent upon the wicked: "And ye are called to bring to pass the gathering of mine elect; for mine elect hear my voice and harden not their hearts; Wherefore the decree hath gone forth from the Father that they shall be gathered in unto one place upon the face of the land [America], to prepare their hearts and be prepared in all things against the day when tribulation and desolation are sent forth upon the wicked." (D&C 29:7-8, I.A.)

Those who choose to stay among the wicked after being told to gather have received this warning: "Come out of her [Babylon], my people, that ye be not partakers of her sins, and that ye receive not of her plagues. For her sins have reached unto heaven, and God hath remembered her iniquities." (Rev. 18:4-5, I.A.)

Apparently this great gathering of Israel does not just include the posterity of Israel who are scattered throughout the world. Moses said that if some have been scattered to the outermost regions of heaven, they will also be gathered home by God: "...thou shalt call them to mind among all nations, whither the Lord thy God hath driven thee, And shalt return unto the Lord thy God, and shalt obey his voice according to all that I command thee this day, thou and thy children, with all thine heart, and with all thy soul. That then the Lord thy God will...gather thee from all nations, whither the Lord thy God hath scattered thee. If any of thine be driven out unto the outmost parts of heaven, from thence will the Lord thy God gather thee, and from thence will be fetch thee:" (Deut. 30:1-4, I.A.). So if any of His people have been driven to the furthest parts of space, the Lord will bring them back.

The prophet Nehemiah also foretold that if the chosen people have been taken to the uttermost part of the heavens, God will gather them back: "If ye transgress, I will scatter you abroad among the nations: But if ye turn unto me, and keep my commandments, and do them; though there were of you cast out unto the uttermost part of the heaven, yet will I gather them from thence, and will bring them unto the place that I have chosen to set my name there." (Neh. 1:8-9, I.A.)

THE PEOPLE OF ZION WILL BE THE ONLY PEOPLE NOT AT WAR

What will be some of the blessings received by those who are obedient and gather to Zion? They will be safe and happy: "And it shall come to pass among the wicked, that every man that will not take his sword against his neighbor must needs flee unto Zion for safety. And there shall be gathered unto it out of every nation under heaven; and it shall be the only people that shall not be at war one with another. And it shall come to pass that the righteous shall be gathered out from among all nations, and shall come to Zion, singing with songs of everlasting joy." (D&C 45:68-69, 71, I.A.)

With civil strife rampant on all sides, Zion will be a place of refuge from the storm and from the wrath that will be poured out upon the earth: "And that the gathering together upon the land of Zion, and upon her stakes, may be for a defense, and for a refuge from the storm, and from wrath when it shall be poured out without mixture upon the whole earth." (D&C 115:6, I.A.)

THE WATERS WILL BE CURSED

What will prevent the wicked from gathering to America? The Lord has cursed the waters through John, so that the wicked will not be able to gather to America: "Behold, I, the Lord, in the beginning blessed the waters; but in the last days, by the mouth of my servant John, I cursed the waters. Wherefore, the days will come that no flesh shall be safe upon the waters. And it shall be said in days to come that none is able to go up to the land of Zion [America] upon the waters, but he that is upright in heart." (D&C 61:14-16, I.A.)

Jesus told His disciples that before His coming, the times of the Gentiles would be fulfilled, and there would be signs in the sun, moon and stars. Then he said that the earth will be troubled and the waters of the oceans: "Master, tell us concerning thy coming? And he answered them, and said, In the generation in which the times of the Gentiles shall be fulfilled, there shall be signs in the sun, and in the moon, and in the stars; and upon the earth distress of nations with perplexity, like the sea and the waves roaring. The earth shall be troubled, and the waters of the great deep;" (JST Luke 21:24-25, I.A.).

It sounds like perhaps the only means of transportation that people will have to travel to the Americas at the time of the gathering will be on the water.

THE RIGHTEOUS WILL BE SEPARATED FROM THE WICKED

The preaching of the gospel in all the world along with the gathering of Israel to the lands of their inheritance will cause a separation between the wicked and the righteous: "For the time speedily cometh that the Lord God shall cause a great division among the people, and the wicked will he destroy; and he will spare his people, yea, even if it so be that he must destroy the wicked by fire." (2 Ne. 30:10, I.A.)

The elect will have to flee out of Babylon or out from the wicked in order to deliver their souls: "Flee out of the midst of Babylon, and deliver every man his soul: be not cut off in her iniquity; for this is the time of the Lord's vengeance; he will render unto her a recompence." (Jer. 51:6, I.A.)

Those who have not heeded the warning of the Lord through His servants will be cut off: "And the arm of the Lord shall be revealed; and the day cometh that they who will not hear the voice of the Lord, neither give heed to the words of the prophets and apostles, shall be cut off from among the people;" (D&C 1:11-12, 14, I.A.).

The Lord has warned that those who remain in Babylon or among the wicked will not be spared: "For after today cometh the burning--this is speaking after the manner of the Lord--for verily I say, tomorrow all the proud and they that do wickedly shall be as stubble; and I will burn them up, for I am the Lord of Hosts; and I will not spare any that remain in Babylon." (D&C 64:24, I.A.) The Lord gave this scripture during the sixth seal which would be the sixth day to Him or "today". On the seventh day or during the seventh seal, which is "tomorrow" to the Lord, the wicked will be burned.

It is always wise to heed the counsel of God's chosen servants. Those who decide to ignore the warning they will receive to leave Babylon or the wicked will burn with them when Christ returns.

SYMBOLS AND INTERPRETATIONS

WAR IN HEAVEN

(Rev. 12:7.) Michael is Adam, the father and prince of all, the ancient of days (D&C 27:11.)

(Rev. 12:7.) Michael fights the dragon who is the old serpent, the devil and Satan (Rev. 12:9.)

(Rev. 12:8-9.) The dragon is cast down with his angels called the third part of the stars of heaven (Rev. 12:4.)

(Rev. 12:4.) The stars of heaven which were cast down to the earth were the third part of the hosts of heaven that the devil turned away from God. They were thrust down and became the devil and his angels (D&C 29:36-37.)

THE CHURCH OF GOD

An Ecclesiastical and spiritual organization--
Governed by priesthood and revelation from God.
Members worship the Father, Son and Holy Ghost.
(Rev. 12:1.) Called a woman clothed with the sun and moon with a crown of twelve stars--She is the Church of God (JST Rev. 12:7.)
(Rev. 12:6.) The woman flees into the wilderness--the Church during the apostasy (D&C 86:2-3, JST Rev. 12:13-17.)
(Rev. 7:1.) Four angels--they restore the gospel (D&C 77:8 and Rev. 14:6.)
(Rev. 7:2.) Another angel ascends from the east--John the Revelator gathers Israel and restores all things (D&C 77:9,14.)
(Rev. 7:4-8.) 144,000 are sealed--they are virgin men who serve Christ (Rev. 14:1-5.)
(Rev. 19:7-9.) The marriage supper of the Lamb is held--the Church is the bride, the marriage is the union of Christ and the woman or the Church (D&C 109:73:74.)
(Rev. 19:8.) The fine linen, clean and white worn by the woman at the marriage supper is the righteousness of the saints (Rev. 19:8.)
Only baptized members are in the Church.

THE CHURCH OF THE DEVIL

An Ecclesiastical and spiritual organization--
Governed by false priesthood and revelation from the devil.
Members worship the devil.
(Rev. 17:1-6.) Called a whore--the church of the devil (1 Nephi 14:9-10.)
(Rev. 17:1.) Called a whore--because the kings of the earth commit spiritual fornication with the whore (Rev. 17:2.)
(Rev. 14:8,16:19,17:5, D&C 86:3.) The whore is called Babylon--the church of the devil and wickedness (1 Nephi 14:3,10, D&C 133:14.)
Babylon is also the great city that reigns over the kings of the earth (Rev. 17:18,14:8.)
(Rev. 18:23.) Sorceries used in the church deceive all nations
(Rev. 13:1-12.) Another beast is the false prophet (Rev. 19:20, Rev. 16:13-14.) He ex er cises great evil through religious power. He performs great miracles, forces the worship of an idol (idolatry) and his followers receive a seal in the hand or forehead which is the mark of the beast (Rev. 13:11-18.)
(Rev. 14:9-11.) Those with the mark of the beast are destroyed--the beast and false prophet are destroyed (Rev. 19:20.)
(Rev. 18:2, Rev. 14:8,10, D&C 1:16.) Babylon is destroyed by fire
(Rev. 17:16.) The city of Babylon is burned with fire by the ten horns or kings
(Rev. 17:12 and 18:9-19.)

SYMBOLS AND INTERPRETATIONS

THE KINGDOM OF GOD

The Kingdom of God already rules in heaven and among the righteous dead

It will be a political organization on the earth

It will be a product of or be brought forth by the Church of God

(Rev. 12:5.) A man child--he is the Kingdom of our God and His Christ (JST Rev. 12:7.)

(Rev. 12:4-5.) The man child is brought forth by the woman--she is the Church of God (JST Rev. 12:7.)

(Rev. 12:5.) The man child was caught up unto God--during the apostacy

(Dan. 7:9,13-14 and D&C 116.) A council will be held at Adam-ondi-Ahman--where political power will be given to Christ and saints (Dan. 7:22,27 and D&C 78:15-16.)

(Rev. 11:15 and JST Rev. 19:15.) The kingdoms of the world become the kingdoms of God and Christ

All people (both members and non-members of the Church of God) will be subject to the rule of Christ and His saints.

THE KINGDOM OF THE DEVIL

The kingdom of the devil is the political power that the devil exercises over the kingdoms of the earth, the 1/3 of the fallen spirits and the wicked dead

(Rev. 12:3.) A great red dragon--the old serpent, the devil and Satan (Rev. 12:9.)

(Rev. 12:13.) The devil persecutes the Church of God which tries to bring forth the Kingdom of God (JST Rev. 12:7.)

(Rev. 12:17.) The devil makes war with the saints

(Rev. 13:1.) A beast--the likeness of the kingdoms of the earth (JST Rev. 13:1.)

(Rev. 13:1.) Seven heads of the beast--seven mountains on which the whore sits and seven kings: five are fallen, and one is, and the other is not yet come; and when he comes, he must continue a short space (Rev. 17:9-10.)

(Rev. 13:1.) The beast has ten horns and upon them ten crowns--they are ten kings which have received no kingdom as yet; but receive power as kings one hour with the beast (Rev. 17:12.)

(Rev. 13:3,12,14.) One of the heads of the beast (one of the kings) is wounded by a sword unto death, his deadly wound is healed, his image is worshipped--the church and kingdom of the devil combine power (Rev. 13.)

(I Nephi 22:22-23.) The kingdom of the devil rules over all churches but the Church of God

(Rev. 17:16-18.) The ten horns (or ten kings) hate the whore (the great and wicked city that reigns over the kings of the earth) and help destroy her by fire.

(Rev. 17:14.) The kingdom of the devil will make war against the Lamb and will be defeated

(Rev. 20:2-3.) The devil will be bound for 1000 years and will have no more political power until the end of the millenium when he will be loosed for a little season

14

THE CHURCH AND KINGDOM OF GOD,

THE CHURCH AND KINGDOM OF THE DEVIL

In the Book of Revelation, John the Revelator received visions which have an overview of the war between God and Satan or the devil. This war started in the pre-mortal life with war in heaven. John was given a great deal of detail about this conflict between the followers of God and the followers of the devil in the last days. Special emphasis was made on the time period after the opening of the seventh seal.

The war began in the pre-mortal life (Rev. 12:7): "The contention in heaven was--Jesus said there would be certain souls that would not be saved; and the devil said he could save them all, and laid his plan before the grand council, who gave their vote in favor of Jesus Christ. So the devil rose up in rebellion against God, and was cast down, with all who put up their heads for him." (Teachings, p. 357, I.A.)

John used symbolic imagery frequently in the Book of Revelation. Each scripture that includes a symbol will be cited along with the scripture that gives the interpretation of what the symbol means: "And there was war in heaven: Michael [Adam] and his angels [followers] fought against the dragon [Satan]; and the dragon [Satan] fought and his angels [followers], And prevailed not; neither was their place found any more in heaven. And the great dragon [Satan] was cast out, that old serpent, called the Devil, and Satan, which deceiveth the whole world: he was cast out into the earth, and his angels [the one third of the spirit children of God who followed him] were cast out with him [to the earth]. Woe to the inhabiters of the earth and of the sea! for the devil is come down unto you, having great wrath [great bitterness because of defeat], because he knoweth that he hath but a short time [before he is bound for 1000 years]." (Rev. 12:7-9, 12, I.A., and D&C 27:11, D&C 29:36-37, Rev. 20:2-3) "And there appeared another wonder in heaven; and behold a great red dragon [Satan], having seven heads and ten horns and seven crowns upon his heads. And his tail drew the third part of the stars of heaven [one third of God's spirit children who rebelled with him] and did cast them to the earth:" (Rev. 12:3-4, I.A., and D&C 29:36-37).

THE CHURCH OF GOD

The Church of God, which is an ecclesiastical and spiritual organization, is governed by the priesthood and receives revelation from God. Its members worship Heavenly Father, His Son Jesus Christ and the Holy Ghost. Jesus Christ established His Church when He was on the earth in the meridian of time. Only baptized members are part of the Church of God. The following scripture refers to the Church of God that was established during the lifetime of Jesus. The Church attempted to establish the Kingdom of God but was thwarted by Satan and there was an apostasy: "And there appeared a great wonder in heaven; a woman [the Church of God] clothed with the sun, and the moon under her feet, and upon her head a crown of twelve stars: And she being with child cried, travailing in birth, and pained to be delivered...and the dragon [Satan] stood before the woman [the Church of God] which was ready to be delivered, for to devour her child [the Kingdom of God] as soon as it was born. And she brought forth a man child [the Kingdom of God], who was to rule all nations with a rod of iron [the word of God]: and her child [the Kingdom of God] was caught up unto God, and to his throne. And the woman [the Church of God] fled into the wilderness [during the apostasy], where she hath a place prepared of God, that they should feed her there a thousand two hundred and threescore days." (Rev. 12:1-2, 4-6, I.A., and JST Rev. 12:7, Rev. 12:9, 1 Ne. 11:25, D&C 86:2-3, JST Rev. 12:13-17)

The Church of God was again restored to the earth after the apostasy and during the sixth seal: "I saw four angels [four angels sent forth from God to whom is given power over the four parts of the earth, to save life and to destroy; these have the everlasting gospel to commit to every nation, kindred, tongue, and people; having power to shut up the heavens, to seal up unto life, or to cast down to the regions of darkness] standing on the four corners of the earth, holding the four winds of the earth, that the wind should not blow on the earth, nor on the sea, nor on any tree. And I saw another angel ascending from the east, having the seal of the living God [this angel is John the Revelator to whom is given the seal of the living God over the twelve tribes of Israel; wherefore, he crieth unto the four angels having the everlasting gospel], to whom it was given to hurt the earth and the sea, Saying, Hurt not the earth, neither the sea, nor the trees, till we have sealed the servants of our God in their foreheads [the 144,000]. [And, if you will receive it, this is Elias, John the Revelator, which was to come to gather together the tribes of Israel and restore all things.]" (Rev. 7:1-3, I.A., and D&C 77:8-9, 14, Rev. 7:4-8)

With the help of the 144,000 who are sealed (Rev. 7:4-8, 14:1, 3-5) and the missionary effort of the Church, the gospel of the Church of God will be preached in all the world. Nephi saw the latter-day Church of God: "And it came to pass that I beheld the church of the Lamb of God, and its numbers were few, because of the wickedness and abominations of the whore [the great and abominable church] who sat upon many waters [the peoples of the earth]; nevertheless, I beheld that the church of the Lamb, who were the saints of God, were also upon all the face of the earth; and their dominions upon the face of the earth were small, because of the wickedness of the great whore [the great and abominable church] whom I saw." (1 Ne. 14:12, I.A., and 1 Ne. 14:9-10, Rev 17:15)

How will the great power of the devil be overcome? The testimonies and sacrifices of the saints and the atonement of Jesus Christ will overcome him: "And they overcame him [the devil] by the blood of the Lamb, and by the word of their testimony; and they loved not their lives unto death." (Rev. 12:11, I.A., and Rev. 12:9-10)

When the Bridegroom, who is Jesus Christ, returns again, the marriage supper of the Lamb will take place. His wife, who is the Church of God, will be dressed in fine linen which will be clean and white. The clean and white linen symbolizes the righteousness of the saints. This marriage is symbolic of the unity between the Savior and the faithful people of His Church forever. (Only five of the ten virgins or one-half of the members of the Church will be prepared to attend the marriage supper. D&C 109:73-74, 65:3, JST Rev. 12:7, Matt. 25:1-12, Faith, pp. 253-254) "Let us be glad and rejoice, and give honour to him: for the marriage of the Lamb is come, and his wife [the Church of God] hath made herself ready. And to her was granted that she should be arrayed in fine linen, clean and white: for the fine linen is the righteousness of saints. And he saith unto me, Write, blessed are they [the righteous and prepared saints] which are called unto the marriage supper of the Lamb [the union of Christ and the Church of God]. And he saith unto me, these are the true sayings of God." (Rev. 19:7-9, I.A.)

THE KINGDOM OF GOD

The Kingdom of God is a political organization which already rules in heaven and among the righteous dead.

The early Church tried to bring forth the Kingdom of God (or the political reign) upon the earth as was symbolized by the woman (who symbolized the Church of God) in labor who finally brings forth a man child (who symbolized the Kingdom of God). But Satan, who enjoys his power over earthly kingdoms, caused through the wickedness of the people, the child (the Kingdom of God) to flee unto God and the woman (the Church of God) to flee into the wilderness or to go into apostasy. (Rev. 12:1, 4-6, JST Rev. 12:7, 13-17, D&C 86:3)

The Church of God has been established again in our day. Once again the Church is trying to bring forth the Kingdom of God on the earth with Christ as the political ruler and King of Kings.

A great priesthood council at Adam-ondi-Ahman will be held prior to the second coming, and Christ and the saints will be given the political power over the earth. (Dan. 7:13-14, 22, 27) Then will come the triumphant day when Christ will rule on the earth, "The kingdoms of this world are become the kingdoms of our Lord, and of his Christ; and he shall reign forever and ever." (Rev. 11:15, I.A.)

When the Kingdom of God comes, it will rule and reign over all people and nations regardless of whether or not they are members of the Church of God.

THE CHURCH OF THE DEVIL

The church of the devil, which is an ecclesiastical and religious organization, is governed by false priesthoods (sorcery, etc.) and revelation from Satan and his followers. It members follow the devil and often worship him. This church will grow in power especially at the beginning of the seventh seal or seventh thousand year period which will be between the approximate year of 2000 A.D. and 3000 A.D.

This church is symbolized by a woman who is a "whore" because the kings of the earth commit spiritual fornication with her. A whore is a prostitute. This whore causes men to commit idolatry and to stray in false devotion. Satan's church is also referred to as "Babylon". (Babylon is also the name of the great city which reigns over the kings of the earth.) This whore sits upon many waters which represents the fact that where she sits is among peoples, multitudes, nations and tongues. (Rev. 17:1-6, 15, 18, 16:19, 1 Ne. 14:3, 9-10, D&C 86:3, 133:14)

John was shown the future of this evil church in the beginning of the seventh seal or time period. The kingdoms of the devil will combine with the church of the devil in a powerful alliance. Their evil power will be used to force people through threat of death and economic isolation to worship the image of a king. A false prophet will work miracles through the power of Satan and deceive people into worshipping an image and committing idolatry: "And I beheld another beast [this beast exercises great evil through religious power and is referred to as the false prophet] coming up out of the earth; and he had two horns like a lamb, and he spake as a dragon. And he [the false prophet] exerciseth all the power of the first beast [the likeness of the kingdoms of the earth] before him, and causeth the earth and them which dwell therein to worship the first beast, whose deadly wound was healed. [the first beast will be one of the seven heads, or kings, of the beast and he will be wounded to death by a sword so the one they worship must be one of the seven kings.] And he [the false prophet] doeth great wonders, so that he maketh fire come down from heaven on the earth in the sight of men, And deceiveth them that dwell on the earth by the means of those miracles which he had power to do in the sight of the beast [the kingdoms of the world]; saying to them that dwell on the earth, that they should make an image to the beast [one of the seven kings]; which had the wound by a sword, and did live. And he [the false prophet] had power to give life unto the image of the beast [one of the seven kings], that the image of the beast [the king] should both speak, and cause that as many as would not worship the image of the beast [king] should be killed. [Satan is still trying to take away free agency.] And he causeth all, both small and great, rich and poor, free and bond, to receive a mark in their right hand, or in their foreheads: And that no man might buy or sell, save he that had the mark, or the name of the beast [the king], or the number of his name. Here is wisdom, Let him that hath understanding count the number of the beast: for it is the number of a man; and his number is Six hundred threescore and six [666]." (Rev. 13:11-18, I.A., and Rev. 13:1-3, 16:13-14, 17:9-10, 19:20, JST Rev. 13:1-3)

During John's day, many worshipers of heathen gods would mark their foreheads with the name or symbol of their god to show devotion and servitude. The worshipers of the beast will likewise put a mark in their right hand or in their forehead to show their allegiance. This mark might be a tattoo of the number or name of the king.

The magicians in Pharaoh's court had the power through sorcery to perform several of the miracles that Moses was able to perform by the power of God. (Ex. 7-8) This false prophet will have an extraordinary command of the powers of black magic and sorcery as he will be able to call down fire from heaven and cause the image of the beast or king to live and speak.

John has told us which people will be deceived into worshipping the idol which will be the image of the king: "And all that dwell upon the earth shall worship him, whose names are not written in the book of life of the Lamb slain from the foundation of the world." (Rev. 12:8, I.A.)

Hopefully, during the time when Satan has such

great power over his dominions and kingdoms, we will have gathered to Zion where God's power, glory and protection will be for we are promised, "the devil shall have power over his dominion. And also the Lord shall have power over his saints, and shall reign in their midst," (D&C 1:35-36, I.A.) "And the glory of the Lord shall be there, and the terror of the Lord also shall be there, insomuch that the wicked will not come unto it, and it shall be called Zion. And it shall be said among the wicked: Let us not go up to battle against Zion, for the inhabitants of Zion are terrible; wherefore we cannot stand." (D&C 45:67, 70, I.A.)

THE KINGDOM OF THE DEVIL

The kingdom of the devil is the political power and rule that Satan exercises over the kingdoms of the earth, the one-third of the spirit children that followed him and the wicked dead. His power and influence will also be over all the churches except the Church of God. (1 Ne. 22:22-23) Some of the power he exercises through the other churches is that they satisfy the inner spiritual needs of the people and lead their members away from the saving ordinances of the gospel of Jesus Christ.

John was shown the history of the political power of the devil. These kingdoms overcame the early saints causing the apostasy. The power of his combined kingdoms during the beginning of the seventh seal and time period will be so great that people will worship the image of one of its kings. Many in the world have a great fear of nuclear war. If this combined kingdom could propose a plan for world peace and security from nuclear war, some may accept it regardless of the price they may have to pay or the wickedness of its leaders.

John saw a vision about the kingdoms of Satan: "And I stood upon the sand of the sea, and saw a beast [the likeness of the kingdoms of the earth] rise up out of the sea, having seven heads [seven mountains on which the woman, Babylon, sitteth and seven kings] and ten horns, and upon his horns ten crowns [ten kings, which have received no kingdom yet; but receive power as kings one hour with the beast, who is the likeness of the kingdoms of the earth], and upon his heads the name of blasphemy. And the beast [the kingdoms of the earth] which I saw was like unto a leopard, and his feet were as the feet of a bear, and his mouth as the mouth of a lion: and the dragon [the devil] gave him his power, and his seat, and great authority. And I saw one of his heads [one of the seven kings] as it were wounded to death; and his deadly wound was healed: and all the world wondered after the beast [the kingdoms of the earth]. And they worshipped the dragon [the devil] which gave power to the beast [the kingdoms of the earth]: and they worshipped the beast [the kingdoms of the earth], saying, Who is like the beast [the kingdoms of the earth]? Who is able to make war with him? And there was given unto him a mouth speaking great things and blasphemies, and power was given him to continue forty and two months [three and a half years]. And he opened his mouth in blasphemy against God, to blaspheme his name, and his tabernacle, and them that dwell in heaven. And it was given unto him to make war with the saints, and to overcome them [the apostasy]: and power was given him over all kindreds, and tongues, and nations." (Rev. 13:1-7, I.A., and Rev. 12:3, 9, 17:9-10, 12, JST Rev. 12:13-17, 13:1, D&C 86:3.

This combined political kingdom of the devil will commit blasphemy. Blasphemy is contempt or irreverence toward God or claiming the attributes of God. These evil kingdoms will have irreverent contempt for God, His name, His dwelling and those who are with Him in heaven.

Joseph Fielding Smith taught about Satan's power in the governments or kingdoms of the world: "Satan has control now. No matter where you look, he is in control, even in our own land. He is guiding the governments as far as the Lord will permit him." (Doctrines, 3:315, I.A.)

The political power of Satan has been great in the past and will continue to grow in strength and dominion until the Savior comes and Satan is bound.

THE VICTORY

Those who have died and were faithful to God and have not received the mark of the beast were shown to John in vision. He saw that they would be in heaven enjoying their victory as they will sing the song of the Lamb: "Great and marvellous are thy works, Lord God Almighty; just and true are thy ways, thou King of saints. Who shall not fear thee, O Lord, and glorify thy name? for thou art holy: for all nations shall come and worship before thee; for thy judgments are made manifest." (Rev. 15:3-4, I.A.)

In the next chapter, we will study the seven judgments that God will send upon those who receive the mark of the beast. (These include members of Satan's Church, the false prophet, the king whose image will be worshipped and the wicked governments of Satan's power.) These judgments culminate in the burning of the wicked, the destruction of all political kingdoms and the return of Jesus Christ with the powers of heaven. Finally, Christ will rule as King of Kings with his saints, for the Church of God will triumphantly bring forth the Kingdom of God on the earth.

THE SEVEN JUDGMENTS

In Revelation 8:1, at the opening of the seventh seal, there is silence in heaven for one-half hour (which possibly equals a time period of almost twenty-one years on the earth). Then in Revelation 8:2, John tells of seven angels who stand before God. They will be given seven trumpets that will break the silence in heaven. Each of these seven trumpets will sound an alarm before each of the seven judgments take place on the earth.

Just before the seven angels take turns sound their trumpets, John saw that another angel at the golden altar which is before the throne has a golden "censer". A censer is a metal vessel which was used anciently to receive burning charcoal from the altar and in which incense was sprinkled by a priest. (Rev. 8:3-5, Lev. 16:12-13, 1 Kgs. 7:50) A lot of incense is given to this angel, and he is to offer it with the prayers of all saints. The smoke from the incense along with the prayers of the saints will ascend up before God out of the angel's hand. Then the angel will fill the censer with fire (probably burning coals from the altar) and cast it to the earth. This will cause four things to happen on the earth: voices, thunderings, lightnings and an earthquake. (Rev. 8:4-5) The Lord has referred to the noise made by thunder, lightning, tempests and tidal waves as "voices" when He said, "And also cometh the testimony of the voice of thunderings, and the voice of lightnings, and the voice of tempests, and the voice of waves heaving themselves beyond their bounds." (D&C 88:90, I.A.)

This very powerful "censer" filled with fire will cause some upheavals on the earth. Then seven angels will sound their trumpets and announce seven judgments upon the wicked. Those who have gathered to Zion will be spared these judgments. The gathering to Zion will be a defense and refuge from God's wrath. In Zion His people will be prepared for the day of tribulation and desolation: "Verily I say unto you all: Arise and shine forth, that thy light may be a standard for the nations; And that the gathering together upon the land of Zion, and upon her stakes, may be for a defense, and for a refuge from the storm, and from wrath when it shall be poured out without mixture upon the whole earth." (D&C 115:5-6, I.A.) "And ye are called to bring to pass the gathering of mine elect; for mine elect hear my voice and harden not their hearts; Wherefore the decree hath gone forth from the Father that they shall be gathered in unto one place upon the face of this land [America], to prepare their hearts and be prepared in all things against the day when tribulation and desolation are sent forth upon the wicked." (D&C 29:7-8, I.A.)

THE FIRST JUDGMENT

HAIL AND FIRE

"The first angel sounded, and there followed hail and fire mingled with blood, and they were cast upon the earth: and the third part of trees was burnt up, and all green grass was burnt up." (Rev. 8:7, I.A., and Ex. 9:23-25)

Ice hail does not usually fall with fire mingled with blood. But meteorites have fallen in the past with gases like naptha or sticky, burning fluid that can ignite and burn in the atmosphere and on the earth. Real blood could fall or perhaps red dust could cover the meteorites or fall with them that could combine with moisture or water to look like blood.

What a tragedy it will be to have one third of all the trees burned up and all the green grass burned up.

THE SECOND JUDGMENT

A BURNING MOUNTAIN

"And the second angel sounded, and as it were a great mountain burning with fire was cast into the sea: and the third part of the sea became blood; And the third part of the creatures which were in the sea, and had life, died; and the third part of the ships were destroyed." (Rev. 8:8-9, I.A., and Ex. 7:17-21)

What John saw falling to the earth resembled "as it were" a great burning mountain which fell into the sea. (When he says "as it were", he probably means that is what it reminded him of.) This caused one third of the sea to become like blood. If this huge meteorite or comet falls with ferric oxide or red dust on it or in its tail, it could make the water look like blood. This fouled water will kill the living creatures that are in one-third of the seas. All the ships in the third part of the sea will be destroyed also.

THE THIRD JUDGMENT

A BURNING STAR

"And the third angel sounded, and there fell a great star from heaven, burning as it were a lamp, and it fell upon the third part of the rivers, and upon the fountains of waters; And the name of the star is called Wormwood: and the third part of the waters became wormwood, and many men died of the waters, because they were made bitter." (Rev. 8:10-11, I.A.)

John saw that what would look like a great star will fall from heaven. (We call meteorites that fall at night and burn up in the atmosphere, "falling stars".) The falling star reminded John of a lamp probably because it gave off great light. This bright, falling body will cause one third of the rivers and fountains of water or springs to become bitter or poisonous. Many people will die when they will attempt to drink from the contaminated river and springs.

The star is named "Wormwood". Wormwood was a plant with an extremely bitter taste. Drinking water with wormwood in it would be fatal.

THE FOURTH JUDGMENT

PARTIAL DARKNESS

"And the fourth angel sounded, and the third part of the sun was smitten, and the third part of the moon, and the third part of the stars; so as the third part of them was darkened, and the day shone not for a third part of it, and the night likewise." (Rev. 8:12, I.A., and Ex. 10:21-22)

If we put the five events together that are listed in Revelation 8:5-12, a definite pattern develops. To start with there is "a censer of fire" thrown to the earth. This "censer" will then cause an earthquake, thunder, lightning and voices. Then the first angel casts a meteorite shower mingled with fire and blood upon the earth which burns up one-third of the trees and all the green grass. The second angel throws a fiery meteor into the sea causing one-third of the seas to turn to blood and become poisonous. The third angel casts another great and bright meteor or comet to the earth which poisons one-third of the fresh water of the rivers and springs. The fourth angel announces that one-third of the usual light from the sun, moon and stars is darkened causing a third of the day and night to be without any light. The dirt and pollution that would be forced up into the atmosphere during an earthquake, meteorite shower (along with the smoke from the burning trees and grass) and the impact of two huge meteors or comets hitting the waters of the earth would automatically cause darkness over the one-third part of the earth that would be affected. It sounds like perhaps only one-third of the earth will receive these first four judgments (with the exception of all the green grass being burned up). It would not be surprising if these judgments happened quite close together. Moses, through the power of God, turned the water into blood which killed the fish, and he then caused a plague of hail and fire which was followed by three days of darkness. (Ex. 7:17-21, 9:23-24, 10:21-22)

THE FIFTH JUDGMENT

MANKIND IS TORMENTED

"And the fifth angel sounded, and I saw a star fall from heaven unto the earth: and to him was given the key to the bottomless pit." (Rev. 9:1, I.A.)

Just after telling us that a star will fall from heaven, John then refers to the star as "him". Sometimes in the scriptures, a star refers to an important person just as it does today. The greatest person to fall from heaven was Lucifer or Satan. (D&C 76:25-27, Isa. 14:12)

Anciently, locks were extremely expensive and protected only the most valuable possessions. Keys were generally worn on a chain around the neck. Anyone having a key was assumed to be a person of wealth, power and authority. Keys were a symbol of great power and authority. So this important man is given the key to "the bottomless pit". What is the bottomless pit? John gave us a good description of what it is in Rev. 20:1-3: "And I saw an angel come down from heaven, having the key of the bottomless pit and a great chain in his hand. And he laid hold on the dragon, that old serpent, which is the Devil, and Satan, and bound him a thousand years, And cast him into the bottomless pit, and shut him up, and set a seal upon him, that he should deceive the nations no more, till the thousand years should be fulfilled:".

So the bottomless pit is a prison or hellish abyss that is secured with a certain key. It is probably located beneath the surface of the earth because a pit means a hole or cavity in the ground. So this important person who falls from heaven is given the key to this hellish prison, and he opens it and releases the prisoners: "And he opened the bottomless pit; and there arose a smoke out of the pit, as the smoke of a great furnace; and the sun and the air were darkened by reason of the smoke of the pit." (Rev. 9:2, I.A.)

Smoke is often associated with hell. King Benjamin spoke of those with evil works who are consigned to hell where smoke ascends up: "And if they be evil they are consigned to an awful view of their own guilt and abominations, which doth cause them to shrink from the presence of the Lord into a state of misery and endless torment,...And their torment is as a lake of fire and brimstone, whose flames are unquenchable, and whose smoke ascendeth up forever and ever." (Mosiah 3:25, 27, I.A., and Jacob 6:10)

So far in the vision, John was shown the spiritual forces that are the influence behind the physical forces that are shown to him next. As we analyze his description of what he saw, remember that John is describing vehicles with powers completely foreign to anything from his own experience since they had no machines in his ancient culture.

In Revelation 9:3-10, John recounted what he saw coming out of the sky when it was full of smoke: (1) He called them locusts. But they could not literally have been locusts since what he sees does not hurt the grass or any green thing, but only the people who do not have the seal of God in their foreheads (all except those who have gathered to Zion and the 144,000 missionaries). Real locusts devour everything that is green which they can find. (2) He compared their power to hurt with the torment that is inflicted by a scorpion's sting. The sting of a scorpion is painful but not fatal. These do not have the power to kill but only to torment men five months. In fact, men will desire to die, but will not. He said their tails reminded him of a scorpion's tail, and their sting or power to hurt was likewise in their tail. (3) John described these flying "locusts" as follows: They have something similar to gold "crowns" on their heads. Their faces were the "faces of men". Their hair was like "the hair of women". Their teeth were as "the teeth of lions" (which are sharp and pointed). Their "breastplates" appeared like they were "made of iron". Their wings made a sound similar to the "noise of chariots of many horses running to battle". The following is an illustration of what John might have seen.

HELICOPTERS

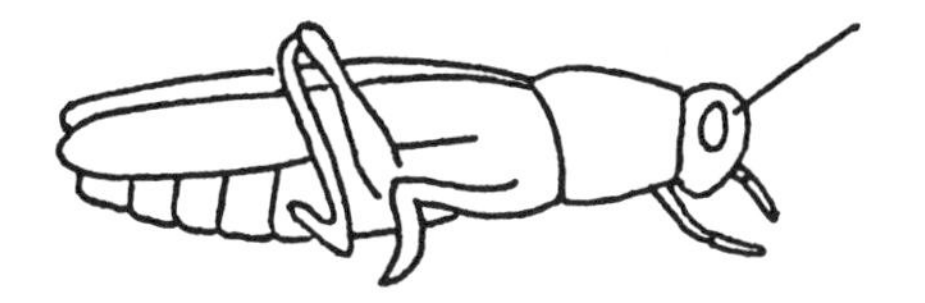

They resembled locusts
(Revelation 9:3.)

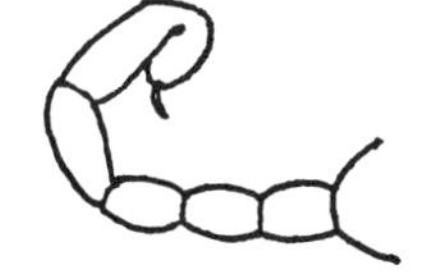

Their tails were like
the tails of scorpions
(Revelation 9:10.)

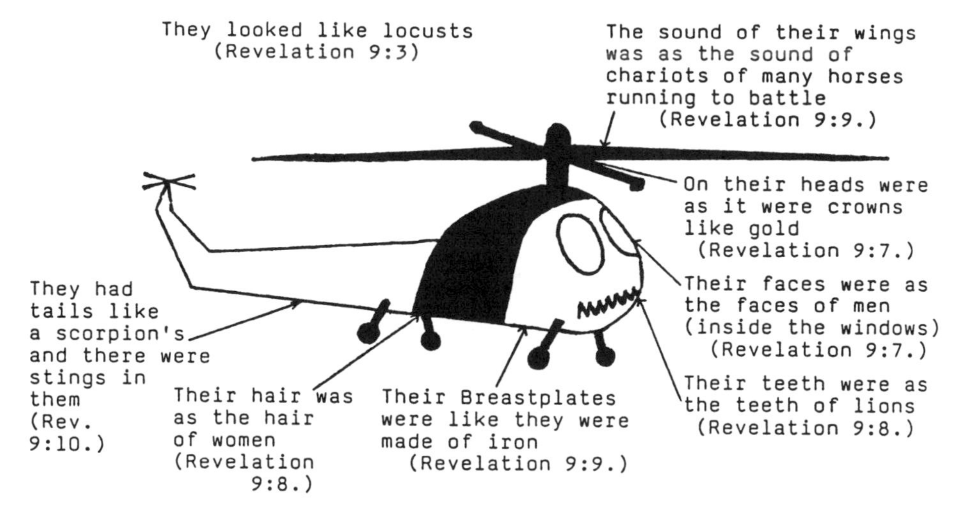

They were like unto horses prepared for battle. Anciently horses were sometimes covered with a drape of heavy material with holes for their eyes to protect their bodies during battle. Horses were also a symbol of the ability to move rapidly and power in war. (Rev. 9:7.)

Could John have been trying to describe helicopters? These vehicles will not be allowed to kill people but only to torment them for five months. (Rev. 9:5) Generally in battles, the purpose is to kill the enemy. What would cause intense suffering but would not kill, and also would harm only men and not grass, trees and green things? We know that chemicals can do that. Helicopters can drop chemicals and bombs. Why would God allow them to torment men? Probably because He is hoping they will repent and not be burned at His coming which would result in them being in torment with Satan for 1000 years. But they do not repent even after five months of torment. (Rev. 9:20-21)

John foretold that these forces will have a king: "And they had a king over them which is the angel of the bottomless pit, whose name in the Hebrew tongue is Abaddon, but in the Greek tongue hath his name Apollyon." (Rev. 9:11, I.A.) Abaddon, a Hebrew word, and Apollyon, a Greek word, mean "the destroyer". Perdition means destruction or utter loss and has been used as a name for Lucifer or Satan. (D&C 76:26) So it is possible that Abaddon and Apollyon are names for the devil who is also called the angel of the abyss.

THE SIXTH JUDGMENT

ONE THIRD OF MANKIND IS KILLED

"And the sixth angel sounded and I heard a voice from the four horns of the golden altar which is before God, Saying to the sixth angel which had the trumpet, Loose the four angels which are bound in the great river Euphrates [in the bottomless pit]. And the four angels were loosed, which were prepared for an hour, and a day, and a month, and a year to slay the third part of men." (Rev. 9:13-15, JST Rev. 9:14, I.A.)

The Joseph Smith Translation of the Bible clarifies that these four angels are bound in the bottomless pit not in the river Euphrates. Again John was shown the spiritual forces (the four evil spirits from the bottomless pit or hellish prison) that influence the physical army that will kill one-third of mankind in a little over a year.

Again, John tried to describe modern flying machines with ancient terminology of almost 2000 years ago when they had no flying machines. Revelation 9:16-19 has given us many details. This war will have an army of 200,000,000 which slays a third part of men. What they sat on were described as "horses". In John's day, horses were a symbol of power in war and the ability to travel rapidly. Their heads were "the heads of lions". They had "breastplates of fire, of jacinth" (an orange or brown gem) "and brimstone". Their tails were like "serpents" or large snakes and had heads. They had power in their tails to hurt. Out of their mouths issued "fire, smoke and brimstone" which killed the third part of men. The following is an attempt to illustrate what John described.

AIRPLANES

John said they sat on horses. Horses were a symbol of power in war and represented the ability to travel rapidly. (Revelation 9:17.)

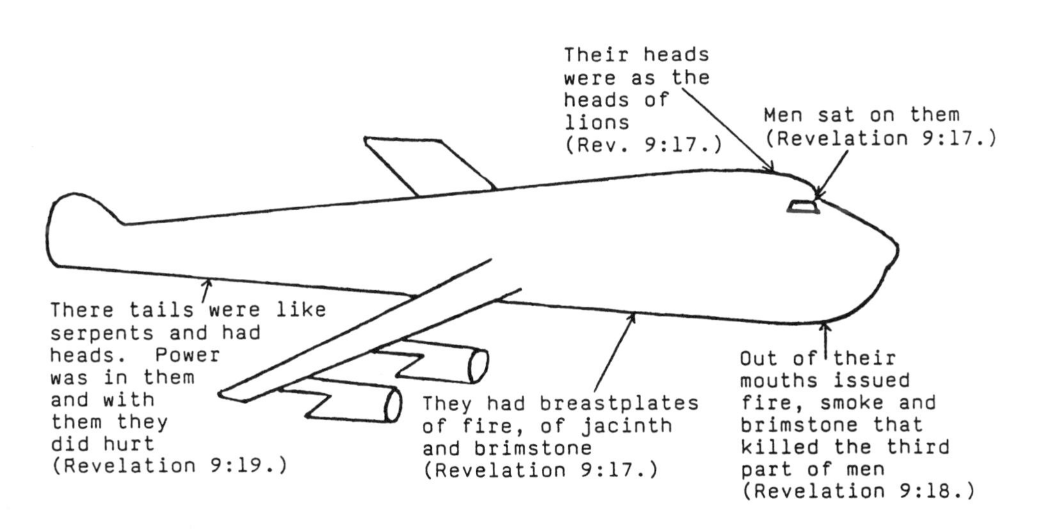

Did John see our modern airplanes dropping bombs? Even after a terrible war that will kill a third part of the people, they still do not repent of their idolatry, murders, sorceries, immorality or thefts. "And the rest of the men which were not killed by these plagues yet repented not of the works of their hands, that they should not worship devils, and idols of gold, and silver, and brass, and stone, and of wood: which neither can see, nor hear, nor walk: Neither repented they of their murders, nor of their sorceries, nor of their fornication, nor of their thefts." (Rev. 9:20-21, I.A.)

While it was still during the time of the sixth judgment, John was told to measure the temple in Jerusalem, and he saw what was happening in the holy city.

TWO PROPHETS IN JERUSALEM

John foretold, "the holy city shall they tread under foot forty and two months. And I will give power unto my two witnesses, and they shall prophesy a thousand two hundred and threescore days, clothed in sackcloth. These are the two olive trees, and the two candlesticks standing before the God of the earth." (Rev. 11:2-4, I.A.)

So Jerusalem will be under assault for three and a half years. Two witnesses or prophets will be given special power from God and will prophesy for almost three and a half years (3.45 years).

These two prophets are compared to olive trees and candlesticks. The candlestick (or prophet) is not the source of the light but holds up the light (who is Jesus Christ) for all to see.

During this almost three and a half year time period, God will give these two witnesses great power over plagues: "And if any man will hurt them, fire proceedeth out of their mouths, and devoureth their enemies: and if any man will hurt them, he must in this manner be killed. These [the two witnesses] have power to shut heaven, that it rain not in the days of their prophesy: and have power over waters to turn them to blood, and to smite the earth with all plagues, as often as they will." (Rev. 11:5-6, I.A.)

Most likely what is meant by "fire proceedeth out of their mouth, and devoureth their enemies" is that by the power of their word that comes out of their mouth (through the power of the Priesthood), they will be able to command fire to devour their enemies. There were times in the Old Testament when fire from the Lord consumed men. Nadab and Abihu performed sacrifices that were unauthorized, "And there went out fire from the Lord, and devoured them, and they died before the Lord." (Lev. 10:2, I.A.) Two hundred and fifty men who rebelled against Moses were consumed by the Lord: "And there came out a fire from the Lord, and consumed the two hundred and fifty men that offered incense." (Num. 16:35, I.A.)

These two prophets will also "have power over waters to turn them to blood, and to smite the earth with all plagues". We will now discuss, during the sixth judgment, the seven final plagues that these two witnesses have been given power over. When Joseph Smith was asked about these two prophets, he said that they will be raised up to the Jewish nation: "Q. What is to be understood by the two witnesses, in the eleventh chapter of Revelation? A. They are two prophets that are to be raised up to the Jewish nation in the last days, at the time of the restoration and to prophesy to the Jews after they are gathered and have built the city of Jerusalem in the land of their fathers." (D&C 77:15, I.A.)

THE SEVEN FINAL PLAGUES

These seven vials or plagues that are poured out

by seven angels are the wrath or divine chastisement of God: "And I heard a great voice out of the temple saying to the seven angels, Go your ways, and pour out the vials of the wrath of God upon the earth." (Rev. 16:1, I.A.)

Those who have gathered to Zion will not receive these plagues because they will not have partaken of the sins of Babylon or the wicked: "And I heard a voice from heaven, saying, Come out of her [Babylon], my people, that ye be not partakers of her sins, and that ye receive not of her plagues. For her sins have reached unto heaven, and God hath remembered her iniquities." (Rev. 18:4-5, I.A.)

God's wrath and punishment will be poured out on those with the mark of the beast: "If any man worship the beast and his image, and receive his mark in his forehead, or in his hand, The same shall drink of the wine of the wrath of God, which is poured out without mixture into the cup of his indignation;" (Rev. 14:9-10, I.A.).

THE FIRST VIAL AND PLAGUE

"And the first went, and poured out his vial upon the earth; and there fell a noisome [Greek: bad, evil] and grievous sore upon the men which had the mark of the beast, and upon them which worshipped his image." (Rev. 16:2, I.A.)

Judgment will then come upon the followers of the devil, the evil king and his false prophet who practice sorcery. A bad sore that will cause intense suffering will come upon those with the mark of the beast.

THE SECOND VIAL AND PLAGUE

"And the second angel poured out his vial upon the sea; and it became as the blood of a dead man: and every living soul died in the sea." (Rev. 16:3, I.A.)

The redness of the sea will look like or be similar to blood for John said it was "as the blood of a dead man". This poisonous water will kill all the living souls in the sea that John saw.

THE THIRD VIAL AND PLAGUE

"And the third angel poured out his vial upon the rivers and fountains of waters; and they became as blood." (Rev. 16:4, I.A.)

The same plague of red-colored water that looks like blood will affect the rivers and springs that John saw. The Lord might cause this plague by red dust from space infiltrating our atmosphere and falling into the water.

THE FOURTH VIAL AND PLAGUE

"And the fourth angel poured out his vial upon the sun; and power was given unto him to scorch men with fire. And men were scorched with great heat, and blasphemed the name of God, which hath power over these plagues: and they repented not to give him glory." (Rev. 16:8-9, I.A.)

The sun will scorch men with fire and great heat, but still the wicked are unrepentant. This terrific heat could be caused by the earth temporarily stopping in its rotation so that half of the earth would receive uninterrupted sunshine for a period of time. The gravitational pull from a close encounter with a planet or comet could be the natural means the Lord might use to stop the earth's rotation as the planet or comet went by.

THE FIFTH VIAL AND PLAGUE

"And the fifth angel poured out his vial upon the seat of the beast; and his kingdom was full of darkness; and they gnawed their tongues for pain, And blasphemed the God of heaven because of their pains and their sores, and repented not of their deeds." (Rev. 16:10-11, I.A.

The wicked will still refuse to repent of their sins. In the fourth plague, the kingdom of the beast will get too much sun and in the fifth plague it will not get any as darkness will reign. They will have so much pain that they will bite their tongues. Again, darkness could reign for a period of time on half of the earth if our planet's rotation were temporarily stopped again.

These five plagues must happen fairly close together since those with the sign of the beast will receive sores in the first plague, and they are still suffering from those sores during the fifth plague.

THE SIXTH VIAL AND PLAGUE--ARMAGEDDON

"And the sixth angel poured out his vial upon the great river Euphrates; and the water thereof was dried up, that the way of the kings of the east might be prepared." (Rev. 16:12, I.A.)

After the events of great heat and great darkness, the river Euphrates will be dried up. The Euphrates is an important river that provides a natural line between the east and west. It marks one of the boundaries to the land that was given to Abraham. With that natural barrier dried up, it will greatly facilitate the movement of troops from the eastern countries to the Palestine area for the great battle which is going to take place.

"And I saw three unclean spirits like frogs come

out of the mouth of the dragon, and out of the mouth of the beast, and out of the mouth of the false prophet. For they are <u>the spirits of devils, working miracles</u>, which do go forth unto <u>the kings</u> of the earth and <u>of the whole world</u>, to gather them to <u>the battle</u> of that great day God Almighty. And he gathered them together into a place called in the Hebrew tongue <u>Armageddon</u>." (Rev. 16:13-14, 16, I.A.)

It will be these three prominent evil spirits that will have the power to work miracles, who will use their spiritual influence and power with the leaders of the world to bring the armies of these leaders to battle against Israel. This great war has come to be called the battle of Armageddon. During the sixth judgment and the sixth plague, the momentous battle of Armageddon will be fought.

Gog of the land of Magog, the chief prince of Mechech and Tubal, was seen by Ezekiel in vision as the leader of the army that will come up against Israel. (Ezek. 38:1-3) Gog is symbolic of the name of the leader or combination of leaders of the evil forces that will arise. Ezekiel named Persia, Ethiopia, Libya, Gomer and Togarmah as those countries which will be in alliance with Gog. (Ezek. 38:2-6) Gomer, Magog, Tubal and Meshech are descendants of Noah through his son Japheth. (Gen. 10:2) The ancient country of Magog would include areas north and east of the Black Sea including Crimea today. These lands are part of the USSR or her satellites at this time. Meshech would now be territory that is under the control of the USSR. The ancient land of Tubal would now probably include the area around the Black Sea in Georgia and modern Turkey. Persia would be modern Iran. Ethiopia would include the southern part of the African continent. The ancient country of Libya would today be the northern countries of Africa (except Egypt) like Libya, Tunisia, Morocco and Algeria. Gomer would now include most of modern Europe with some parts of Asia Minor. The old land of

Togarmah would today be Asia Minor including Armenia, part of southern USSR, Turkey and Syria. ("The Old Testament: 1 Kings--Malachi",Student Manual (Religion 302), Church publication, pp. 285-286)

Jeremiah added to the list of countries that will fight against Israel by naming many countries in the Middle East. (Jer. 25:15-25) All nations will be joined in alliance in one way or another in this war. (Rev. 16:14, Jer. 25:26, Zech. 14:2, Joel 3:1-2)

Armageddon is another name for the valley of Esdraelon which is in southern Galilee about sixty miles north of Jerusalem. An ancient fortress city called Megiddo (it means "the place of troops") was used to guard the entrance to the valley because of the many great battles that have taken place in this strategically placed valley of Armageddon. The last great war before the second coming will occur in this famous valley: "Multitudes, multitudes in the valley of decision: for the day of the Lord is near in the valley of decision." (Joel 3:14, I.A.)

So how does the small nation of Israel defend itself against the combined armies of much of the world? The two prophets in Jerusalem, who have power over fire and plagues, will stop them for the period of their ministry which is almost three and one-half years.

THE TWO PROPHETS ARE KILLED

"And when they [the two prophets] shall have finished their testimony, the beast that ascendeth out of the bottomless pit shall make war against them, and shall overcome them, and kill them. And their dead bodies shall lie in the street of the great city, which spiritually is called Sodom and Egypt, where also our Lord was crucified. And they of the people and kindreds and tongues and nations shall see their dead bodies three days and an half, and shall not suffer their dead bodies to be put in graves. And they that dwell upon the earth shall rejoice over them, and make merry, and shall send gifts one to another; because these two prophets tormented them that dwelt on the earth." (Rev. 11:7-10, I.A.)

In supposed triumph, the Gentile armies will celebrate. The people of these nations will view the dead bodies (possibly through television) and will exchange presents. For the two prophets, who had smitten them with plagues and prevented their victory over Israel, will be dead.

WAR CASUALTIES IN ISRAEL

During this horrible war, two-thirds of the nation of Israel will perish and one-third will be refined through their tribulations and will be prepared to accept the Lord. (Zech. 13:8-9) One half of Jerusalem will be taken captive along with "the houses rifled, and the women ravished". (Zech. 14:2, Zech. 1-2)

THE TWO PROPHETS RESURRECT

"And after three days and an half the Spirit of life from God entered into them [the two prophets], and they stood upon their feet; and great fear fell upon them which saw them. And they heard a great voice from heaven saying unto them, Come up hither. And they ascended up to heaven in a cloud; and their enemies beheld them." (Rev. 11:11-12, I.A.)

The wicked Gentile armies will have enjoyed their victory party for three and a half days, but then their celebrating will come to an abrupt end. They will witness the Messiah of the Jews, the King of Israel, as He will come down from heaven to defend His covenant people.

THE MESSIAH STANDS ON THE MOUNT OF OLIVES

In the same hour as the two prophets will resurrect, a great earthquake will occur in the Holy Land: "And the same hour was there a great earthquake, and the tenth part of the city fell, and in the earthquake were slain of men seven thousand: And the remnant were affrighted, and gave glory to the God of heaven." (Rev. 11:13, I.A.)

This earthquake will split the mount of Olives in two as Jesus Christ will appear upon the mount: "And his [the Lord's] feet shall stand in that day upon the mount of Olives, which is before Jerusalem on the east, and the mount of Olives shall cleave in the midst thereof toward the east and toward the west, and there shall be a very great valley; and half of the mountain shall remove toward the north, and half of it toward the south. And ye shall flee to the valley of the mountains; for the valley of the mountains shall reach unto Azal: Yea, ye shall flee, like as ye fled from before the earthquake in the days of Uzziah King of Judah:" (Zech. 14:4-5, I.A.). "And then shall the arm of the Lord fall upon the nations. And then shall the Lord set his foot upon this mount, and it shall cleave in twain," (D&C 45:47-48, I.A.).

The Jewish people will be saved from the Gentile armies by running through the huge valley created when the mount of Olives will divide into two parts by the earthquake.

THE JEWS ARE CONVERTED TO CHRIST

It will be a special and sad time when the Jews finally meet their long-awaited Messiah and find that He came to Israel once before: "And then shall the Jews look upon me and say: What are these wounds in thine hands and in thy feet? Then shall they know that I am the Lord; for I will say unto them: These wounds are the wounds with which I was wounded in the house of my friends. I am he who was lifted up. I am Jesus that was crucified. I am the Son of God. And then shall they weep because of their iniquities; then shall they lament because they persecuted their king." (D&C 45:51-53, I.A., and Zech. 12:10-14, 13:6)

What a bittersweet experience for the Jewish people. Their Messiah will have come, and He will be Jesus of Nazareth whom their ancestors crucified, and whom they have refused to accept until they will see Him.

THE SEVENTH JUDGMENT

IT IS DONE

"But in the days of the voice of the seventh angel, when he shall begin to sound, the mystery of God should be finished, as he hath declared to his servants the prophets." (Rev. 10:7, I.A.)

Right after the two prophets resurrect and an earthquake rocks Jerusalem (Rev. 11:12-14), John saw this in vision: "And the seventh angel sounded; and there were great voices in heaven, saying, The kingdoms of this world are become the kingdoms of our Lord, and of his Christ; and he shall reign for ever and ever. And the nations were angry, and thy wrath is come, and the time of the dead, that they should be judged, and that thou shouldest give reward unto thy servants the prophets, and to the saints, and them that fear thy name, small and great; and shouldest destroy them which destroy the earth. And the temple of God was opened in heaven, and there was seen in his temple the ark of his testament: and there were lightnings, and voices, and thunderings, and an earthquake, and great hail." (Rev. 11:15, 18-19, I.A., and Ezek. 38:18-22)

Jesus Christ, the King of Kings, will take His rightful place as ruler of this earth. He will reward the righteous and will destroy the wicked, who will have stubbornly refused to repent and who will have brought ruin to the earth. There will be lightning, voices (D&C 88:90), thunder, an earthquake and great hail.

THE SEVENTH VIAL AND PLAGUE

Right after Armageddon (Rev. 16:16), John related what would happen when the seventh vial is poured out. The same things are mentioned as are part of the seventh judgment as the temple in heaven is seen and there are voices, thunders, lightnings, an earthquake and great hail. "And the seventh angel poured out his vial into the air; and there came a great voice out of the temple of heaven, from the throne, saying, It is done. And there were voices, thunders, and lightnings; and there was a great earthquake, such as was not since men were upon the earth, so mighty an earthquake, and so great. And the great city was divided into three parts, and the cities of the nations fell: and great Babylon came in remembrance before God, to give unto her the cup of the wine of the fierceness of his wrath. And there fell upon men a great hail out of heaven, every stone about the weight of a talent: and men blasphemed God because of the plague of the hail; for the plague thereof was exceeding great." (Rev. 16:17-19, 21, I.A., and Ezek. 38:22)

It appears that both the seventh judgment and the seventh vial and plague are describing the same event. It will happen right after the battle of Armageddon. Voices will be heard from heaven proclaiming Christ's reign and the end of the world. (Compare Rev. 10:7, Rev. 11:12-14, with Rev. 16:17-19, 21)

In the seventh plague, more details are given about the earthquake and the great hail. It will be the greatest earthquake in the history of the world which will divide Jerusalem into three parts and level the cities of the nations. A great hail will fall out heaven. The weight of each stone or meteorite from heaven will be about the weight of a talent. (A talent was 57.85 pounds in ancient times.)

DESTRUCTION OF FIVE-SIXTHS OF THE GENTILE ARMIES

The armies that will come against Israel will then begin to fight among themselves. (Ezek. 38:21, Zech. 14:13) Then many of them will be killed by the pestilence, overflowing rain, great hailstones, fire and brimstone. "And I will plead against him [Gog] with pestilence and with blood; and I will rain upon him, and upon his bands, and upon the many people that are with him, an overflowing rain, and great hailstones, fire, and brimstone." (Ezek. 38:22, I.A.)

Only one-sixth of the armies of Gog will be left when this destruction is finished. (Ezek. 39:1-6, Rev. 19:17-21) Ezekiel prophesied that it would take seven months for Israel to bury the dead from Gog and his multitude. They will be buried in a valley that will be called Hamon-gog. The weapons and shields which will be left from the armies will give Israel fuel for seven years. (Ezek. 39:9-16)

The seven judgments and seven plagues that God will send upon the wicked through His angels will be finished. The wicked and Babylon will have been given plenty of time to repent of their sins after feeling these divine chastisements from God. The fate of the wicked will be sealed as all that are living witness the end of the world.

BABYLON AND THE WICKED ARE BURNED

THE END OF THE WORLD

"The destruction of the wicked is the end of the world." (JS-M 1:4, I.A.) The end of the world means the end or destruction of wickedness. This should not be confused with the end of the earth which will happen at the end of the millenium when the earth will die and be resurrected. (D&C 88:25-26, 101)

What will the wicked say when the thunders and lightnings call them to repentance? Our compassionate Lord will remind the sinners at His coming of all His efforts to save them with an everlasting salvation, but they would not repent of their iniquities. Jesus has warned, "...what will ye say when the day cometh when the thunders shall utter their voices from the ends of the earth, speaking to the ears of all that live, saying--Repent, and prepare for the great day of the Lord? Yea, and again, when the lightnings shall streak forth from the east unto the west, and shall utter forth their voices unto all that live, and make the ears of all tingle that hear, saying these words--Repent ye, for the great day of the Lord is come? And again, the Lord shall utter his voice out of heaven, saying: Hearken, O ye nations of the earth, and hear the words of the God who made you. O, ye nations of the earth, how often would I have gathered you together as a hen gathereth her chickens under her wings, but ye would not! How oft have I called upon you by the mouth of my servants, and by the ministering of angels, and by mine own voice, and by the voice of thunderings, and by the voice of lightnings, and by the voice of tempests, and by the voice of earthquakes, and great hailstorms, and by the voice of famines and pestilences of every kind, and by the great sound of a trump, and by the voice of judgment, and by the voice of mercy all the day long, and by the voice of glory and honor and the riches of eternal life, and would have saved you with an everlasting salvation, but ye would not! Behold, the day has come, when the cup of the wrath of mine indignation is full. Behold, verily I say unto you, that these are the words of the Lord your God." (D&C 43:21-27, I.A., compare with 3 Ne. 10:3-6)

Noah warned the people of his day for one hundred and twenty years to repent or be destroyed. (Moses 8:17) Those who were righteous and would listen "were caught up by the powers of heaven into Zion" (Moses 7:27), except for Noah's immediate family who stayed on the earth. All of the rest of the people who were wicked died in the flood. Again, the Lord has been warning the world through His prophets for over one hundred and fifty years to repent, or they will be destroyed. And again the righteous will be caught up by the powers of heaven and the wicked will be destroyed. (D&C 88:96, JST 1 Thes. 4:17)

John was shown in vision the whore who is called Babylon: "Come hither; I will shew unto thee the judgment of the great whore that sitteth upon many waters: With whom the kings of the earth have committed fornication," (Rev. 17:1-2, I.A.).

The whore represents that great and abominable church: "And upon her forehead was a name written, MYSTERY, BABYLON THE GREAT, THE MOTHER OF HARLOTS AND ABOMINATIONS OF THE EARTH. And I saw a woman drunken with the blood of saints, and with the blood of the martyrs of Jesus:" (Rev. 17:5-6, I.A.).

The kings of the earth will commit idolatry with the whore to gain power. Then they will make war against the Lord and will be defeated: "These [the ten kings and the beast] shall make war with the Lamb, and the Lamb shall overcome them: for he is Lord of lords, and King of kings: and they that are with him are called, and chosen, and faithful." (Rev. 17:14, I.A.)

Even though the kings will be in alliance with the whore, they will hate Babylon which will be the great city that will reign over the kings of the earth. They will burn the city with fire. (Rev. 17:16-18) Babylon will be destroyed: "And after these things I saw another angel come down from heaven, having great power; and the earth was lightened with his glory. And he cried mightily with a strong voice, saying, Babylon the great is fallen, is fallen," (Rev. 18:1-2, I.A., and D&C 88:105). "For her sins have reached unto heaven, and God hath remembered her iniquities. Therefore shall her plagues come in one day, death, and mourning, and famine; and she shall utterly burned with fire: for strong is the Lord God who judgeth her...for by thy sorceries were all nations deceived. And in her was found the blood of prophets, and of saints, and of all that were slain upon the earth." (Rev. 18:5, 8, 23-24, I.A.)

The evil king and the false prophet will receive the reward for their wickedness also: "And the beast was taken, and with him the false prophet that wrought miracles before him, with which he deceived them that had received the mark of the beast, and them that worshipped his image. These both were cast alive into a lake of fire burning with brimstone. And the remnant were slain." (Rev. 19:20-21, I.A., and Dan. 7:11)

The prophet Joseph Smith explained what is meant by "a lake of fire and brimstone". "A man is his own tormenter and his own condemner. Hence the saying, They shall go into the lake that burns with fire and brimstone. The torment of disappointment in the mind of man is as exquisite a lake burning with fire and brimstone. I say, so is the torment of man." (Teachings, p. 357, I.A.)

The Lord has sometimes used the allegory of the wheat and the tares when speaking of the end of the world. Tares is another name from darnel grass which is a poisonous weed. When the tares are young and before they come into ear, they look like wheat. It is difficult to tell young tares from wheat. But as the tares mature, it becomes easy to distinguish between the poisonous tares and the valuable wheat. After the wheat has been gathered out from among the tares, the tares will be burned: "Therefore, let the wheat and the tares grow together until the harvest is fully ripe; then ye shall gather out the wheat from among the tares, and after the gathering of the wheat, behold and lo, the tares are bound in bundles, and the field remaineth to be burned." (D&C 86:7, I.A.)

The harvest is the end of the world: "The harvest is the end of the world, or the destruction of the wicked. The reapers are the angels, or the messengers sent of heaven. As, therefore, the tares are gathered and burned in the fire, so shall it be in the end of this world, or the destruction of the wicked. For in that day, before the Son of Man shall come, he shall send forth his angels and messengers of heaven. And they shall gather out of his kingdom all things that offend, and them which do iniquity, and shall cast them out among the wicked; and there shall be wailing and gnashing of teeth. For the world shall be burned with fire." (JST Matt. 13:39-44, I.A., and JST 2 Pet. 3:10, 12)

ALL CORRUPTIBLE MEN AND CREATURES ARE CONSUMED

The wicked will have refused to repent and will have enjoyed their evil ways. By blaspheming their Maker and scorning the righteous, their doom will be fixed. "And the Lord shall utter his voice, and all the ends of the earth shall hear it; and the nations of the earth shall mourn, and they that have laughed shall see their folly. And calamity shall cover the mocker, and the scorner shall be consumed; and they that have watched for iniquity shall be hewn down and cast into the fire." (D&C 45:49-50, I.A.)

The proud and the wicked will be burned so that righteousness can be on the earth, "...all the proud and they that do wickedly shall be as stubble; and I will burn them up, saith the Lord of Hosts, that wickedness shall not be upon the earth;" (D&C 29:9, I.A., and JST Heb. 6:7-8, 1 Ne. 22:15).

The Lord spoke of those who are living a telestial law as those who will be burned when He comes and that are not "caught up" (D&C 76:98-102). "Last of all these all are they who will not be gathered with the saints, to be caught up into the church of the Firstborn, and received into the cloud. These are they who are liars, and sorcerers, and adulterers, and whoremongers, and whoso loves and makes a lie. These are they who suffer the vengeance of eternal fire. These are they who are cast down to hell and suffer the wrath of Almighty God," (D&C 76:102-106, I.A.).

Everything that is of a telestial nature whether it be men, beasts, birds or fish will burn: "And every corruptible thing, both of man, or of the beasts of the field, or of the fowls of the heavens, or of the fish of the sea, that dwells upon all the face of the earth, shall be consumed; And also that of element shall melt with fervent heat;" (D&C 101:24-25, I.A., and 2 Pet. 3:10).

Unfortunately, Isaiah foresaw that after this burning there will be few men left compared to the present population: "Therefore hath the curse devoured the earth, and they that dwell therein are desolate: therefore the inhabitants of the earth are burned, and few men left." (Isa. 24:6, I.A., and Zech. 5:1-4)

THE TITHED ARE NOT BURNED

Speaking of those who pay their tithing, the Lord promised: "Behold, now it is called today until the coming of the Son of Man, and verily it is a day of sacrifice, and a day for the tithing of my people; for he that is tithed shall not be burned at his coming. For after today cometh the burning--this is speaking after the manner of the Lord--for verily I say, tomorrow all the proud and they that do wickedly shall be as stubble; and I will burn them up, for I am the Lord of Hosts; and I will not spare any that remain in Babylon." (D&C 64:23-24, I.A., and Mal. 3:11, 4:1)

When the Lord gave this scripture, it was the sixth day or "today" to Him. The seventh day or time period will be "tomorrow" to the Lord, and He will burn the wicked who remained in Babylon.

The earth was baptized at the time of the worldwide flood. At the second coming of the Lord, the earth will receive the Holy Ghost by fire. At the end of the millenium, the earth will die and be resurrected. (D&C 88:26)

17

THE KINGDOM OF GOD REIGNS OVER THE EARTH

THE COUNCIL AT ADAM-ONDI-AHMAN

Three years before his death, Adam called together all of his righteous posterity and gave them his last blessing. The location for this grand council was the valley of Adam-ondi-Ahman. The Lord appeared at this council and blessed Adam and called him Michael, the Archangel. The Lord comforted Adam and made him a prince over his posterity. Under the influence of the Holy Ghost, Adam prophesied about all that would befall his posterity to the last generation. (D&C 107:53-57)

The Lord has revealed the modern location of the ancient valley of Adam-ondi-Ahman, "Spring Hill is named by the Lord Adam-ondi-Ahman, because, said he, it is the place where Adam shall come to visit his people, or the Ancient of Days shall sit, as spoken by Daniel the prophet." (D&C 116, I.A., and Dan. 7:9, 13) Spring Hill is in Daviess County, Missouri.

It was Adam or Michael who waged war against Satan in the pre-mortal life. (Rev. 12:7) Adam is also called "the Ancient of Days" because he was the first and therefore the oldest man. (Teachings, p. 157)

Daniel the prophet told us about Adam: "I beheld till thrones were cast down, and the Ancient of days did sit, whose garment was white as snow, and the hair of his head like the pure wool: his throne was like the fiery flame, and his wheels as burning fire." (Dan. 7:9, I.A.)

Daniel beheld down through history until the political kingdoms of the world will be destroyed at the second coming of Christ. Daniel saw Adam sitting upon a fiery throne and he also saw his brilliant wheels.

Adam will participate in the judgment of the dead at the end of the world: "A fiery stream issued and came forth from before him: thousand thousands ministered unto him, and ten thousand times ten thousand stood before him: the judgment was set, and the books were opened." (Dan. 7:10, I.A.) At least one hundred million will come before him for judgment.

Sometime prior to the second coming, another momentous priesthood council will be held at Adam-ondi-Ahman. Jesus Christ will appear to Adam at this grand assembly and receive His Kingdom: "I saw in the night visions, and, behold, one like the Son of man came with the clouds of heaven, and came to the Ancient of days, and they brought him near before him. And there was given him dominion, and glory, and a kingdom, that all people, nations, and languages, should serve him: his dominion is an everlasting dominion, which shall not pass away, and his kingdom that which shall not be destroyed." (Dan. 7:13-14, I.A.)

When Jesus comes to Adam in the valley of Adam-ondi-Ahman during this great Priesthood council, Adam will deliver up his stewardship to the Lord: "He [Adam] is the father of the human family, and presides over the spirits of all men, and all that have had keys must stand before him in this grand council...The Son of Man stands before him, and there is given him glory and dominion. Adam delivers up his stewardship to Christ, that which was delivered to him as holding the keys of the universe, but retains his standing as head of the human family." (Teachings, p. 157, I.A.)

THE SAINTS ARE GIVEN THE KINGDOM

Also at this same priesthood council, the saints will be given the political rule over the earth under the leadership of the Savior: "...the Ancient of days came, and judgment was given to the saints of the most High; and the time came that the saints possessed the kingdom. And the kingdom and dominion, and the greatest of the kingdom under the whole heaven, shall be given to the people of the saints of the most High, whose kingdom is an everlasting kingdom, and all dominions shall serve and obey him." (Dan. 7:22, 27, I.A.)

What great blessings await those saints who are faithful and righteous. But His people must be tested and tried through the furnace of affliction to prove their worthiness for such great blessings. Those who keep the commandments will be crowned with power and great authority: "...notwithstanding the tribulation which shall descend upon you,...That you may come up unto the crown prepared for you, and be made rulers over many kingdoms, saith the Lord God, the Holy One of Zion, who hath established the foundations of Adam-ondi-Ahman; Who hath appointed Michael [Adam] your prince, and established his feet, and set him upon high, and given unto him the keys of salvation under the counsel and direction of the Holy One, who is without beginning of days or end of life." (D&C 78:14-16, I.A.)

At the second coming, the saints will inherit the earth: "And then shall the angels be crowned with the glory of his might, and the saints shall be filled with his glory, and receive their inheritance and be made equal with him." (D&C 88:107, I.A., and D&C 45:58-59, 103:7) John the Revelator saw that the resurrected saints would live and reign with Christ for a thousand years. (Rev. 20:4-6)

God has decreed that there will be a "full end of all nations" (D&C 87:6), at His second coming. Then finally, the King of Kings and Lord of Lords will return and reign over the earth with His saints.

18

THE MARRIAGE SUPPER OF THE LAMB

HE COMES AS A THIEF IN THE NIGHT

When Jesus comes again, it will be a surprise to many, and they will not be prepared. No one knows exactly when the Savior will return. Jesus has said, "...but the hour and the day no man knoweth, neither the angels in heaven, nor shall they know until he comes." (D&C 49:7, I.A.) "But of that day and hour knoweth no man, no, not the angels of heaven, but my Father only." (Matt. 24:36, I.A., and D&C 39:21)

We know how unexpected and shocking a burglar in our home would be in the middle of the night. Jesus said that His coming will be a surprise like that to some as He comes "as a thief in the night". (1 Thes. 5:2) "Watch therefore: for ye know not what hour your Lord doth come. But know this, that if the goodman of the house had known in what watch the thief would come, he would have watched, and would not have suffered his house to be broken up. Therefore be ye also ready: for in such an hour as ye think not the Son of man cometh." (Matt. 24:42-44, I.A.)

Just as it was in the days before the flood, people will be eating, drinking and marrying right up until the day of His coming. (Matt. 24:37-39)

There will be some servants who will say in their hearts that the Lord will delay His coming for a while, so it is alright to live as the wicked do. That servant who does this will receive his reward with the hypocrites in hell. (Matt. 24:48-51)

Those who have the gospel but have not lived it are under more condemnation than those who have not had the light of the gospel and have erred out of ignorance, "For unto whomsoever much is given, of him shall much be required;" (Luke 12:48, I.A.).

The saints who have proved themselves faithful and wise, will reign with the Lord on the earth during the millenium: "Who then is a faithful and wise servant, whom his lord hath made ruler over his household, to give them meat in due season? Blessed is that servant, whom his lord when he cometh shall find so doing. Verily I say unto you, That he shall make him ruler over all his goods." (Matt. 24:45-47, I.A.) It would be wise to always be prepared to meet our Lord.

THE TEN VIRGINS ARE CALLED TO ATTEND THE SUPPER

"Let us be glad and rejoice, and give honour to him: for the marriage of the Lamb is come, and his wife hath made herself ready. And to her was granted that she should be arrayed in fine linen, clean and white: for the fine linen is the righteousness of the saints. And he saith unto me, Write, Blessed are they which are called unto the marriage supper of the Lamb." (Rev. 19:7-9, I.A.) Jesus Christ is the Bridegroom. (D&C 65:3) The Church of God is His wife. (D&C 109:73-74) The marriage supper takes place when the Lord returns again. Only those with the proper attire which is clean and white linen (symbolic of the righteousness of the saints) can attend the wedding feast. Jesus told a parable about someone trying to come to the marriage feast without the proper attire: "And when the king came in to see the guests, he saw there a man which had not on a wedding garment: And he saith unto him, Friend, how camest thou in hither not having a wedding garment? And he was speechless. Then said the king to the servants, Bind him hand and foot, and take him away, and cast him into outer darkness; there shall be weeping and gnashing of teeth. For many are called, but few are chosen wherefore all do not have on the wedding garment." (Matt. 22:11-14, JST Matt. 22:14, I.A.)

Before this great wedding supper, all nations will be invited to attend without discrimination. "Yea, a supper of the house of the Lord, well prepared, unto which all nations shall be invited. First, the rich and the learned, the wise and the noble; And after that cometh the day of my power; then shall the poor, the lame, and the blind, and the deaf, come in unto the marriage of the Lamb, and partake of the supper of the Lord, prepared for the great day to come," (D&C 58:9-11, I.A.).

A marriage supper of the Lord is to be held and His servants will be sent to get guests for it. (Luke 14:16-17) What will be the reaction of some to an invitation to the marriage feast? They will find all sorts of excuses for why they cannot attend. (Luke 14:18-20) Some will love a family member more than the Lord. (Luke 14:26) Others will not be willing to give their life to Jesus Christ. (JST Luke 14:26) Some will be unwilling to "bear his cross" and suffer for the Lord's sake. (Luke 14:27) Others will decide not to keep His commandments. (JST Luke 14:28) Some will begin to come but then will be unable to finish what they began. (Luke 14:31, JST Luke 14:31) And finally, others will be unwilling to forsake the world to be a disciple. (Luke 14:33)

Many are familiar with the Parable of the Ten Virgins. President Kimball told us who the Ten Virgins represent: "I believe that the Ten Virgins represent the people of the Church of Jesus Christ and not the rank and file of the world." (Faith, pp. 253-254, I.A.)

When the Savior returns, half of the Church members will be prepared for Him and half will not.

When the cry is made, "Behold, the bridegroom cometh; go ye out to meet him" (Matt. 25:6), half of the Church members will have oil in their lamps and half will have let their oil run out. (Matt. 25:7-9) What does the oil represent? "And at that day, when I shall come in my glory, shall the parable be fulfilled which I spake concerning the ten virgins. For they that are wise and have received the truth, and have taken the Holy Spirit for their guide, and have not been deceived--verily I say unto you, they shall not be hewn down and cast into the fire, but shall abide the day." (D&C 45:56-57, I.A.) The oil represents being wise and following the Holy Spirit in obedience.

It is only Church members who have received the truth and who can take the Holy Spirit for their guide after confirmation, not the world at large. Therefore, the ten virgins represent Church members. The foolish virgins want to borrow oil from the wise virgins, but you cannot borrow faithfulness and righteousness. (Matt. 25:8-9)

Then the foolish virgins try to immediately repent and come in to the marriage supper, but the door is shut. (Matt. 25:10) This is one wedding feast that will be very important to be on time to: "Afterward came also the other virgins, saying, Lord, Lord, open to us. But he answered and said, Verily I say unto you, I know you not." (Matt. 25:11-12, I.A.)

Then what happens to the five foolish virgins or one-half of the members of the Church? At the second coming of the Lord, they will be cast into hell. Those who have the blessings of the gospel can receive the greatest rewards but also the greatest cursings: "Hearken and hear, O ye my people, saith the Lord and your God, ye whom I delight to bless with the greatest of all blessings, ye that hear me; and ye that hear me not will I curse, that have professed my name, with the heaviest of all cursings." (D&C 41:1, I.A.)

At this time there are wise and foolish members of the Church. When the Lord comes, there will be a complete separation between the righteous and the wicked. Those who have not kept their sacred covenants will be damned: "And until that hour [the day of the coming of the Son of Man] there will be foolish virgins among the wise; and at that hour cometh an entire separation of the righteous and the wicked; and in that day will I send mine angels to pluck out the wicked and cast them into unquenchable fire." (D&C 63:54, I.A., and D&C 45:56-57, Teachings, pp. 96-97)

The righteous or wise virgins will be "caught up" and the unwise or wicked virgins will be burned and cast into hell. (Matt. 24:40-41) The saints will need to be purified to abide the day of His coming, "But the day soon cometh that ye shall see me, and know that I am; for the veil of darkness shall soon be rent, and he that is not purified shall not abide the day. Wherefore, gird up your loins and be prepared." (D&C 38:8-9, I.A.)

We must never be ashamed of God or His words no matter what the world may say, otherwise the Lord will be ashamed of us when He comes again. "Whosoever therefore shall be ashamed of me and of my words in this adulterous and sinful generation; of him also shall the Son of man be ashamed, when he cometh in the glory of his Father with the holy angels." (Mark 8:38, I.A.)

We cannot afford to be unprepared. The saints must follow the guidance of the Holy Spirit and not be deceived by the world. This is one wedding feast that it will be worth every sacrifice to attend.

19

CATACLYSMIC EVENTS AT THE LORD'S APPEARANCE

THE MOUNTAINS ARE BROKEN DOWN

At about the same time as the Savior will stand upon the mount of Olives, his armies will also be upon the ocean, the islands and Zion or the New Jerusalem. Then the voice of the Lord "as the voice of many waters" will be heard worldwide. The prophet Ezekiel said that the noise of the wings of the cherubims is like the noise of great waters, which is as the voice of the Almighty and the voice of speech. (Ezek. 1:24) "For behold, he [Jesus Christ] shall stand upon the mount of Olivet [Olives], and upon the mighty ocean, even the great deep, and upon the islands of the sea, and upon the land of Zion. And he shall utter his voice out of Zion, and he shall speak from Jerusalem, and his voice shall be heard among all people; And it shall be a voice as the voice of many waters, and as the voice of a great thunder, which shall break down the mountains, and the valleys shall not be found." (D&C 133:20-22, I.A.)

This great noise will break down the mountains of the earth. Sound is a form of energy which is given off by a vibrating body. When an object vibrates, it makes the air that surrounds it vibrate. A sound wave is a vibration in the air. The sound waves are detected by our ears, and then are classified and interpreted by the brain. Loud noises can break things. Supersonic airplanes (that can fly faster than the speed of sound) can cause sonic booms that sometimes result in damage on the ground. Therefore, this great thunder and noise like many waters (caused by the noise of the cherubim's wings) will be heard by all people and will have the power to break down the mountains of the earth and make it more level.

There will be a tremendous change in the topography of the earth as the surface becomes more level. We are told that this will take place so that the glory of the Lord may fill the earth: "...thou shalt unveil the heavens, and cause the mountains to flow down at thy presence, and the valleys to be exalted, the rough places made smooth; that thy glory may fill the earth." (D&C 109:74, I.A., and JST Luke 3:10-11)

After this happens, much more of the surface of the earth will be habitable, but the mountains will be missed by those who love them. "The mountains quake at him [the Lord], and the hills melt, and the earth is burned at his presence, yea, the world, and all that dwell therein." (Nahum 1:5, I.A.)

THE HEAVENS AND EARTH SHAKE

At the time when the Lord will set his foot on the mount of Olives, the earth will reel to and fro and the heavens will also shake: "And then shall the Lord set his foot upon this mount, and it shall cleave in twain, and the earth shall tremble, and reel to and fro, and the heavens also shall shake." (D&C 45:48, I.A.)

This trembling of the earth and the shaking of the heavens will also occur at the same time that the Lord's "voice" roars from Zion and Jerusalem: "The Lord also shall roar out of Zion, and utter his voice from Jerusalem; and the heavens and the earth shall shake:" (Joel 3:16, I.A.).

Not only will the earth reel to and fro, but she will be removed out of her place: "Behold, the day of the Lord cometh...and he shall destroy the sinners thereof out of it. Therefore I will shake the heavens, and the earth shall remove out of her place, in the wrath of the Lord of hosts, and in the day of his fierce anger." (Isa. 13:9, 13, I.A.) So when the Lord returns, the heavens and the earth will shake and the earth will be removed out of her place.

ONE LAND MASS

Even more massive changes will take place on the earth as all the continents will come together into one land: "He [the Lord] shall command the great deep, and it shall be driven back into the north countries, and the islands shall become one land; And the land of Jerusalem and the land of Zion shall be turned back into their own place, and the earth shall be like as it was in the days before it was divided." (D&C 133:23-24, I.A., and Rev. 16:20, Gen. 10:25)

Apparently, the Atlantic Ocean will be driven back to the north, and the continents will come together to form one land mass and the earth will appear again as it was in the beginning.

THE SUN AND MOON WITHHOLD THEIR LIGHT

Along with all the other tremendous changes in the earth when Christ returns, the sun and moon will be darkened and the stars will be hurled from their places. "And so great shall be the glory of his presence that the sun shall hide his face in shame, and the moon shall withhold its light, and the stars shall be hurled from their places." (D&C 133:49, I.A., Joel 3:15, Isa. 13:10)

Some of the massive physical changes that will take place when the Savior returns will be the land becoming smooth and turning back into one land mass again. The earth and the heavens will shake and the earth will be removed out of her place. Also the sun and the moon will be darkened and the stars will fall at the glory of His presence.

THE RIGHTEOUS ARE CAUGHT UP TO BE WITH CHRIST

THE HEAVENS ARE OPENED

At the second coming, the heavens will be opened and the face of the Lord will be unveiled, "...and immediately after shall the curtain of heaven be unfolded, as a scroll is unfolded after it is rolled up, and the face of the Lord shall be unveiled;" (D&C 88:95, I.A., and Rev. 19:11, JST Rev. 6:14).

The Lord will unveil the heavens and men will no longer be limited in their vision, and they will see the heavens as they really are as God and His angels will be revealed. (D&C 109:74)

THE RIGHTEOUS WHO ARE ALIVE ARE CAUGHT UP TO MEET HIM

When the Lord comes a second time, those righteous saints who are alive will be caught up to meet the Savior: "And the saints that are upon the earth, who are alive, shall be quickened and be caught up to meet him." (D&C 88:96, I.A.)

Those who are of the Church of Christ will be taken up in a cloud and will receive their rewards for the good they have done: "For ye are the church of the Firstborn, and he will take you up in a cloud, and appoint every man his portion." (D&C 78:21, I.A.)

The righteous who are alive at His coming will be caught up in the clouds to meet the Lord in the air along with those who remain asleep or dead until the coming of the Lord. "Then they who are alive, shall be caught up together into the clouds with them who remain, to meet the Lord in the air; and so shall we be ever with the Lord." (JST 1 Thes. 4:17, I.A., and JST 1 Thes. 4:15) Those who are fortunate enough to be caught up in the clouds will be with their Lord and God forever.

SOME SAINTS ARE GATHERED BY ANGELS PRIOR TO THE SECOND COMING

Apparently after the worldwide earthquake and the Sign of the Son of Man, some people will be gathered by angels: "Immediately after the tribulation of those days shall the sun be darkened, and the moon shall not give her light, and the stars shall fall from heaven, and the powers of the heavens shall be shaken: And then shall appear the sign of the Son of man in heaven: and then shall all the tribes of the earth mourn, and they shall see the Son of man coming in the clouds of heaven with power and great glory. And he shall send his angels with a great sound of a trumpet, and they shall gather together his elect from the four winds, from one end of heaven to the other. Now learn a parable of the fig tree; When his branch is yet tender, and putteth forth leaves, ye know that summer is nigh: So likewise ye, when ye shall see all these things, know that it is near, even at the doors. Verily I say unto you, this generation shall not pass, till all these things be fulfilled." (Matt. 24:29-34, I.A.)

When we see the signs in the sun, moon and stars, the powers of heaven shaken, the sign of the Son of man and the elect gathered by angels, then we will know that all that has been prophesied to occur in the twenty-fourth chapter of Matthew will be fulfilled in that generation.

Mark recorded what Jesus said in similar words: "But in those days, after that tribulation, the sun shall be darkened, and the moon shall not give her light, And the stars of heaven shall fall, and the powers that are in heaven shall be shaken. And then shall they see the Son of man coming in the clouds with power and glory. And then shall he send his angels, and shall gather together his elect from the hour winds, from the uttermost part of the earth to the the uttermost part of heaven. Now learn a parable of the fig tree; When her branch is yet tender, and putteth forth leaves, ye know that summer is near: So ye in like manner, when ye shall see these things come to pass, know that it is nigh even at the doors. Verily I say unto you, that this generation shall not pass, till all these things be done." (Mark 13:24-30, I.A.) According to Mark, Jesus said the angels would gather the elect from the earth to the heavens.

At the second coming, "the remainder" of the saints or the elect will be gathered to where the other saints already are: "I tell you, in that night there shall be two men in one bed: the one shall be taken, and the other shall be left. Two women shall be grinding together; the one shall be taken, and the other left. Two men shall be in the field; the one shall be taken, and the other left. And they answered and said unto him, Where, Lord, shall they be taken. And he said unto them, Wheresoever the body is gathered; or in other words, whithersoever the saints are gathered, thither will the eagles be gathered together; or, thither will the remainder be gathered together. This he spake, signifying the gathering of his saints; and of angels descending and gathering the remainder unto them; the one from the bed, the other from the grinding, and the other from the field, withersoever he listeth." (Luke 17:34-36, JST Luke 17: 36-38, I.A.)

Angels will descend and the remainder of the saints will be gathered to where the other saints already are at the second coming. We are told that those who are alive when He comes or the remainder will be caught up into the clouds in the air. (JST 1 Thes. 4:17) Therefore, the saints who will be gathered previously must be in the clouds in the air if the remainder are gathered unto them.

Again, we are told that "the remainder" of the elect will be gathered at the second coming of Christ, which means that the angels must have gathered some of the elect previously: "...the Son of Man shall come, and he shall send his angels before him with the great sound of a trumpet, and they shall gather together the remainder of his elect from the four winds, from one end of heaven to the other." (JS-M 1:37, I.A., and D&C 124:10)

QUICKENED

In D&C 88:96, the Lord said that "the saints that are upon the earth, who are alive, shall be quickened and be caught up to meet him". Why would they need to be quickened? Because mankind cannot see God unless they are quickened, and these saints are being taken up to be with God. "For no man has seen God at any time in the flesh, except quickened by the Spirit of God." (D&C 67:11, I.A.) So it is "the Spirit of God" that quickens men.

The "Spirit of the Lord" quickened Adam also: "And it came to pass, when the Lord had spoken with Adam, our father, that Adam cried unto the Lord, and he was caught away by the Spirit of the Lord, and was carried down into the water, and was laid under the water, and was brought forth out of the water. And thus he was baptized, and the Spirit of God descended upon him, and thus he was born of the Spirit, and became quickened in the inner man." (Moses 6:64-65, I.A.) Ezekiel said that the spirit was in the wheels. (Ezekiel 1:20)

What might it feel like to be "quickened"? Joseph Smith described this somewhat in an account of the First Vision that was recorded by Orson Pratt. Joseph was prepared through the power of God to see

Heavenly Father and Jesus: "And, while thus pouring out his soul, anxiously desiring an answer from God, he, at length, saw a very bright light in the heavens above,...It continued descending slowly, until it rested upon the earth, and he was enveloped in the midst of it. When it first came upon him, it produced a peculiar sensation throughout his whole system; and immediately, his mind was caught away, from the natural objects with which he was surrounded; and he was enwrapped in a heavenly vision," (Taken from a pamphlet by Orson Pratt entitled, "Interesting Account of Several Remarkable Visions, and the Late Discovery of Ancient American Records", I.A.). So when a person is quickened, it produces a peculiar sensation and change in their entire system.

How bitter will be the disappointment for those saints who are among the "foolish virgins". They will be left to burn while the faithful and righteous are quickened and caught up to heaven to be with their God forever and to enjoy eternal bliss.

THE DEAD ARE CAUGHT UP TO MEET HIM

A trumpet will announce the resurrection of the dead at the Lord's second coming. (D&C 29:13) The saints who are dead will come forth into the cloud to meet the Savior: "But before the arm of the Lord shall fall, an angel shall sound his trump, and the saints that have slept shall come forth to meet me in the cloud." (D&C 45:45, I.A.)

All of those who have given their life for the gospel will be in the cloud of glory on the right hand of Jesus Christ when He returns: "For verily I say unto you, That he shall come; and he that layeth down his life for my sake and the gospel's, shall come with him, and shall be clothed with his glory in the cloud, on the right hand of the Son of Man." (JST Mark 8:43, I.A.)

In the inspired prayer which Joseph Smith offered at the dedication of the Kirtland Temple, the heartfelt desire of every true latter-day saint was expressed: "That when the trump shall sound for the dead, we shall be caught up in the cloud to meet thee, that we may ever be with the Lord;" (D&C 109:75, I.A.).

We must be worthy to earn the right to be caught up into the cloud to meet the Lord and to dwell with Him forever. "And the graves of the saints shall be opened; and they shall come forth and stand on the right hand of the Lamb, when he shall stand upon Mount Zion, and upon the holy city, the New Jerusalem; and they shall sing the song of the Lamb, day and night forever and ever." (D&C 133:56, I.A.)

Apparently the dead saints will be caught up first before the saints who are alive are taken up. "For this we say unto you by the word of the Lord, that they who are alive at the coming of the Lord, shall not prevent them who remain unto the coming of the Lord, who are asleep [the dead]. For the Lord himself shall descend from heaven with a shout, with the voice of the archangel, and with the trump of God: and the dead in Christ shall rise first: Then they who are alive, shall be caught up together into the clouds with them who remain [the dead], to meet the Lord in the air; and so shall we be ever with the Lord. Wherefore comfort one another with these words." (JST 1 Thes. 4:15, 1 Thes. 4:16, JST 1 Thes. 4:17, 1 Thes. 4:18, I.A.)

21

THE FIRST RESURRECTION

THE RESURRECTION OF THE JUST

Those that are dead who have accepted the gospel and have kept the commandments will take part in the first resurrection or the resurrection of the just. (D&C 76:50-53) These were seen in vision: "These are they whom he shall bring with him, when he shall come in the clouds of heaven to reign on the earth over his people. These are they who shall have part in the first resurrection. These are they who shall come forth in the resurrection of the just." (D&C 76:63-65, I.A.) The just will be brought with Christ in the clouds of heaven when He comes to reign.

King Mosiah said that those who were resurrected at the time when Jesus Christ was included prophets, the saints, those who died in ignorance and little children who had died. He taught that those who had rebelled against God and had died in their sins would not have part in that resurrection. (Mosiah 15:20-26) That was called the first resurrection for those who had lived before the resurrection of Jesus Christ. For those who have lived after the Lord's resurrection, the first resurrection will be at the second coming.

First of all, the saints who are dead will be caught up into the midst of the pillar of heaven to meet the Lord. Then the dead who have been in spirit prison and received the gospel will be redeemed: "And the saints that are upon the earth, who are alive, shall be quickened and be caught up to meet him. And they [the saints] who have slept in their graves shall come forth, for their graves shall be opened; and they also shall be caught up to meet him in the midst of the pillar of heaven--They are Christ's, the first fruits, they who shall descend with him first, and they who are on the earth and in their graves, who are first caught up to meet him; and all this by the voice of the sounding of the trump of the angel of God. And after this another angel shall sound, which is the second trump; and then cometh the redemption of those who are Christ's at his coming; who have received their part in that prison which is prepared for them, that they might receive the gospel, and be judged according to men in the flesh." (D&C 88:96-99, I.A., and Moses 7:38-39, 57)

Some of those who have their part in the prison are terrestrial people. They did not accept the gospel while they were alive but received a testimony in the spirit world. They are honorable people who were deceived. These are also those who have a testimony of Jesus but have not been valiant in their faith: "...these are they who are of the terrestrial,...Behold, these are they who died without law. And also they who are the spirits of men kept in prison, whom the Son visited, and preached the gospel unto them, that they might be judged according to men in the flesh; Who received not the testimony of Jesus in the flesh, but afterwards received it. These are they who are honorable men of the earth, who were blinded by the craftiness of men. These are they who receive of his glory, but not of his fulness. These are they who receive of the presence of the Son, but not of the fulness of the Father. These are they who are not valiant in the testimony of Jesus; wherefore, they obtain not the crown over the kingdoms of our God." (D&C 76:71-77, 79, I.A.)

Although the terrestrial people will be resurrected, they will not obtain the crown over the kingdom of God or, in other words, they will not rule with Christ over the earth.

THE HEATHEN WILL BE REDEEMED

The heathen nations and those who have known no law will be resurrected at the second coming of Jesus: "And then shall the heathen nations be redeemed, and they that knew no law shall have part in the first resurrection; and it shall be tolerable for them." (D&C 45:54, I.A., and Ezek. 37:28, 39:7, Ps. 98:1-3)

THOSE WHO ARE NOT PART OF THE FIRST RESURRECTION

The dead who are still sinners when the Lord comes again will not come forth at the first resurrection. "For the day cometh that the Lord shall utter his voice out of heaven; the heavens shall shake and the earth shall tremble, and the trump of God shall sound both long and loud, and shall say to the sleeping nations: Ye saints arise and live; ye sinners stay and sleep until I shall call again." (D&C 43:18, I.A.)

Those who have lived telestial lives will not be caught up into the cloud during the first resurrection: "And the glory of the telestial...these all are they who will not be gathered with the saints, to be caught up into the church of the Firstborn, and received into the cloud. These are they who are liars, and sorcerers, and adulterers, and whoremongers, and whosoever loves and makes a lie." (D&C 76:98, 102-103, I.A.) A whoremonger is a lecher who goes to prostitutes and is promiscuous. He can also be one who is an idolater and worshiper of idols.

Those who do not take part in the first resurrection because they are still under condemnation will have to wait one thousand years to be resurrected: "And again, another trump shall sound, which is the third trump; and then come the spirits of men who are to be judged, and are found under condemnation; And these are the rest of the dead; and they live not again until the thousand years are ended; neither again, until the end of the earth." (D&C 88:100-101, I.A., and Rev. 20:5)

22

JESUS CHRIST'S SECOND COMING

The Lord Jesus Christ will return to the earth and will usher in a millenium of peace and righteousness. What a blessed and long-awaited day that will be.

HIS RED APPAREL

Jesus will not be wearing white when He returns as some paintings depict, but his apparel will be blood-red. "And I saw heaven opened, and behold a white horse; and he that sat upon him was called Faithful and True, and in righteousness he doth judge and make war. His eyes were as a flame of fire, and on his head were many crowns; and he had a name written, that no man knew, but he himself. And he was clothed with a vesture dipped in blood: and his name is called The Word of God. And the armies which were in heaven followed him upon white horses, clothed in fine linen, white and clean. And he hath on his vesture and on his thigh a name written, KING OF KINGS, AND LORD OF LORDS." (Rev. 19:11-14, 16, I.A., and Isa. 63:1-4, D&C 133:51) Anciently a horse was a symbol of power in war and the ability to travel rapidly. Christ will come swiftly to judge and to wage war.

Because this will be the day when He takes vengeance upon the wicked, His garments will be the color of blood: "Who is this that cometh down from God in heaven with dyed garments; yea, from the regions which are not known, clothed in his glorious apparel, traveling in the greatness of his strength? And he shall say: I am he who spake in righteousness, mighty to save. And the Lord shall be red in his apparel, and his garments like him that treadeth in the wine-vat." (D&C 133:46-48, I.A.)

HIS APOSTLES WILL BE ON HIS RIGHT HAND

The twelve apostles who were with Christ in His ministry will stand on his right hand in a pillar of fire in great glory. They will judge only those of the House of Israel who have loved the Lord and kept His commandments. Jesus said, "...mine apostles, the Twelve which were with me in my ministry at Jerusalem, shall stand at my right hand at the day of my coming in a pillar of fire, being clothed in robes of righteousness, with crowns upon their heads, in glory even as I am, to judge the whole house of Israel, even as many as have loved me and kept my commandments, and none else."(D&C 29:12, I.A.)

HE WILL COME IN HIS GLORY WITH THE ANGELS IN THE CLOUDS OF HEAVEN

When the Savior returns, He will come in a cloud with power and great glory: "For behold, verily, verily, I say unto you, the time is soon at hand that I shall come in a cloud with power and great glory." (D&C 34:7, I.A.)

This cloud which is also called "the glory of the Lord" will be seen by all people: "And the glory of the Lord shall be revealed, and all flesh shall see it together: for the mouth of the Lord hath spoken it." (Isa. 40:5, I.A.)

The righteous will call Him blessed when He returns in the clouds of heaven with his angels: "Blessed is he who cometh in the name of the Lord, in the clouds of heaven, and all the holy angels with him." (JS-M 1:1, I.A.)

Those saints who are watching will be overjoyed to see the Lord in the clouds of heaven, but those who are not ready will be cut off. "And then they shall look for me, and behold, I will come; and they shall see me in the clouds of heaven, clothed with power and great glory; with all the holy angels; and he that watches not for me shall be cut off." (D&C 45:44, I.A.)

Everyone will see Him come with clouds, but the wicked will mourn: "Behold, he cometh with clouds; and every eye shall see him, and they also which pierced him: and all kindreds of the earth shall wail because of him." (Rev. 1:7, I.A.)

The clouds of heaven that the Lord and his angels will come in have also been called chariots. His rebuke of the wicked will be with flames of fire. "For, behold, the Lord will come with fire, and with his chariots like a whirlwind, to render his anger with fury, and his rebuke with flames of fire." (Isa. 66:16, I.A.)

The Savior will be accompanied by His armies of angels. (Rev. 19:14, Matt. 16:27, D&C 45:44) The Lord has a very great army of heavenly chariots and thousands of angels: "The chariots of God are twenty thousand, even thousands of angels: To him that rideth upon the heaven or heavens,...Ascribe ye strength unto God: his excellency is over Israel, and his strength is in the clouds. O God, thou art terrible out of thy holy places:" (Ps. 68:17, 33-35, I.A.).

What will His coming look like to those who are on the earth? "For as the light of the morning cometh out of the east, and shineth even unto the west, and covereth the whole earth, so shall also the coming of the Son of Man be." (JS-M 1:26, I.A.)

Wearing red apparel, the Lord Jesus Christ will

come out of the east on His throne in the glory of the Lord. His apostles and angels will accompany Him in the clouds of heaven. His chariots will number at least twenty thousand, and they will cover the whole earth. The righteous will rejoice when they see Him and the wicked will mourn. Because of the brightness of the Lord's glorious return, in the evening of the day when He comes, it will be light. (Zech. 14:5-7)

EVERY KNEE SHALL BOW

When the Lord makes His appearance at the end of the world, every knee will bow and every tongue will confess that Jesus Christ is the Lord. A trumpet will be heard in heaven, in the earth and under the earth calling on all people to bow and confess to the Lord who will sit upon the throne. All will obey: "And this shall be the sound of his *trump*, saying to *all people*, both *in heaven* and *in earth*, and that *are under the earth*--for every ear shall hear it, and *every knee shall bow*, and every tongue shall confess, while they hear the sound of the trump, saying: Fear God, and *give glory to him who sitteth upon the throne*, forever and ever; for the hour of his judgment is come." (D&C 88:104, I.A.)

All people in heaven, in earth and under the earth will confess that Jesus Christ is the Lord to the glory of God: "That at the name of Jesus every knee should bow, of things in heaven, and things in earth, and things under the earth; And that *every tongue should confess that Jesus Christ is Lord, to the glory of God the Father*." (Philip. 2:10-11, I.A.)

Even those in the sea will praise the Lord who sits on the throne: "And every creature which is in heaven, and on the earth, and under the earth, and such as are *in the sea*, and all that are in them, heard I saying, *Blessing, and honour, and glory, and power*, be unto *him that sitteth upon the throne*, and unto *the Lamb* for ever and ever." (Rev. 5:13, I.A.)

Jesus Christ is called "the Lamb" because He was the sacrificial offering that was made to atone for the sins of all people who will repent and accept Him.

As all the living will bow their knees and praise their King of all Kings, Jesus Christ will begin His rule of the earth.

THE SECRET ACTS OF MANKIND REVEALED

How many people feel that those secret things that they do when no one else sees them will always remain hidden? Some people only worry about their public appearance before others while their private life is dark and sinful. Jesus referred to these kinds of people as hypocrites: "...hypocrites! for ye are like unto whited sepulchres, which indeed appear beautiful outward, but are within full of dead men's bones, and of all uncleanness. Even so ye also outwardly appear righteous unto men, but within ye are full of hypocrisy and iniquity." (Matt. 23:27-28, I.A.)

After the Lord returns, all who are hypocrites and are rebellious will be exposed: "And the rebellious shall be pierced with much sorrow; for their iniquities shall be spoken upon the housetops, and their secret acts shall be revealed." (D&C 1:3, I.A.)

Not only will the secret acts of all men be revealed but also the thoughts and intents of the hearts of everyone since Adam. "And then shall the first angel sound his trump in the ears of all living, and reveal the secret acts of men, and the mighty works of God in the first thousand years. And then shall the second angel sound his trump, and reveal the secret acts of men, and the thoughts and intents of their hearts, and the mighty works of God in the second thousand years--And so on, until the seventh angel shall sound his trump;" (D&C 88:108-110, I.A.).

We should always keep in mind that God sees everything we do whether it is in public or private. The day will come when everyone will know our thoughts and deeds.

THERE WILL BE TIME NO LONGER

One of the changes that will take place after Christ returns is that there will no longer be time: "...the seventh angel shall sound his trump; and he shall stand forth upon the land and upon the sea, and swear in the name of him who sitteth upon the throne that there shall be time no longer; and Satan shall be bound," (D&C 88:110, I.A., and Rev. 10:6, D&C 84:100).

We get our time from the light of the sun as the earth rotates upon its axis and revolves around the sun. One possible reason why there will no longer be time during the millenium is because when Jesus Christ dwells on the earth, His glory will be the light. The Lord will be an everlasting light and the earth will not rely upon the sun any longer. After the terrible war of Armageddon, Israel was promised by the Lord that there will be no more violence in the land and He will be their light, "...they shall call thee, The city of the Lord, The Zion of the Holy One of Israel. Violence shall no more be heard in thy land, wasting nor destruction with thy borders; The sun shall be no more thy light by day; neither for brightness shall the moon give light unto thee: but the Lord shall be unto thee an everlasting light, and thy God thy glory. Thy sun shall no more go down; neither shall thy moon withdraw itself: for the Lord shall be thine everlasting light, and the days of thy mourning shall be ended." (Isa. 60:14, 18-20, I.A.)

SATAN WILL BE BOUND

Right now, Satan has the power to tempt mankind.

He will be bound in such a way that this power will be taken away from him: "And in that day [the second coming] Satan shall not have power to tempt any man." (D&C 101:28, I.A.)

What a marvelous day it will be when Satan can no longer tempt or deceive the people on the earth for a thousand years: "And I saw an angel come down from heaven, having the key of the bottomless pit and a great chain in his hand. And he laid hold on the dragon, that old serpent, which is the Devil, and Satan, and bound him a thousand years, And cast him into the bottomless pit, and shut him up, and set a seal upon him, that he should deceive the nations no more, till the thousand years be fulfilled: and after that he must be loosed a little season." (Rev. 20:1-3, I.A.)

The devil will no longer have a place in the hearts of men during the millenium of righteousness, "And Satan shall be bound, that he shall have no place in the hearts of the children of men." (D&C 45:55, I.A., and D&C 84:100, 1 Ne. 22:15, 2 Ne. 30:18)

After a thousand years of being bound, Satan will be loosed again for a short time, "For Satan shall be bound, and when he is loosed again he shall only reign for a little season, and then cometh the end of the earth." (D&C 43:31, I.A.)

Why would the Lord allow Satan to be loosed again at the end of the millenium? One reason will be so that he can gather his armies for the final battle: "...and Satan shall be bound, that old serpent, who is called the devil, and shall not be loosed for the space of a thousand years. And then he shall be loosed for a little season that he may gather together his armies. And Michael [Adam], the seventh angel, even the archangel, shall gather together his armies, even the hosts of heaven. And the devil shall gather together his armies; even the hosts of hell, and shall come up to battle against Michael [Adam] and his armies. And then cometh the battle of the great God;

and the devil and his armies shall be cast away into their own place, that they shall not have power over the saints any more at all. For Michael [Adam] shall fight their battles, and shall overcome him who seeketh the throne of him who sitteth upon the throne, even the Lamb." (D&C 88:110-115, I.A., and D&C 27:11)

One reason Satan will not be given power during the millenium will be because of the righteousness of the people. (1 Ne. 22:26) Perhaps another purpose for loosing the devil for a short time is because of the fact that some people will become wicked at the end of the millenium: "And again, verily, verily, I say unto you that when the thousand years are ended, and men again begin to deny their God, then will I spare the earth but for a little season." (D&C 29:22, I.A.)

THE CITY OF ENOCH RETURNS

Before the great flood, the City of Enoch was translated and taken into heaven until a day of righteousness would come upon the earth, "...the God of Enoch, and his brethren, Who were separated from the earth, and were received unto myself--a city reserved until a day of righteousness shall come--a day which was sought for by all holy men, and they found it not because of wickedness and abominations;" (D&C 45:11-12, I.A., and Moses 7:21, 69, D&C 84:100).

The rainbow is a sign of the covenant that God made to Enoch that the City of Enoch would return to the earth: "And the bow shall be in the cloud; and I will look upon it, that I may remember the everlasting covenant, which I made unto thy father Enoch; that, when men should keep all my commandments, Zion should again come on the earth, the city of Enoch which I have caught up unto myself. And this is mine everlasting covenant, that when thy posterity shall embrace the truth, and look upward, then shall Zion look downward, and all the heavens shall shake with gladness, and the earth shall tremble with joy. And the general assembly of the church of the first-born shall come down out of heaven, and possess the earth, and shall have place until the end come. And this is mine everlasting covenant, which I made with thy father Enoch." (JST Gen. 9:21-23, I.A.)

When the City of Enoch returns to the earth and they greet the people of Zion, there will be great rejoicing, "...it shall be called Zion, a New Jerusalem. And the Lord said unto Enoch: Then shall thou and all thy city meet them there, and we will receive them into our bosom, and they shall see us; and we will fall upon their necks, and they shall fall upon our necks, and we will kiss each other; And there shall be mine abode, and it shall be Zion, which shall come forth out of all the creations which I have made; and for the space of a thousand years the earth shall rest." (Moses 7:62-64, I.A.)

THE LORD REVEALS ALL THAT HAS BEEN HIDDEN

Apparently there are a lot of things which have been kept hidden that will be revealed at the beginning of the millenium: "Wherefore, the things of all nations shall be made known; yea, all things shall be made known unto the children of men. There is nothing which is secret save it shall be revealed; there is no work of darkness save it shall be made manifest in the light; and there is nothing which is sealed upon the earth save it shall be loosed. Wherefore, all things which have been revealed unto the children of men shall at that day be revealed; and Satan shall have power over the hearts of the children of men no more, for a long time." (2 Ne. 30:16-18, I.A.)

When the Lord comes again all hidden things will be revealed along with many mysteries about the earth and its creation. "Yea, verily I say unto you, in that day when the Lord shall come, he shall reveal all things--Things which have passed, and hidden things which no man knew, things of the earth, by which it was made, and the purpose and the end thereof--Things most precious, things that are above, and things that are beneath, things that are in the earth, and upon the earth, and in heaven." (D&C 101:32-34, I.A.) For those with a curious mind, that will be a fantastic history lesson.

THE SAVIOR WILL REIGN PERSONALLY UPON THE EARTH

The earth will be crowned with the presence of Jesus Christ during the millenium. "And the Lord, even the Savior, shall stand in the midst of his people, and shall reign over all flesh." (D&C 133:25, I.A., and D&C 43:29, 29:11, Rev. 20:4, 10th A of F)

Jesus will reign over the earth from two world capitols, the New Jerusalem and the Old Jerusalem (Isa. 24:23), "and the Lord shall be king over all the earth:" (Zech. 14:9, I.A.).

GLORIOUS CONDITIONS DURING THE MILLENIUM

A NEW HEAVENS AND A NEW EARTH

Spencer W. Kimball taught that our world is very sick and is failing fast: "Our world is in turmoil. It is aging toward senility. It is very ill. Long ago it was born with brilliant prospects. It was baptized by water, and its sins were washed away. It was never baptized by fire, for that is still to come. It has had shorter periods of good health but longer ones of ailing. Most of the time there have been pains and aches in its anatomy, but now that it is growing old, complications have set in, and all the ailments seem to be everywhere." ("Conference Report", Oct. 1961, p. 30, I.A.)

After Jesus told his ancient disciples that the saints would be taken up at the second coming, He proclaimed: "For verily there shall be new heavens, and a new earth, wherein dwelleth righteousness. And there shall be no unclean thing; for the earth becoming old, even as a garment, having waxed in corruption, wherefore it vanisheth away, and the footstool remaineth sanctified, cleansed from all sin." (JST Luke 17:39-40, I.A.) The earth is old and filled with corruption. The evil will be purged away, and the earth will be sanctified and renewed.

The Lord has given us even more details as to how the earth will be made new. "But the day of the Lord will come as a thief in the night, in the which the heavens shall shake, and the earth also shall tremble, and the mountains shall melt, and pass away with a great noise, and the elements shall be filled with fervent heat; the earth also shall be filled, and the corruptible works which are therein shall be burned up. If then all these things shall be destroyed, what manner of persons ought ye to be in holy conduct and godliness, Looking unto, and preparing for the day of the coming of the Lord wherein the corruptible things of the heavens being on fire, shall be dissolved, and the mountains shall melt with fervent heat? Nevertheless, if we shall endure, we shall be kept according to his promise. And we look for a new heavens, and a new earth wherein dwelleth righteousness." (JST 2 Pet. 3:10-13, I.A., and D&C 101:25)

If the earth were moved to another part of the galaxy, we would have a new heavens. Indeed, the prophet Isaiah said that the earth will be removed out of the place she is now in when the Lord comes: "Behold, the day of the Lord cometh, cruel both with wrath and fierce anger, to lay the land desolate: and he shall destroy the sinners thereof out of it. Therefore I will shake the heavens, and the earth shall remove out of her place, in the wrath of the Lord of hosts, and in the day of his fierce anger." (Isa. 13:9, 13, I.A., and 2 Ne. 23:9, 13)

If the earth were removed from her present location then the inhabitants of the earth would see a new and different heavens: "...the foundations of the earth do shake. The earth is utterly broken down, the earth is clean dissolved, the earth is moved exceedingly. The earth shall reel to and fro like a drunkard, and shall be removed like a cottage;...when the Lord shall reign in mount Zion, and in Jerusalem, and before his ancients gloriously." (Isa. 24:18-20, 23, I.A.)

Apostle Orson Hyde taught that at the second coming the earth will be removed from its present orbit: "...it will be removed out of its present orbit. The earth will have to be removed from its place,...The fact is, it has got to leave the old track in which it has roamed in time passed, and beat a new track...where the sun will shine upon it continually, and there shall be no more night there;...but when the earth is taken out of this orbit, it will come in contact with the rays of other suns" (J.D. 1:130, I.A.).

However, the new heavens and the new earth will resemble the old heavens and the old earth: "And there shall be a new heaven and a new earth; and they shall be like unto the old save the old have passed away, and all things have become new." (Ether 13:9, I.A.)

The old earth and heavens will be forgotten. "For, behold, I create new heavens and a new earth: and the former shall not be remembered nor come into mind." (Isa. 65:17, I.A., and Isa. 66:22)

Imagine an earth with no corruption or wickedness. It will be a paradise indeed.

THE EARTH CHANGED FROM A TELESTIAL TO A TERRESTRIAL PLANET

Joseph Fielding Smith taught that our telestial planet will become a terrestrial planet during the millenium with terrestrial people living on it: "We discover from the word of the Lord that the earth, like mankind upon it, is passing through various stages of development, or change. It was created and pronounced good. It partook of the decree of mortality coming through the fall. It is now passing through the telestial condition, in which telestial beings predominate and rule. It will then pass into the 'renewed', or restored state, for a thousand years as a terrestrial earth and the abode of terrestrial inhabitants. Then comes the end. The earth like all creatures living on it must die. Then it will, like all creatures, receive its resurrection and be celestialized because it obeys its law." (Church

History, p. 295, I.A.)

To renew means to make new spiritually or to regenerate. To restore means to bring back into the original state. The earth was once a paradise before the fall of Adam and Eve. Another word for this future renewed and restored state of the earth is that she will be "transfigured". "Nevertheless, he that endureth in faith and doeth my will, the same shall overcome, and shall receive an inheritance upon the earth when the day of transfiguration shall come; When the earth shall be transfigured, even according to the pattern which was shown unto mine apostles upon the mount; of which account the fulness ye have not yet received." (D&C 63:20-21, I.A.)

A transfiguration is a supernatural or glorious change in appearance. This change will make the earth a paradise. "We believe in the literal gathering of Israel and in the restoration of the Ten Tribes; that Zion (the New Jerusalem) will be built upon the American continent; that Christ will reign personally upon the earth; and that the earth will be renewed and receive its paradisiacal glory." (10th A of F, I.A.)

Paradisiacal refers to the earth being like it was in the Garden of Eden. The earth will become like it was before it was cursed after the fall of Adam and Eve. "For the Lord shall comfort Zion: he will comfort all her waste places; and he will make her wilderness like Eden, and her desert like the garden of the Lord; joy and gladness shall be found therein, thanksgiving, and the voice of melody." (Isa. 51:3, I.A., and 2 Ne. 8:3, Isa. 35:1-2)

At the time of the Tower of Babel, the Lord confounded the language of mankind causing many different tongues to be spoken on the earth. As part of the restoration of all things at the second coming, the Lord will re-establish a pure language and all men will pray to him in one tongue. "For then will I turn to the people a pure language, that they may all call upon the name of the Lord, to serve him with one consent." (Zeph. 3:9, I.A.)

ENMITY CEASES, NO SORROW AND NO DEATH

Many other glorious blessings will be enjoyed upon this new earth during the millenial era. All hatred and hostility will cease. Mankind will ask for blessings and then receive them. There will be no sadness, because there will be no death. People will live to a certain age and then be changed in the twinkling of an eye. "And also that of element shall melt with fervent heat; and all things shall become new, that my knowledge and glory may dwell upon all the earth. And in that day the enmity of man, and the enmity of beasts, yea, the enmity of all flesh, shall cease from before my face. And in that day whatsoever any man shall ask, it shall be given unto him. And in that day Satan shall not have power to tempt any man. And there shall be no sorrow because there is no death. In that day an infant shall not die until he is old; and his life shall be as the age of a tree; And when he dies he shall not sleep, that is to say in the earth, but shall be changed in the twinkling of an eye, and shall be caught up, and his rest shall be glorious." (D&C 101:25-31, I.A., and D&C 63:49-51)

It is necessary for all of the corruption and wickedness of the earth to be burned and destroyed so that this new age of enlightenment and peace can be ushered in.

What a splendid time this will be to live on the earth. Isaiah foresaw that the age which mankind would like to before being changed in the twinkling of an eye during the millenium will be one hundred years old. (Isa. 65:20)

Many will be delighted to realize that there will also be no pain during the millenium. "And I heard a great voice out of heaven saying, Behold, the tabernacle of God is with men, and he will dwell with them, and they shall be his people, and God himself shall be with them, and be their God. And God shall wipe away all tears from their eyes; and there shall be no more death, neither sorrow, nor crying, neither shall there be any more pain: for the former things are passed away. And he that sat upon the throne said, Behold, I make all things new." (Rev. 21:3-5, I.A., and Isa. 33:24)

THE EARTH IS FULL OF THE KNOWLEDGE OF GOD

There are so many misconceptions in the world today about God. Many are unsure and unknowledgeable about the nature of the Being they worship. During the millenium, all of these falsehoods and misconceptions will be replaced with an understanding of the true nature of the Lord. "The wolf shall dwell with the lamb, and the leopard shall lie down with the kid; and the calf and the young lion and the fatling together; and a little child shall lead them. And the cow and the bear shall feed; their young ones shall lie down together: and the lion shall eat straw like the ox. And the suckling child shall play on the hole of the asp, and the weaned child shall put his hand on the cockatrice' den. They shall not hurt nor destroy in all my holy mountain: for the earth shall be full of the knowledge of the Lord, as the waters cover the sea." (Isa. 11:6-9, I.A.) It will be wonderful to have the true knowledge of God cover the earth.

The faithful saints are promised great blessings during the millenium along with their children. "And the earth shall be given unto them for an inheritance; and they shall multiply and wax strong, and their children shall grow up without sin unto salvation. For the Lord shall be in their midst, and his glory shall be upon them, and he will be their king and their lawgiver." (D&C 45:58-59, I.A.)

With the wickedness that is rampant now, raising children can be very difficult. It would certainly be a paradise for parents to have their children grow up without sin.

During the millenium, people will enjoy a new heaven and a new earth. This beautiful and restored earth will be free from enmity, sorrow, death, pain and temptation from Satan. It will truly be a paradise on earth.

24

WILL PEOPLE ON THE EARTH BE TRANSLATED BEINGS DURING THE MILLENIUM?

The changes that will take place on the earth and with mankind during the millenium when the earth becomes a terrestrial planet sound very much like what has happened to people who have been translated. The five similarities between translation and the millenial era on the earth are discussed next.

FIVE EVIDENCES THAT THEY WILL

The following are five evidences that those people who inhabit the earth during the millenium will be translated beings.

(1) The first evidence is that in the past, mortals who were translated were caught up into heaven by angels as in the case of the City of Enoch, Elijah and probably Alma.

Speaking of the City of Enoch: "Zion, in process of time, was taken up into heaven. And Enoch beheld angels descending out of heaven, bearing testimony of the Father and Son; and the Holy Ghost fell on many, and they were caught up by the powers of heaven into Zion." (Moses 7:21, 27, I.A.)

When Elijah was translated, "...there appeared a chariot of fire;...and Elijah went up by a whirlwind into heaven." (2 Kgs. 2:11, I.A.)

After Alma disappeared without a trace, the

people said, "Behold, this we know, that he was a righteous man; and the saying went abroad in the church that he was taken up by the Spirit," (Alma 45:19, I.A.).

The righteous who are on the earth at the time of the Lord's second coming will likewise be caught up by angels. "Then they who are alive, shall be caught up together into the clouds with them who remain [the dead], to meet the Lord in the air:" (JST 1 Thes. 4:17, I.A.). "And the saints that are upon the earth, who are alive, shall be quickened and be caught up to meet him." (D&C 88:96, I.A., and Luke 17:34-36, JST Luke 17:36-38)

(2) The second evidence is that those who were translated in the past were promised that they would not die but would be changed in the twinkling of an eye from mortality to immortality.

Jesus promised the Three Nephites: "And ye shall never endure the pains of death; but when I shall come in my glory ye shall be changed in the twinkling of an eye from mortality to immortality;" (3 Ne. 28:8, I.A.). That was one of the blessings of being translated.

Enoch had the same promise, "By faith Enoch was translated that he should not see death; and was not found, because God had translated him:" (Heb. 11:5, I.A., and D&C 7:2).

Conditions during the millenium will be such that there will be no death, but each person will be changed in the twinkling of an eye when 100 years old. "And in that day Satan shall not have power to tempt any man. And there will be no sorrow because there is no death. In that day an infant shall not die until he is old; and his life shall be as the age of a tree; And when he dies he shall not sleep, that is to say in the earth, but shall be changed in the twinkling of an eye," (D&C 101:28:31, I.A., and Isa. 65:20, D&C 63:49-51).

(3) A third evidence is that translated beings in the past have not suffered from pain or sorrow (except for the sins of the world).

When the Three Nephites were translated, "...that they might not taste of death there was a change wrought upon their bodies, that they might not suffer pain nor sorrow save it were for the sins of the world." (3 Ne. 28:38, I.A.)

During the millenium, people will not suffer from pain or sorrow either. "And God shall wipe away all tears from their eyes; and there shall be no more death, neither sorrow, nor crying, neither shall there be any more pain." (Rev. 21:4, I.A., and D&C 101:29, Isa. 33:24)

(4) The fourth evidence is that in the past, God has dwelt among translated beings.

God was among the City of Enoch, "Zion, in process of time, was taken up into heaven. And the Lord said unto Enoch: Behold mine abode forever." (Moses 7:21, I.A., and Moses 7:69)

When the Lord comes to reign on the earth during the millenium, he will dwell among men. "And the Lord, even the Savior, shall stand in the midst of his people, and shall reign over all flesh." (D&C 133:25, I.A., and Isa. 24:23, 10th A of F)

(5) In the past, translated beings were terrestrial beings.

Joseph Smith taught, "...and Enoch walked with God, and he was not, for God took him. (Gen. 5:22) Now this Enoch God reserved unto Himself, that he should not die at that time, and appointed unto him a ministry unto terrestrial bodies, of whom there has been but little revealed...Many have supposed that the doctrine of translation was a doctrine whereby men were taken immediately into the presence of God, and into an eternal fullness, but this is a mistaken idea. Their place of habitation is that of the terrestrial order, and a place prepared for such characters He held in reserve to be ministering angels unto many planets," (Teachings, p. 170, I.A.).

The earth is now a telestial planet and will be changed to a terrestrial planet when the Savior returns. This was plainly taught by Joseph Fielding Smith: "We discover from the word of the Lord that the earth, like mankind upon it, is passing through various stages of development, or change. It was created and pronounced good. It partook of the decree of mortality coming through the fall. It is now passing through the telestial condition, in which telestial beings predominate and rule. It will then pass into the 'renewed', or restored state, for a thousand years as a terrestrial earth and the abode of terrestrial inhabitants." (Church History, p. 295, Vol. 1, I.A.)

There is sometimes joking among Church members about a person getting so good that he or she might be translated. That may not be a joke at all during the millenium. In light of the five evidences given, it is very possible that the people who live during the millenium will be translated beings.

TRANSLATION IS PART OF THE RESTORATION OF ALL THINGS

We live in the dispensation of the fullness of times when all things will be restored. (Acts 3:19-21, Eph. 1:10, Teachings, pp. 171-172) The children of Israel will be gathered and restored to their inheritance. The earth which fell will be renewed and restored to its paradisiacal glory. Restitution means "a reestablishment of the gospel of Jesus Christ on the earth in the last days, with the powers, ordinances, doctrines, offices, and all things as they have existed in former ages." (Bible Dictionary, The Holy Bible, published by the Church, p. 761, I.A.)

President John Taylor taught that our dispensation must include all of the spiritual blessings that have been available in all other dispensations which would include the power of translation. He said, "We are living in the dispensation which is emphatically called the dispensation of the fulness of times, which we are informed from the scriptures has been 'spoken of by all the holy prophets since the world was;' and this being the case, the dispensation in which we live embraces necessarily all that was contained in any and all of the other dispensations that have existed in all the ages preceding ours; and that consequently whatever organizations, manifestations, revelations or communications that have ever come from God to the human family in their times and dispensations, we may consistently expect to be embodied in this one...The power of translation was a principle that existed in the Church in that dispensation. There is something very peculiar in these things." (J.D. 21:242-243, I.A.)

The five similarities that exist between translated beings and those who will dwell on the earth during the millenium are amazing. Both are caught up to heaven first, do not suffer death as a separation of the body and spirit, have no pain or sorrow, have God dwell with them and are terrestrial beings. In order for all things to be restored in this dispensation, the power of translation must also be utilized in our day because it was a power that existed in previous dispensations.

THE CONCLUSION

There is great pain, discomfort and difficulty suffered during labor and in the delivery of a child. It helps to keep in mind the purpose for the anguish, and the blessed reward that comes after the tribulation.

Similarly, we live in the last days before the end of the world. Wickedness will be everywhere and will multiply. There will be times of great hardship and trial as the Lord pleads with mankind to repent before the great and dreadful day of the Lord.

To survive the last days physically and spiritually, it is critical that we follow the Lord's prophets, understand the scriptures and take the Holy Spirit for our guide. We must always keep in mind that after the tribulations come the blessings. These evil and difficult times will culminate in the birth of a new earth with conditions as glorious as the Garden of Eden, when righteousness will be amply rewarded.

The coming of the Lord Jesus Christ will be a great day if we have endured to the end and been faithful. On the other hand, it will be a dreadful day if we are among the half of the Church members who will not be prepared, who have been deceived and who will burn with the wicked.

We make our own choices daily and will live with the consequences eternally; may we choose wisely. The Lord and his prophets have repeatedly warned us to keep the commandments and to be prepared. Jesus promised His saints: "What I the Lord have spoken, I have spoken, and I excuse not myself, and though the heavens and the earth pass away, my word shall not pass away, but shall all be fulfilled, whether by mine voice or by the voice of my servants, it is the same." (D&C 1:38, I.A.)

BIBLIOGRAPHY

Church History and Modern Revelation. By Joseph Fielding Smith. Deseret Book Co.: Salt Lake City, Utah. Two volumes.

Doctrines of Salvation. By Joseph Fielding Smith. Bookcraft: Salt Lake City, Utah. 1954-56. Three Volumes.

Faith Precedes the Miracle. By Spencer W. Kimball. Deseret Book Co.: Salt Lake City, Utah. 1973.

History of the Church of Jesus Christ of Latter-day Saints. By Joseph Smith Jr. and Edited by B. H. Roberts. Deseret Book Co.: Salt Lake City, Utah. 1949. Seven Volumes.

The Hollow Earth. By Raymond Bernard, Ph.D. Citadel Press: Secaucus, New Jersey. 1969.

Journal of Discourses. Latter-day Saints' Book Depot: London, England. 1854-86. Twenty-six Volumes.

The Lost Books of the Bible and the Forgotten Books of Eden. The World Publishing Co.: Cleveland and New York. 1963.

Mormon Doctrine. By Bruce R. McConkie. Bookcraft: Salt Lake City, Utah. 1958.

Teachings of the Prophet Joseph Smith. Compiled by Joseph Fielding Smith. Deseret Book Co.: Salt Lake City, Utah. 1967.

Unpublished Revelations of the Prophets and Presidents of the Church of Jesus Christ of Latter Day Saints. Compiled by Fred C. Collier. Collier's Publishing Co.: Salt Lake City, Utah. Vol. 1.

Wilford Woodruff. By Matthais F. Cowley. Deseret News: Salt Lake City, Utah. 1916.

The World Book Encyclopedia. World Book--Childcraft International, Inc. 1980.

A

Aaron, 58, 65, 123
Aaronic Priesthood, 73
Abominable church, 95, 96, 156, 157
Abominations, 5, 95, 221
Abraham, 106, 125, 147
Adam, 68, 123, 193-195, 208, 218, 220-221, 227
Adam-ondi-Ahman, 158, 193-194
Affliction, 97
Airplanes, 174, 175
Albany, 83
Alma, 51, 71, 141, 231
Almalthea, 139
Amber, 38, 54, 55
America(n), 7, 26, 34, 75, 83-86, 94-95, 97, 116, 121, 131, 135, 140, 147-150, 165, 227
Amos, 8
Ancient of Days, 68, 193-194
Angel(s), 4, 12, 28, 30, 31, 50, 60, 62, 68-72, 74-76, 79, 81, 86, 95, 106, 113-114, 117-118, 142, 144, 156, 164-166, 168, 172-173, 177, 184, 186-187, 189-190, 197, 201, 206-207, 209, 212, 216-220, 231-232
Animals, 30
Apocrypha, 118, 122, 126
Apostasy, 3, 155-156, 158, 161-162
Apostles, 66, 69, 215, 217
Apparel, 214
Armageddon, 144, 179-181, 185, 219
Ark, 102, 104-105
Armies, 30, 108, 202, 214, 216, 220, 221
Arsareth, 119, 127, 133
Aser (Asher), 113
Assyria, 119
Atonement, 111
Aurora Borealis, 135
Auroras, 139
Axis, 15-16

B

Babylon, 147-148, 150-151, 159, 162, 177, 185-189, 192
Bands, 95
Baptize(d), 30, 49, 155, 208, 224
Beast, 41
Benjamin, King, 113, 169
Benson, Ezra Taft, 105
Beryl, 43
Bethlehem, 75
Bible, 73-79, 124, 130, 173
Black magic, 160

Blasphemy, 15, 162, 190
Blood, 24-25, 33, 87-88, 92, 95, 111 119, 132, 157, 165-168, 176-178, 186, 188-189, 214
Bloodshed, 86, 92-93, 103, 110, 116, 134
Boston, 83
Brass, 38, 40
Bridegroom, 31, 157, 198, 200
Burn(ed), 34-35, 101, 144, 151, 187, 190-192, 225, 228
Byrd, Richard E., 136-137

C

Caiaphas, 69
Cain, 7
Calamities, 13, 105
Canaan, 108
Canada, 140
Candlesticks, 175
Celestial(ized), 30, 72, 226
Censer, 164-165, 167
Chaldea, 48
Chambers, 67
Chapels, 90
Chariot(s), 30, 36, 67-68, 73-76, 79, 81, 84, 216, 231
Cherub(ims), 37, 44-47, 51-52, 54-56, 202
Christian Church, 12, 13
Church(es), 3, 90, 95
Church (of Jesus Christ of Latter-day Saints), 4, 11, 96, 103, 140, 155-158, 161, 163, 198-201, 205, 236
Civil War, 10, 92-93
Clothing, 106
Cloud(s) (of heaven), 32-33, 36-38, 56-58, 61, 63-65, 67-73, 110-112, 182, 191, 194, 205-211, 213, 215-217
Coal(s), 44, 46-47
Columbus, 135, 140
Comet, 33, 168
Commandments, 90, 199, 215
Communism, 7, 92
Congregation, 58
Constitution, 96-97, 103
Covenant, 90, 221
Cowdery, Oliver, 28, 53
Creation, 48, 133, 222
Creature(s), 38, 40-41, 44-45, 47, 51-53, 129, 226
Crime, organized, 7
Crops, 87
Cross, 199
Crown(s), 195, 212, 214
Curse, 5, 80-81, 149, 200

D

Daniel, 68, 193-194
Darkness, 167-168, 199
David, 46, 74, 79, 106, 125
Dead, 51, 72, 209-211
Dead Sea, 145
Death, 87, 228, 230, 232
Delusion, 106
Desert, 59
Desolation, 90, 93, 106, 148, 165
Destruction, 21, 83-84, 93, 186-187, 190

Devil(s), 6, 34, 49, 88, 91, 95, 155, 157-158, 161-162, 169, 177
Dimensions, 28
Disappointment, 189
Disaster, 85, 105
Disease, 87, 89
Doctrine and Covenants, 1, 4, 57, 70
Dome of the Rock, 98
Door in heaven, 50
Dreams, 4

E

Eagle, 39-41
Earthquake, 2-3, 9, 13-15, 19-22, 26-27, 31, 33-34, 69, 83, 85, 88-89, 98, 100, 102, 105, 132, 164, 167, 183-185, 187
East, 34, 57, 100, 216-217
Eden, 46
Egypt, 67, 80, 101, 106, 121-122
Elders, 96-97
Elect, 97, 206-208
Elias, 117-118, 156
Elijah, 4-5, 48, 73, 79, 103, 231
Elisha, 30, 48, 73-74, 106
Endowments, 122
Enoch, 51, 110, 221-222, 231-233
Enoch, City of, 126-127, 132, 221-222, 231, 233
Ephraim, 116, 122
Eternal life, 188
Euphrates, 119, 172-173
Europe, 119, 135
Exaltation, 37
Extra-terrestrials, 37
Extravagance, 11-12
Ezekiel, 8, 33, 37-39, 44-45, 51-52, 54, 56-57, 78-79, 145, 202, 208

F

Face(s), 38, 40
Faith, 25, 28, 87
False Christs, 99, 100
False prophet(s), 99, 100, 180, 189
Famine, 85, 102, 105, 116, 187, 189
Fear, 21-22, 26, 30, 182
Fig tree, 34-35
Fire, 23-26, 38, 46, 54-55, 58-59, 62-63, 66-67, 74, 83, 150, 165, 167-168, 173, 175-176, 178, 181, 186, 189-193, 215
Firstborn, 191, 205, 222
Flies, 87-88
Flood, 84, 102, 188, 192, 197
Flying roll, 80-81
Flying saucer, 37
Food, 102-106
Fuel, 102

G

Gad, 113
Garden(s), 22, 102, 104-106

Garden of Eden, 46, 227, 236
Garment, 198-199, 214-215
Gather, 8
Genealogy, 5
Gentile(s), 3, 8, 12, 35, 67, 84-85, 89, 94-95, 108, 117, 124, 150, 182, 186
Glory, 130, 229
Glory of the Lord, 32, 54-62, 73, 111, 161, 203, 215, 217
God the Father, 4
Gog, 180, 186
Gospel, 3, 12-13, 68, 117, 146, 150, 155-156, 161, 198, 200, 212, 234

H

Habakkuk, 74
Hail(storm), 23-24, 85, 116, 165, 168, 184-185, 187
Hailstones, 186
Heathen, 213
Heaven(s), 16, 23-25, 31, 44, 48, 59, 67, 70
Heavenly Father, 49, 60, 77, 155, 209
Heavens opened, 4, 27-32, 214
Helaman, 16, 141
Helicopters, 171-172
Hell, 169, 201
Herod, 75, 76
Highway, 121-122, 134
Hispanic, 94
Hollow earth, 127-128, 135-136
Holy Ghost, 155, 192
Holy land, 90, 125
Holy places, 90
Holy Spirit, 200-201, 236
Homes, 90
Hyde, Orson, 225
Hypocrites, 218

I

Idols, 213, 159-161
Idumea, 7
Incense, 164
Indians, 94, 140
Inheritance, 195
Iniquity, 5-6, 120, 189, 191, 218
Inspiration, 86
Io, 139
Isaac, 106, 125
Issachar, 113
Isaiah, 59, 67, 74, 80, 191, 225, 228
Israel(ites), 8, 12-13, 48, 57, 62-63, 65, 73, 80-81, 85, 97, 106, 108, 156, 180-183, 186, 215-216, 219, 227, 234

J

Jackson County, 107-108
Jacob, 80, 94-95, 106, 125, 141
James, 68
Japeth, 180
Jared, brother of, 28, 32, 71

Jaredite(s), 7, 71, 84, 86, 91-92
Jeremiah, 68, 106, 181
Jerusalem, 56, 66, 70-71, 76, 80, 83, 97-99, 117, 119, 125, 141, 145, 147, 175, 181-182, 184-185, 203, 215, 223, 225
Jesus Christ, 3-4, 6, 8-9, 15, 26, 28, 30-34, 49, 52-53, 60, 69, 72, 75-78, 84-86, 94, 100, 111, 114-116, 119-120, 124, 129-131, 140-142, 144-145, 150, 157-158, 161, 163, 175, 183-184, 188, 194-195, 197-199, 202, 205-207, 209-212, 214-219, 223, 234, 236
Jews, 8, 12-13, 97-99, 120, 124, 134, 141, 145-147, 176, 182-183
Joel, 4, 145
John the Baptist, 73
John the Revelator, 1-3, 11, 14, 19, 29, 31, 49, 53, 68, 70, 113-116, 118, 129-130, 147, 149, 156, 159-161, 166-170, 173, 175, 178, 188
Joseph, 75, 108, 113, 147
Joshua, 108
Juda(h), 113, 116, 124, 145
Judgment(s), 14, 87, 89, 93, 106, 163-168, 180, 185-186, 188
Jupiter, 138-139
Just, 211

K

Key(s), 168-169
Kimball, Heber C., 11
Kimball, Spencer W., 105, 224
King(s), 8, 125, 172, 177, 180, 188-189, 223
Kingdom, 195
Kingdom of God, 87, 155, 157, 163, 193-194, 212
King of Kings, 142, 158, 184, 189, 196, 214, 218
Kirtland Temple, 5, 28, 53, 61, 66, 72, 120
Knee, 129-130, 217-218
Knowledge, 28, 228
Kolob, 143

L

Lamanites, 13, 93-95, 106, 108, 117, 120, 140-141
Lamb, 31-32, 50, 100, 111, 114, 116, 129, 156-157, 160, 188, 197-199, 217-218
Lamp(s), 33, 37-38, 44-45, 50, 56
Land of the north, 119-121, 124
Language, 227
Last days, 3-4, 6, 8, 11-12, 102, 236

Lehi, 30, 65, 140-141
Levi, 113, 123
Levi, sons of, 123
Liberty, 97
Lightnings, 14, 21-22, 26, 51-52, 63, 164, 167, 184-185, 187
Lion, 39-40, 94-95
Logan, 83
Lord of Hosts, 192
Lord of lords, 188-189, 196, 214
Lost Tribes, 85, 116, 120, 124, 126, 132, 134, 146
Love, 5
Lucifer, 168, 172

M

Maggots, 88
Magog, 180
Malachi, 4-5
Man, 38-39, 41, 54-55, 100
Manasses(h), 113, 116
Man of Holiness, 32
Mark (of the beast), 160, 177, 189
Mark, 206-207
Marks, William, 74-75
Marriage Supper, 157, 197-199
Mars, 138
Mary, 75-76
Matthew, 206
Mediterranean Sea, 145
Melchizedek, 30
Mercy, 188
Messiah, 182-184
Meteorites, 20, 23-24, 88, 167-168, 186
Methuselah, 106
Microscope, 28
Millenium, 2, 67, 131, 187, 192, 198, 214, 219-235
Miracles, 3, 99-100, 121, 159
Miriam, 65
Missionaries, 13-14, 31, 35, 146, 156
Missouri, 107-109, 123
Moon, 19-23, 25, 32-33, 87, 132-133, 137, 139, 150, 204
Moriancumer, 71
Mormon, 6, 93-94, 141
Moroni, 93, 106, 127
Moses, 51, 57-59, 62-65, 78-79, 81, 101, 122, 168
Mosiah, 141, 211
Mosiah, sons of, 71
Mosque, 98
Mountain(s), 49-51, 53, 57, 62, 68, 202-203
Mount of Olives, 183, 202-203
Mystery, 131, 184

N

Nehemiah, 65
Nephi, 12, 30, 50, 119, 129, 141
Nephite(s), 7, 52, 71, 84, 91-93, 106, 117, 120, 124, 131, 140-141
Nephthalim (Naphtali), 113
New age, 228
New Jerusalem, 60-62, 64, 66, 108, 110-112, 122-123, 147, 202, 210, 222-223, 227
New York, 83

Noah, 102-105, 180, 188
North country (countries), 117, 119, 121, 125-127, 133, 147, 204
Northern Lights, 135
North Pole, 133, 136

O

Obadiah, 48
Obedience, 90, 200
Ocean, 52, 121, 202, 204
Offering, 123
Oil, 200
One hundred forty-four thousand, 113-118, 156
Orbit, 226
Ox, 39-41

P

Pacific Islands, 140
Pain, 228-230, 233, 235
Parable, 34-35
Paradise, 87, 227, 230
Parents, 6, 230
Paul, 33
Peace, 6, 10, 149, 214, 228
Pearl Harbor, 93
Pearl of Great Price, 1-4, 57, 70, 76
Pentecost, 61-62
Pestilence, 14, 85, 87, 106, 116, 186-187
Peter, 4, 8, 30, 68, 143
Pillar, 36, 62-66, 70, 76-78, 110-111, 211-212, 215
Pit, 168-169, 173
Plague(s), 87-88, 168, 175-181, 185-186, 189
Planet(s), 33, 137-139
Poor, 3
Powers of heaven, 25-26, 32, 35, 111, 188, 206
Pratt, Orson, 77, 208
Prepared, 197-201, 236
Pride, 3, 12
Prison, 211-212
Priestcrafts, 3
Priesthood, 89, 108, 120-121, 123, 155, 158, 176, 194
Prophesy, 4
Prophet(s), 70, 175
Punishment, 89-90, 177
Purified, 201

Q

Quickened, 208-209

R

Rainbow, 17, 54-55, 70, 221
Red Sea, 121
Remainder, 207-208
Restitution, 234
Restoration, 3, 117, 131, 227
Resurrection, 209-213, 226
Reuben, 113
Revelation(s), 4, 86, 155, 235
Revelation, Book of, 1, 100, 114, 117, 129
Rigdon, Sidney, 60
Righteous(ness), 87, 90, 120, 123, 149-150, 157, 185, 188, 193, 198, 200, 205, 214, 217
Rings, 42-43, 45

S

Sabbath, 80
Sacrifice, 123, 192, 201
Saints, 7, 11, 14, 70, 72, 86-87, 89, 95, 102, 108, 111-112, 146, 161-162, 164, 188-189, 191, 195-196, 198, 205-211, 213, 216, 229
Samson, 48-49
Samuel the Lamanite, 75
Sapphire stone, 54-55
Satan, 131, 155, 158-163, 168-169, 172, 219-220, 230, 232
Saturn, 137
Saul, 106
Saved, 6, 24-25, 187
Savior, 10, 15, 28, 34, 53, 59, 62, 87-88, 99, 102, 112, 157, 163, 197, 199, 202, 204, 209, 216, 223, 233-234
Scandinavia, 119
Scourge, 88-91
Scroll, 29, 205
Seal(s), 1-3, 11, 19, 21, 26, 100, 116-117, 129, 142-143, 151, 158-159, 164, 217
Sealing of 144,000, 2-3, 113-115
Seasons, 15-16
Second coming, 1-2, 9, 34-35, 53, 70, 99-101, 129-130, 145, 192, 199, 206-207, 209, 211, 214-217, 220, 232, 236
Secret acts, 218
Seraphims, 80
Shepherds, 60
Sickle, 70
Sickness, 88-89
Sign(s), 1, 17, 22-25, 27, 35, 44, 61, 99, 119, 132-133, 150
Sign of the Son of Man, 27, 31-35, 56, 69, 95, 100, 142, 206
Silence in heaven, 142-144
Simeon, 113
Sinai, 58, 63-64, 74
Slaves, 92
Smith, George A., 62
Smith, Joseph, 1, 4, 10, 28, 33-34, 53, 60-62, 66, 70, 73-74, 76-79, 83, 91, 96, 106, 108, 114, 116-118, 123, 125, 127, 145, 176, 189, 208, 210
Smith, Joseph F., 51
Smith, Joseph Fielding, 114-115, 162, 226, 234
Smoke, 24-25, 63, 169-170, 173
Solomon, 59, 112
Son of Man, 1, 27, 30, 32-33, 60, 68-70, 99, 142, 190, 192, 197, 207, 209, 216
Sorcery, 160, 177, 213
Sore, 177
Soul, 150, 209
South Carolina, 10
Southern Lights, 135, 139
Spaceship, 36
Speculation, 11-12
Spirit, 4, 10, 30, 47-51, 56, 65, 73-74, 173

Spirit of the Lord, 37, 48-49, 51, 208, 232
Spirit prison, 211-212
Spring Hill, 193
Stake, 91
Star(s), 19-23, 25, 32-33, 35-36, 49, 75-76, 87, 132-133, 150, 166-168, 206
Stephen, 30, 60, 78-79
Sun, 16, 19-23, 25, 32-33, 35, 70, 76, 87, 132-133, 137-139, 150, 167, 178, 204, 206, 219

T

Tabernacle, 28, 58, 64, 110, 229
Tares, 96, 190
Taylor, John, 14, 66, 86, 93, 96-97, 235
Telescope, 28
Telestial, 72, 191, 213, 226, 234
Tempests, 22, 26, 164, 187
Temple, 28, 62, 67, 70, 79-80, 83, 90, 98, 110, 123-124, 145, 175, 184-185, 210
Temple mount, 98
Temple ordinances, 5
Ten Tribes, 116, 118-122, 124-127, 133-134, 227
Terrestrial, 212, 226, 233-234
Tested, 2
Testimony, 88, 157
Three witnesses, 88
Throne, 31-32, 55-56, 60, 79-80, 194, 217, 219
Thunder(ings), 14, 21-22, 26, 53, 63, 71, 164, 167, 184-185, 187
Tidal waves, 14, 21-22, 33, 83, 164
Time(s), 15, 219
Tithing, 192
Token, 17
Tongues, 62
Torment, 168-169, 172, 189
Tower of Babel, 227
Transfigured, 68, 227
Translated, 51, 60, 115, 126
Translation, 127, 231-235
Treasures, 122
Tree of life, 46
Tribulation, 90, 97-99, 105-106, 115-116, 148, 165, 195, 206
Trump(et), 31, 49, 72, 130, 142-144, 164-165, 188, 209-210, 212-213, 217
Twelve tribes, 117-118

U

Under the earth, 129-135, 217
Unidentified Flying Objects, 37
United Order, 110, 112
United States, 96, 116
Universe, 194
Urim and Thummim, 143

V

Valiant, 212
Vehicle(s), 36-38, 52, 169
Veil, 27-28, 30, 98
Vengeance, 14-15, 18, 84, 87, 191, 214
Venus, 138
Violence, 91, 219
Virgin(s), 50, 114, 116, 198-201
Vision(s), 3-5, 28, 30, 33, 48-50, 56, 60, 70, 74, 76-79, 86, 108, 120, 129, 145, 169, 188, 208-209, 211
Voice(s), 14, 164, 167, 184-185
Voice of the Almighty, 37, 40, 52-53, 73, 202

W

War(s), 9-10, 33, 105, 135, 149, 175, 180-182, 188
Warfare, 92-93
Warning, 17, 35, 84, 90, 151
Water(s), 48, 53, 106, 149-150, 166-168, 176, 178, 202
Waterfalls, 52
Weeping, 22
Wheat, 96, 190
Wheel(s), 36-37, 41-47, 51-52, 63, 193-194, 208
Whirlwind, 17-18, 36, 38, 68, 73-74, 216, 231
Wicked, 9-10, 18, 21, 34-35, 61, 84, 87-89, 91-92, 101, 108, 111, 121, 146, 148, 150-151, 161, 165, 177, 182, 185-188, 190-192, 197, 201, 214, 217, 236
Wickedness, 12, 110, 125, 144, 147, 156-158, 221, 228, 236
Wind, 62
Windows, 44
Wings, 38, 40, 52, 57
Wise, 199-201
Wisemen, 75-76
Witnesses, 175-176
Wonder(s), 99-100, 132
Woodruff, Wilford, 33, 44, 56, 83, 86, 110, 122, 134
World Wars, 7
Wormwood, 166-167
Wrath, 17, 149, 191

Y

Year's supply, 22, 102-106
Young, Brigham, 13, 83, 91, 96, 108

Z

Zabulon, 113
Zechariah, 8, 74, 80, 145
Zion, 3, 61, 67, 90, 92, 108, 110, 121-122, 124, 131-132, 147, 149-150, 165, 177, 188, 202-203, 210, 219, 221-222, 225, 227, 231